THIS NARROW
PLACE

THIS NARROW PLACE

SYLVIA TOWNSEND WARNER
AND VALENTINE ACKLAND:
LIFE, LETTERS AND
POLITICS 1930–1951

Wendy Mulford

PANDORA

London, Sydney, Wellington

First published by Pandora Press, an imprint of the
trade division of Unwin Hyman Limited, in 1988

Unwin Hyman Limited
15–17 Broadwick Street
London W1V 1FP

Allen & Unwin Australia Pty Ltd
8 Napier Street, North Sydney, NSW 2060, Australia

Allen & Unwin New Zealand Pty Ltd with the Port Nicholson Press
60 Cambridge Terrace, Wellington, New Zealand

British Library Cataloging in Publication Data
  Mulford, Wendy
    This narrow place : Sylvia Townsend Warner
    and Valentine Ackland : life, letters and
    politics 1930–1951.
    1. English literature.   Interpersonal
    relationships Ackland, Valentine,
    1906–1969
    I. Title
    828'.91 209

    IBSN 0-86358-262-1

Typeset by Columns of Reading
Printed in Great Britain by
Cox and Wyman Ltd, Reading

FOR ANTONIA (9 JUNE 1940–2 AUGUST 1986)

But narrow is this place, narrow is this space
of garlanded sun and leisure and colour,
of return to life and release from living.

(from *Benicasim* by Sylvia Townsend Warner. She notes: 'At Benicasim on the east coast of Spain is the rest home for the convalescent wounded of the Spanish People's Army, and the Villa dedicated to Ralph Fox, supported by the Spanish Medical Aid.')

CONTENTS

Acknowledgments   xi
Preface   xiv
Introduction   1
1 TOWARDS MEETING   6
2 THE PARTNERSHIP – EARLY YEARS   35
3 WRITERS IN ARMS   70
4 SYLVIA: THE NOVELS OF THE 1930s   104
5 WARTIME AND AFTER: PARTNERSHIP
       UNDER PRESSURE   135
6 MATURE ART: SYLVIA – THE WRITINGS
       OF THE 1940s   175
7 VALENTINE ACKLAND, POET   206
EPILOGUE (1951–1978)   229
ABBREVIATIONS   248
NOTES AND REFERENCES   250
BIBLIOGRAPHY   267
INDEX   272

ILLUSTRATIONS

1.1 Family group: Valentine aged 5 at the wheel, 1911   8
1.2 Valentine aged 9, dressed to ride in London   10
1.3 Valentine in the family Austin, Winterton, 1920   11
1.4 Valentine's childhood home in Norfolk: Hill
     House, Winterton-on-Sea (courtesy of Wm. Goffin) 11
1.5 Sylvia during the London years, following the
     success of *Lolly Willowes* (Howard Coster,
     National Portrait Gallery)   17
1.6 Sylvia, from a watercolour by Frank Dobson   19
1.7 Sylvia at Beth-Car, the Powys' home in East
     Chaldon, 1929   25
1.8 Valentine, the hectic years: Winterton, 1926   27
1.9 Valentine with her gun, Winterton, 1928   27
1.10 Valentine with some village boys, Winterton   27
1.11 Chaldon Green, East Chaldon. Miss Green's
     cottage lies out of the picture, on the northern
     edge of the village (picture taken looking west)   31
2.1 Frankfort Manor today, from across the lawns   36
2.2 The façade of Frankfort Manor   36
2.3 Valentine in the doorway of Frankfort Manor,
     1933   38
2.4 Sylvia with one of the kittens at Frankfort Manor   38
2.5 Sylvia sewing in the hall at Frankfort Manor   38
2.6 Valentine aged 29, West Chaldon   41
2.7 Valentine at West Chaldon   42
2.8 Sylvia and Valentine with Julius Lipton   62
2.9 Sylvia with Towser at West Chaldon, 1937   68
5.1 Sylvia wading the Frome   138
5.2 Lower Frome Vauchurch and the River Frome,
     from across the water meadow   139

5.3   Sylvia and Steven Clarke at Lower Frome
      Vauchurch, 1946   172
5.4   Valentine in the garden at Lower Frome
      Vauchurch; early morning, 1948   172
5.5   Sylvia in the garden at Lower Frome Vauchurch
      with a young relative   172
8.1   Great Eye Folly, Salthouse, in Norfolk, where
      Sylvia and Valentine stayed, 1950–51   230
8.2   Lower Frome Vauchurch after the war   232
8.3   Valentine with one of the treasured cats at Lower
      Frome Vauchurch   232
8.4   Sylvia on the front step at Lower Frome
      Vauchurch, 1964   236
8.5   Valentine's snapshot of Sylvia on one of their
      holidays, Berkshire, 1963   236
8.6   Sylvia and Fougère in the upstairs sitting-room,
      at Lower Frome Vauchurch   237
8.7   Sylvia reading, Lower Frome Vauchurch   239
8.8   Sylvia and one of the cats in the garden at Lower
      Frome Vauchurch, 1968   239
8.9   Drawing of Valentine on her death-bed done by
      Joy Finzi at Sylvia's request   242
8.10 Sylvia in the 1970s (photo by Nigel Luckhurst)   245
8.11 Drawing of East Chaldon church – Valentine
      and Sylvia are buried there together. The stone
      reads 'Non omnis moriar'   247

ACKNOWLEDGMENTS

Valentine Ackland & Sylvia Townsend Warner, *Whether A Dove or a Seagull*, Copyright © Valentine Ackland & Sylvia Townsend Warner 1933. Reprinted by permission of William Maxwell and Susanna Pinney and Chatto & Windus. Valentine Ackland *The Nature of the Moment*, Copyright © by Sylvia Townsend Warner 1973, reprinted by permission of William Maxwell and Susanna Pinney, Chatto & Windus, and New Directions Publishing Corporation. Valentine Ackland, *Further Poems*, Copyright © Welmont Publishing 1978. Reprinted by permission of Julius Lipton. Sylvia Towsend Warner, *Letters*, edited by William Maxwell, Copyright © 1982 by Susanna Pinney, William Maxwell, Executors Sylvia Townsend Warner Estate, and William Maxwell (Introduction), reprinted by permission of the Executors, and Viking Penguin Inc. Sylvia Townsend Warner, *Collected Poems*, edited by Claire Harman, Copyright © 1982 by Susanna Pinney, William Maxwell, and Claire Harman Schmidt (Introduction and Notes). Reprinted by permission of Carcanet Press Ltd., and The Viking Press. All other published, periodical, material by either author is reprinted, where relevant, by permission of the Executors of the Sylvia Townsend Warner Estate. Howard Costa, photograph(s) of Sylvia Towsend Warner, and photograph taken from a painting of her by Frank Dobson, reprinted by permission of The National Portrait Gallery. Photograph of drawing by Joy Finzi of Valentine Ackland on her deathbed, reprinted by permission of Joy Finzi. Photograph by Nigel Luckhurst of Sylvia Townsend Warner in Cambridge, reprinted by permission of Nigel Luckhurst.

Every effort has been made to contact owners of copyright. The author and publishers would be grateful for any information regarding inadvertent omissions, for amendment in future editions.

Further acknowledgments and thanks to: The Marx Memorial Library, the Communist Party Archive, George Mathews and Tony Azienta for their assistance; the librarians at the John Johnson Collection, The Bodleian Library for permission to study Spanish Civil War material; Tony Morgan for translations of letters from the Spanish; The Harry Ranson Humanities Research Center, University of Texas at Austin, for permission to quote from Sylvia's letters to Nancy Cunard; Roger Peers for permission to quote from Sylvia's Commonplace Book in his possession; Miss M. Manisty OBE, for permission to quote from Valentine's letters to her sister Joan Woollcombe, and from an unpublished poem by Valentine in her possession; Elizabeth Wade White for permission to quote from a letter from Valentine to her.

I would also like to thank all those who so kindly talked to me, both about Sylvia and Valentine and about the period, including Sylvia's biographer, Claire Harman, and William Goffin, Bea Howe, Yvonne Kapp, Frieda Knight, Jack Lindsay, Roger Miller, and Jim Pitman.

Especial thanks to Jim Fyrth for his memories, and material about the 1936 Bridport Peace Demonstration, and to Margot Heinemann, for a conversation that lasted for four hours and reminded me, in the middle of Thatcherism, of the importance for our future of recovering our resistant past. Ian Patterson and Deborah Thom have both been enthusiastically critical in their support, understanding the terms of the political endeavour, and I am very grateful to Ian in his capacity as bookseller for his generosity and persistence in procuring out-of-the-way books, references and material.

I am most grateful to Julius Lipton for making available to me photocopies of the correspondence from Sylvia and Valentine to him in the thirties, which has been pivotal to my understanding of their political involvement at the time, and for photographs of himself with Sylvia and Valentine. I owe a great debt to Arnold Rattenbury, for photocopies of correspondence between Edgell Rickword and Sylvia and Valentine, and from Sylvia to Sim and himself, as well as for his encouragement, and infectiously good-humoured quickness in cutting through humbug.

I owe a special debt of thanks to Peg Manisty, who allowed me to see a number of Valentine's papers and letters in her possession, for her kindness and hospitality. Her friendship with Antonia formed a special bond for me. I would also like to thank Sylvia's other trustee, Joy Finzi, who offered me assistance of which unfortunately, due to other circumstances, I was unable to avail myself.

Bea Debenham kindly arranged for me to talk to some of those who had known Sylvia and Valentine in Chaldon, and Roger Peers helped me with questions and published material in the Dorset County Museum Archive, in particular in extending my sense of the range of published material by Valentine in the possession of the Dorset County Museum archive.

On a personal note, I would like to thank everyone in Dorset, including Antonia's friends and the members of her family, and Mrs Cleall, who made me feel welcome at Lower Frome Vauchurch. To Mary Deane, for her kindness, I owe a debt I can never repay.

Many women helped me, but I would particularly like to thank my editor Candida Lacey, and Sally Cline, who has suffered more of this book than anyone. I also wish to thank Anthony who helped me through the dark months: his concern and practical support have sustained me and enabled me to begin and to keep on writing.

Last, but not least, my daughter Rhiannon has managed to survive the year of its writing, and her A levels. This book is also for her.

PREFACE

This book would not have been written without Antonia Trauttmansdorff: it is dedicated to her memory. It was begun in Wales at my parents' house: for everything they have done for me, it is also dedicated to them.

Writing about anybody, you come to feel you know them. Writing about two people in whose home you have lived, for however brief a time, the traces of whose lives still overlay that house – their talk, their photographs, pictures, tablecloths, books, jewels, clothes, picnic-baskets, fishing-rods, boots, hats, their trees, herbs and flowers – it is hard to write *about* them, to distance oneself and treat them as the objects of an enquiry.

This study is inevitably shaped by the experience of living in the house which was Sylvia and Valentine's home for thirty-two years. For too short a time, Antonia and I shared it, and dreamed a future.

I began to write in the aftermath of loss. I had hoped the book would have been a collaboration with Antonia, although the political and literary perspectives are entirely mine. Antonia's presence is nonetheless integral to it, as her presence is in my life.

I begin this book with an extract from Antonia's incomplete memoir of Sylvia, which I hope one day to publish together with other extracts from her reviews, articles and letters:

I first met Sylvia Townsend Warner in Dorset in the spring of 1972. She was by then in her seventies, I in my early thirties.

She came to my house through the auspices of a common friend, for Sylvia had expressed a wish to meet me. The friend even went so far as to say she was 'dying' to meet me. I could hardly suppose that she was. When I recounted this to Sylvia much later she replied, 'There was nothing moribund about my desire to meet you.'

Sylvia had no car, so I offered to drive her over the hill to her house. As we drove up the steep beech avenue, leading out of my valley, we started talking about French writers in North Africa. 'Sad for those who love boys,' I said, 'for the young Arabs so quickly lose their sheen.' 'Sad for those who want to be faithful', she replied. 'Yes, an awkward predicament.' I could feel Sylvia looking at me to see if I was being sarcastic, noting that I was merely speaking dryly about possible anguish, and then composing herself. As we reached the top of the hill, I looked across at the sea, feeling as if, in this old woman, I had found a country from which I had been exiled long ago.

I knew through hearsay that Valentine Ackland had lived with Sylvia for many years and that quite recently she had died of cancer. Yet I was far too busy with Sylvia's present and my own to start pitying the past. That Sylvia missed Valentine acutely I knew, but did not want to intrude upon her mourning. We talked to one another easily and quite intimately from the start, but it was many months before I called Sylvia by her Christian name and years before I ever went into her house without ringing the doorbell and then waiting to hear the scrape of Sylvia's writing chair against the floor as she got up to let me in. 'You looked very suspicious when first we met', Sylvia said. I was, for the knowledge that one is captivated makes for wariness.

Now I am sitting in that same writing chair which used to scrape as Sylvia arose. 'I may haunt you', Sylvia said as she was dying. 'Please feel free,' I replied, 'I would be glad of you in any form. But whatever happens, part of you will live on in me.' 'That is the only real answer', Sylvia said.

During that first summer I saw Sylvia as often as I dared. Once she invited herself to tea with a couple of American writing sisters. I made what I hoped was a proper English tea, cucumber sandwiches, scones, but the tea itself streamed from the spout so culpably black that I could not make out what had gone wrong until, later, I found a wedge of cleaning material inside the pot. So distracted was I by this ghastly concoction that, when one of the sisters remarked that their mother had been English, I replied senselessly,

'How nice'. Sylvia sneered at me for that and in my mind's eye I saw monstrous regiments of English mothers marching through century after century.

Early in the New Year I took the unprecedented step of asking Sylvia if she would like to go out for a drive. 'People often take old ladies for drives', I said, 'it is the respectable thing to do.' She accepted. Quite soon I took her again. 'Would you think me unduly morbid if I asked you to drive me to my grave?' 'No', I replied, thinking 'yes'.

Fortunately it was a beautiful day. The rooks were cawing with archaic rustiness above Chaldon churchyard and the sound was steadying, but still I found it hard to watch that old woman looking down on the grave, which was already Valentine's, and was before long to be her's too. So I turned away and sat on a low wall from which I could see a well cultivated kitchen garden. As I did so I heard Sylvia shout to the four winds, 'If I forget Thee, O Jerusalem, may my right hand forget her cunning'; a desolate incantation which still haunts me.

Usually Sylvia and I met à deux and, judging by some of our experiences in wider company, I think this was just as well. We drove about through those romping springs, which seem to have eloped with themselves, into tattered and self-absorbed late summers and then on, with stone hot water bottles, into the autumn and winter gales. We talked a great deal, tippled, toasted crumpets in front of the kitchen stove and considered ourselves fortunate for this lease of serious joy.

By the November of 1977, I knew Sylvia was sinking. Her heart was giving out, but her wits were as sharp as ever. One day she said, 'I am very much afraid that I am going to become bedridden.' 'Never mind,' I replied, 'I have always thought you charming in bed.' Even then Sylvia could laugh, even then when we knew our prospects were limited and to become increasingly grim.

One of the trials of dying is that some visitors look their last with an awestruck solemnity. Others produce a breezy honesty: 'As we will probably never meet again, we had better say goodbye.' Both reactions are rather difficult to manage socially. One trick, which Sylvia and I devised was to introduce a complicated tray of scalding China tea, lemon slices, milk, hot water and small pieces of cake, which the *poor visitor was obliged to manage while paying last respects.*

That spring there was a heavy snow brought by an east wind. The roads were blocked by twelve foot drifts but, after two days, it was possible to walk over the fields from my house to Sylvia's. Dead calves lay by the hedges, beneath a pink and grey sky. The silence was absolute. Meanwhile Sylvia had, in her windswept writing, written instructions for her funeral.

However, she lived on until the morning of 1 May. By that time paperback editions of her books were flooding into the house. One particularly nastily produced edition of The Corner That Held Them *described the work as 'full-blooded'. 'Me? Full-blooded?' Sylvia said. She kept her translation of Proust by her side and read* Vanity Fair. *The Sainte Beuve comforted her, for she knew it to have been well done, and of* Vanity Fair *she said, 'This time I am enjoying the subsidiary characters most.'*

Before Sylvia drifted off to her death she said, 'What is the meaning of all this, Antonia? They assure me there is one.' 'They', the didactic, loomed above us. 'Sylvia, I don't know,' I said. This was hardly the time to start telling lies.

With the light of life extinguished, her face looked composed with firmness enough to rule a rowdy empire. Now that her voice was silenced, her corpse proclaimed indomitability.

The undertakers wrapped her body in a purple blanket hemmed with mauve silk; a detail which I would have hastened to report to her, had we still been in the same world. The habit of sharing information dies as hard, perhaps, as any other. I remembered that Sylvia wanted to tell Valentine that her mortal remains were driven off in a bright blue van. 'She was sardonic, you see', Sylvia had said to me.

When I came up to Chaldon church I walked up to that small gravestone, remembering the times when I had accompanied Sylvia there, beneath the nesting rooks. Once Sylvia had remarked, 'Along with the psalmist, I often wish that the Lord would number my days, for then I would know how many house repairs I needed to do.' They were numbered now and there was her inscription. 'Non omnis

moriar.' Once I had teased her about that. 'If you had been a
film director, whose work you knew would be destroyed
when they planned a remake, you would not have been able
to quote Horace. He was talking about his work, was he not?'

Lying by the grave, stretched out serenely on the grass was
a large, dead vixen. She looked as if she had been in good
condition and I could see no mark on her. Why, I wondered,
had she not dragged herself away to a sheltered place in
which to die? I laid her in the shadow of the wall. It was as if
Sylvia had sent her as a diversion for me, but I would rather
have seen that beautiful animal running away over the Five
Marys. Then I joined that other world in the church, all
ready, all waiting.

I make no claim to academic detachment but I hope I have,
in some measure, succeeded in being dispassionate in this study.
Writing under the level eyes of Sylvia Townsend Warner
demands one's best attempt. Nonetheless, the writer is *subject*,
no less than her Subjects, perhaps more evidently in a study
such as this. Sylvia was a part of our own lives, and at times I
grew infuriated with her, as much as with the encumbering
processes that prevented me from reaching a fuller understanding of both her and Valentine. (Due to the forthcoming
biography of Sylvia by Claire Harman, I was not granted access
to the unpublished papers in the Dorset County Museum
archive.) Private and public circumstances, therefore, propelled
me toward acquiring a kind of slant knowledge, through
osmosis as it were, shovelling coal in the bunker under the
holly-tree, hearing the owls haunting, blitzing cobwebs (Sylvia
hated to disturb them), clearing the Long Room, which remained
a glory-hole fifteen years after Valentine's death, searching
through Valentine's tool-kits for an unrusty screwdriver.

In any writing, the writer is subject to the processes of her
enquiry. In this writing it seems to me that I am subjected to,
possessed by, the spirit of Lower Frome Vauchurch and its
inhabitants more fully than I can render account of here.
Instead I have tried to tell a relatively straightforward tale of
the middle years of their partnership. My way into their lives
was through their political commitment, and this, and my
choice of certain works as key, has shaped my approach. I
began in this way.

INTRODUCTION

Two books of Sylvia Towsend Warner's first aroused my interest in her. Her first novel, *Lolly Willowes* (1926), which caused an 'excited bustle'[1] when it appeared, and her *Letters* (1982), edited and introduced by William Maxwell, a friend and former editor of hers at *The New Yorker*.

From the Introduction to *Letters* I learned amongst other things that Sylvia had lived for nearly forty years with a woman who wrote poetry when she was young, called Valentine Ackland, of whom I had never heard; and that they had both joined the Communist Party in the 1930s and gone out to Spain. The combination of the quality and liveliness of Sylvia's writing, the two writers' political commitment, and their lives together as women living in Dorset, apart from either Grub Street or Bloomsbury, made me want to investigate further. My curiosity grew when I discovered that although Sylvia's reputation had seen something of a revival with the republication of the first three of her novels, all written in the 1920s,[2] there had been very little mention of her political views, except in an article by Arnold Rattenbury in a 'celebration' in honour of her in 1981, four years after she died.[3]

Furthermore, the growth of interest in politically committed writers of the thirties had centred around the male writers of that decade, with 'honourable mentions' for women novelists such as Storm Jameson, Naomi Mitchison and Vera Brittain. But women were clearly not seen to be centrally involved in the cultural revolution that it is no exaggeration to say took place amongst a wide section of British writers between 1933 and 1939, and whose effects continued to be felt until late into the forties. I wanted to discover how two women writers of this period lived their lives: as writers and political people; political, if you like, with a capital P unashamedly and determinedly partisan. My aim was to try to see how this affected their writing, and how their experiences as women living together differed from those passed down to us from the assumed, central, male point of view.

I also felt it was an important debt to recover the truth of that political commitment, since recent republications and reviews have repeatedly stressed Sylvia Townsend Warner's qualities as a stylist. For example, the review of a recent posthumous collection of stories, *One Thing Leading to Another* (1984), pigeon-holes Sylvia as a writer of 'witty, warm-hearted, well-mannered prose, which never assumed greater significance than the giving . . . or sharing . . . of a good deal of quiet enjoyment.' But as Sylvia wrote of Jane Austen,[4] there are lions that lie in the path of this kind of assessment – and many of those lions lie in the writing of the thirties and forties.

Lastly, I wanted to find out what kind of a writer and a person the mysterious Valentine Ackland was. In the University library at Cambridge there are only two books of hers, both written in the thirties, one a forthright exposure and condemnation of the conditions of agricultural workers, the other a subtle, haunting collection of lyrical poems, written with Sylvia Townsend Warner.

I have chosen to restrict the time-span of my study to just twenty-one years of their thirty-nine years together, because I wished to focus upon the period in their lives when they were most politically active. An appraisal of the part of political commitment in their lives overall would have to take into account both the early non-political period of the twenties, and the gradual quietism and moving away from politics of the last decades, both of which are treated summarily in this book.

Valentine moved to the right towards the end of her life, particularly after her reconversion to the Catholic Church, but she never denied her Communist convictions. Writing of the thirties to her sister Joan in January 1957 she said:

> very many people became Communists for reasons which appeared reasonable and were partly founded on transient facts and partly on their own hopes and good intentions . . . certainly we had hopes and took pains to see whether they

were well-founded. Whether they never were, or whether the foundation crumbled I do not know, certainly there is nothing now on which to found our kind of hope. But this type of change of conviction is really not so much a change as a readjustment in the light of changes brought about by history. . . . 'Once myself always myself' is nearer the mark![5]

Sylvia, however, remained unswerving and passionate in her political alignment, although she no longer took any part in politics. Towards the end of her life, writing about the death of her friend Nancy Cunard, she still raged, 'Have you observed . . . that those who stirred as much as a finger for Spain are left for the kites and crows to deal with? And she was a poet too. What can we expect?'[6]

Sylvia Townsend Warner was born in 1893, nine years before Queen Victoria's reign ended. She was the contemporary of Edith Sitwell and Ivy Compton Burnett, eight years younger than D. H. Lawrence, whom she admired, and five years younger than T. S. Eliot.

Sylvia's first published work was an article in *Blackwoods Magazine* in 1916, based on her experiences of working as a 'relief munitions worker' during the First World War. Her first book *The Espalier* (1925) was a collection of poems published by Chatto & Windus, to which firm she was introduced by the novelist David Garnett. Sylvia's father had been a distinguished master at Harrow and had himself written a number of books. He was widely admired and respected by his pupils and from her childhood Sylvia had made friends with many of the brightest of them.

Despite this background, for Sylvia writing was always a matter of economic necessity as well as pleasure. She began life as a music editor in London, at which she worked for ten years after her father's early death in 1916. She wrote later that she had no alternative but penury in London at this time, as otherwise she would have had to live with her mother in Devon, and would always have exasperated her. Nora Townsend Warner was highly critical of her only child.

Once *Lolly Willowes* had been accepted, Sylvia considered making her living as a writer, which she continued to do for the rest of her life. She published in all 7 novels; 5 books of poetry including one joint book with Valentine Ackland; 12 collections of stories; a translation of Proust; a biography of T. H. White, and innumerable articles, stories and poems in periodicals and pamphlets and anthologies, including more than 140 stories in the *New Yorker* over a period of forty years. Well known as an author in the twenties and early thirties, her reputation later suffered an eclipse. By the mid-sixties it had begun to revive, with the acclaim for her biography of T. H. White (1967), and her novels and stories started to be reprinted. She received literary recognition late in life and was made a fellow of The Royal Society of Letters in 1967. Sylvia was characteristically unimpressed by the honour. She commented: 'I suppose they go by alphabetical order. It is the first public acknowledgement I have received since I was expelled from my Kindergarten for being a disruptive influence.'[7] Her last work, *Kingdoms of Elfin*, a collection of fairy-tale stories, appeared in 1977, to wide acclaim.

Valentine's history as a writer is more briefly told. She was born in 1906. Most of her early years were spent writing poems, but her first collection, *Whether a Dove or a Seagull* (a joint book with Sylvia) was not published until she was twenty-eight, in 1934. Two years later her book *Country Conditions* came out, a clear documentary and analytic account of the labourers' conditions as she knew them, which was well received on the Left. During the thirties and forties she contributed poems, articles and stories, but mainly poems, to a wide range of left-wing periodicals.

Soon after the war she became disenchanted with Communism, but continued to write for left-wing papers such as the *Daily Worker* as late as 1948 and did not leave the Communist Party until 1953.[8] Throughout the 1950s she contributed some poems and articles to papers but was not recognised as a writer. Occasionally a poem of hers was broadcast or published during the sixties, but for the most part her writing was unknown. She had published a pamphlet privately in 1957, *Twenty-Eight Poems*, and another collection was published by Sylvia after her death. The first, and, to date, the only major book of her poetry *The Nature of the Moment* (1973), was published posthumously by Sylvia's publishers, Chatto & Windus. In 1978 another collection appeared from a small publisher, Welmont Press, and in 1985 Chatto & Windus published her autobiographical account of her early life, *For*

Sylvia: An Honest Account, written in 1949, when she was forty-three years old.

The imbalance in Sylvia and Valentine's lives as published writers is some measure of the difficulty that arises in attempting to focus upon their partnership as writers. They did not collaborate upon their work, apart from on *Whether a Dove or a Seagull*, but each was central for the other in their lives. The library in their house at Frome Vauchurch was filled with presents exchanged between them, right up to the last weeks of Valentine's life, each bearing a loving dedication and often recollecting places they visited together. When Valentine was going off on a journey – she went more frequently than Sylvia, who did not drive – she would leave a note. When they were parted, they usually wrote to each other twice a day[9]. For Sylvia, after Valentine's death, it was as if:

> my whole raison d'etre [has been] sent out of my bosom; and
> when I turn to any familiar occupation, trying to write,
> cooking my boring meals, listening to music, their familiarity
> catches me in the illusion that she is still here, I shall hear her
> tread, her whistle. . . . But I am resolved to stay here.
> Anything else would be a sham. Here at least I am in the
> reality of my loss.[10]

Overall in this study I have given more space to Sylvia's work, and I have paid greater attention to the novels than the poems. There is a great deal more to be said about this diverse writer, and a great many more aspects to her art than I have dealt with in this study, which concentrates upon that part of her work directly springing from her left-wing political involvement.

Valentine's unpublished poems, when they are finally edited, will certainly result in a re-evaluation of her work, and a gap in the ranks of English women poets of the twentieth century will be filled. I have included some brief discussion of this work, although it lies outside the scope of this book, in the hope of indicating a little of the extent and quality of her poetry.

CHAPTER 1

TOWARDS MEETING

Sylvia Towsend Warner was born in 1893 in Harrow-on-the-Hill, then still a quiet village on the northern outskirts of London, with, she later recalled, 'meadows of a heavy clay . . . massive hawthorn hedges, and a few slouching farm-houses',[1] all of which were soon to disappear under the encroachment of suburban London.

Queen Victoria had still nine years to rule the British Empire on which the sun never set, and Harrow School was still doing its part to prepare young men of the ruling classes to take up their Imperial duties. George Townsend Warner, Sylvia's father, was a master at the school, subsequently a housemaster and head of the 'modern side', which means head of history, as opposed to the ancients or classics.

Sylvia who was an only child, was not sent to school apart from a brief experiment, when very young, which did not work well, for she mimicked the teachers and distracted the pupils. Her father preferred to keep her near him, and she recalled being jealous of the praise she heard him give one of his pupils for an essay she thought she could have written better. She felt, she said, like Cinderella. She was outside the golden circle of his attention. Excluded from formal education by her gender and her father's idiosyncrasy, she was given the run of his library and read widely. She was encouraged to think and question for herself.

Her father was highly esteemed in the community of the 'public school': he had been a fellow at Jesus College, Cambridge, for a short time and wrote books on a wide range of subjects, including history and the writing of English. His pupils adored him, and were in awe of him – later Sylvia wrote that there were always some of these young men about in her family home, and she often became friendly with them and continued to see them when she had left home to work in London.

George Towsend Warner was a passionàte admirer of Voltaire and the Enlightenment, and a convinced atheist, of which Harrow School possessed not a few. His unconventionality and clear mind must certainly have influenced Sylvia in her own rejection of traditional thinking, for she admired him greatly. Another Communist Party member of the thirties, Margot Heinemann, said of Party members of her own generation that in their rejection of established ideas their parents had done a great deal of the thinking for them. Townsend Warner handed on to his daughter an analytic and often satirical outlook on social and political institutions, and the habit of a scrupulously historical sense.

Early on, however, Sylvia made the inevitable comparison between the opportunities of her father's favoured pupils and her own position as a girl. Although she was later to say that her lack of formal education was an advantage, at the time she resented the boys' prior claim on her father's attention. A keen sense of justice and fairness was always a strong constituent in her nature, which can only have been fed by the contrasts between herself and the privileged young men who came to their school-house for tuition.

Sylvia's mother Nora was beautiful, strong-willed and eccentric, and Sylvia was frightened of her when she was young for she could never please her. Once Nora noticed that the butler had a habit of smirking every time he opened the front door to the house. To cure him of the offence, she spent all one morning making him open and shut the door: this was one of the many incidents Sylvia was later to make use of in her whimsical stories for *The New Yorker* concerning the eccentricities of English life.

Nora had almost as little feeling for religion as her husband: she taught Sylvia her letters, from the New Testament and Old Testament stories, and considered most of the characters in them to be little better than cheats and charlatans. Relations between mother and daughter were so bad that when George Townsend Warner died suddenly of a heart attack in 1916, Sylvia escaped as quickly as possible to London: she said that penury in London was preferable to luxury with her mother in Devon. The year was 1917: Valentine was eleven years old.

1.1 Family group: Valentine aged 5 at the wheel, 1911

Valentine Ackland, the second of two daughters, was born Mary Kathleen McCrory Ackland in 1906 in London. Her father was a successful West End dentist and the family spent much of their time at Hill House, the holiday home he had built at Winterton in Norfolk, on a cliff-top overlooking the dunes and the North Sea. It was a life divided between the bracing North Sea air, which was supposed to be good for Mrs Ackland's health, and the fashionable heart of London. Pictures of Valentine as a child show her in immaculate child's clothes, dressed to go out riding in Rotten Row. One of her earliest memories was of being given a little silver key to commemorate the opening of Selfridges department store, which was just opposite their house in Brook Street, and of being dressed for the occasion in 'white velvet with a beaver-edged collar and tricorne velvet and beaver hat':

My nursery window fortunately had bars to it, otherwise I should have been raspberry-jammed on the distant pavement, for the Ecstasy of leaning out to gaze on my darling friend the Porter, in his best gold lace, receiving Potentates almost daily then, there were so many real ones.[2]

But she was happiest at Winterton. For Valentine, Winterton was 'home', and the community of fishermen and their families retained her affection until the end of her life. She always longed to return and on several occasions she and Sylvia looked for a house in Norfolk. Even when old and ill, she said that her heart still 'swirled', 'at the remembrance of the dunes and the sun and the noise of birds and sea.'[3] It was a childhood paradise that could never be wrested from her, and to which in spirit and in her poetry she constantly returned. The solitary-ness she experienced in Norfolk as a child along that bleak coast was to remain a major constituent of her inmost self: 'alone lonely, even at its deepest depth of cold (river or sea, marshes or shore), *that* is where to be lonely.'[4]

Valentine's older sister Joan tormented her greatly as a child, and the picture of her childhood that Valentine paints in her autobiography, *For Sylvia: An Honest Account* is a deeply unhappy one. She emerges as a sensitive, introspective and melancholy child, unable to withstand the taunts of her nurse or her sister, and largely ignored by her mother. (In later life she decided this was all to the good.) Ruth Ackland was an

1.2 Valentine aged 9, dressed to ride in London

1.3   Valentine in the family
Austin, Winterton, 1920

1.4   Valentine's childhood
home in Norfolk: Hill House,
Winterton-on-Sea

energetic, formidable and long-suffering High Anglican, given to organising the village and neighbourhood in 'good works'. While Valentine as a child would escape to the dunes and perch up trees writing poetry, Mrs Ackland found her escapes in motoring backwards and forwards to London (as frequently as twice a week, their ex-chauffeur recalled).[5] It was a happy household, apparently, but Valentine, unsure of herself and beset by guilt, was an easy prey for her tormentors, chiefly her Nanny and her sister, but also the local boys who would throw stones at her. Later she came to love and admire these same boys; a feeling of mutual respect developed between herself and them that was to endure for the rest of her life.

Ruth Ackland endeared herself to the people of Winterton, despite her good works, because she was a generous woman – she lent her books freely and interested herself in everyone's affairs, often rather too much so. When she was widowed (Valentine's father died in 1923) the servants were most solicitous about her, and tried to persuade Valentine and Joan to prevent her from over-working in all her charitable causes. This was clearly impossible, as Mrs Ackland was the kind of person who believed that the well-being of society depended on her alone. No matter what Molly or Joan or the servants at Hill House might do, Ruth Ackland would go her own way.

'Molly' was Valentine's nickname amongst family and friends when she was young, and the name by which she was known until her mid-twenties. McCrory, her third Christian name, was a family name on her mother's side. It was through this side of the family that she was related to Lord Eldon, the Chancellor who persecuted Shelley, and Sylvia enoyed saying that Valentine was related in a 'Chancery-sort-of-way' to the poet. When Valentine came to have serious aspirations as a poet she renamed herself, and from about 1930 on was only ever known by the androgynous, but more usually male, name Valentine Ackland. The name acted partly as a pen-name; it was an effective disguise, and appropriate for the lesbian identity she had by this time come to adopt. Up until 1929 she still signed her name 'Molly' in her books, kept until recently in the library at Lower Frome Vauchurch.

Sylvia's friend, Bea Howe, saw Valentine as essentially a person who needed disguise: she dressed always in natural materials, wearing expensive leather accessories, which Bea

Howe saw as 'a kind of protective clothing such as Nature gives to disguise an animal living in the wild.'[6] After her death, drawers of the fine, soft leather gloves and silk scarves she wore remained undisturbed for many years.

Bea Howe's first impression of Valentine on meeting her in the early 1930s was of the faint, hesitant smile. 'She was wearing a silk shirt and Morocco slippers, and was standing in the shadowy archway of the door . . . silent but watchful' while Sylvia and Bea talked. It was 'the theatrical image of someone waiting in the wings to make an entrance.' Her face was impassive, pale, 'and the full eyes, slightly hooded . . . were sad eyes, I thought. They did not light up.'[7] Bea was intrigued by Valentine's immaculate appearance.

As a child, Valentine was sent to a convent school in London and then to Paris, where she developed a romantic friendship with her English schoolfriend. The story of this relationship and its disastrous consequences for Valentine is told in some detail in *For Sylvia: An Honest Account*. As a punishment for her supposedly heinous misdeeds she was afterwards sent to a domestic training school in Eastbourne, which was ironically, she said, 'given over to unnatural vice'.[8] It was then that her father died, never having forgiven her.

Near the end of her life, looking back on the shock of his unrelenting anger, she said that she was able to understand his feelings: but when she wrote her autobiography (1949), the portrait she painted of him was of venomous, unforgiving patriarch. In a letter to a friend in the 1960s she wrote:

> My father must have been very ill even then [at the time of the Paris incident] . . . he could not have felt so if he had not fastened hope and pride on me . . . [he] was one of those people who are unmitigatedly of one sex. . . . (I believe the majority of people are to some extent bi-sexual in their make-up: which is easier for them and for their near and dear ones alike!)[9]

Sylvia's father died, mainly of grief she said, in the autumn of 1916. Within a year, Nora Townsend Warner had gone to live at Little Zeal in Devon, and Sylvia had escaped to London, where she lived in a gaunt flat over a furrier's on the Bayswater Road. She had been hired by the Carnegie United Kingdom Trust to work on its Tudor Church Music Research Project as a member of its editoral committee, from 'pure inconspicuous merit, or possibly through the unaccountable machinery of fate',[10] she later wrote. Her income consisted of what seemed a generous salary of £3 per week, plus first-class travelling expenses and an allowance from her mother of £100 a year.

Through her work for the Trust Sylvia published her first writings, on the growth of notation in music. Later she contributed to the Oxford History of Tudor Church Music, under the general editorship of Dr Percy Buck, a distinguished teacher of music at Harrow School.

The Carnegie Trust job involved a considerable amount of travelling around the country, poring over manuscripts of old music in cathedral archives. Both the travelling and the first-class expenses must have come in useful, for Sylvia and Dr Buck conducted a liaison under the name of Arbuthnot in the various cathedral towns of England, which lasted for ten years. Although few of her friends knew of the relationship, she would briskly dismiss them from her flat when he was about to call, and she would probably have married him, had he not already had a wife. As it was, the relationship finally ended because they were both too fond of his wife.

Writing of this time later on, Sylvia said that she was as 'happy and self-sufficient as a lark', and lived with 'economic trimness' on £160 a year: 'From time to time I felt hungry, and in winter I often felt cold. But I never felt poor.'[11] The flat was 'draughty and incommodious', but it had ample room for the grand piano: it cost £90 a year to rent.

The most vivid picture of Sylvia in London in the twenties comes from the anecdotes of her friends. Bea Howe described her as having 'a strong maternal streak in her compassionate and essentially *caring* character. She always needed someone to cherish and protect.'[12] David Garnett, in his autobiography gives a picture of her manner and conversation:

> Sylvia is dark, lean and eager with rather frizzy hair. She wears spectacles and her face is constantly lighting up with amusement and intelligence and the desire to interrupt what I am saying and to cap it with something much wittier of her own. . . . She cannot restrain herself from snatching my uncompleted sentence out of my mouth and giving it a much better ending. . . . In her company I soon come to think I am witty, though vicariously witty, it is true.[13]

There are revealing incidents, too, which later became incorporated into short stories and sketches for *The New Yorker*, such as when she decided she could not resist throwing 'economic trimness' to the winds by buying a pair of linen sheets: the purchase was justified on the grounds that they 'would do to shroud me in'.[14] Or, on another occasion, unable to resist a volume of Crabbe from a bookstall, she made do with bread and tomatoes for the rest of the day, and never did tomatoes taste so sweet, she wrote. Or one catches a glimpse of her, sitting in a teashop after the war thinking about Freud, 'as one often did at that period'.[15] In other words, a heroine very much like Miriam in Dorothy Richardson's *Pilgrimage*: hard-working, independent, gregarious, drinking endless cups of black coffee and talking to the young men who frequented her flat (and whom she partly mothered) late into the night before they all set off to stride round the deserted streets of East London.

Making ends meet, relishing her freedom and the stimulus that living in London gave her, Sylvia's life at this time was divided between music and writing. She had originally been going to study composition under Schoenberg in Vienna, and evidently continued to compose for some time after she left Harrow. The composer Ralph Vaughan Williams who knew her in London asked why she gave up composing and she replied that it was because she didn't think she did it authentically enough, whereas when she wrote she never had any doubts as to what she intended to say. She lingered at the second-hand bookstalls and bookshops such as Harold Monro's famous Poetry Bookshop to which Valentine was also a frequent visitor. There, readers could buy broadsides of poems, roughly decorated with woodcuts to tack to the walls of their rooms.

The young woman writer Bryher (Winifred Ellermann) was also living in London at this time. She describes a London of the post-war literary and artistic world that was rather different from the one Sylvia inhabited. All that generation, however, shared a common background of loss to their lives, from the deaths of friends and family in the war. To Bryher the effect was to create them all as exiles from the country in which they lived:

We were all exiles. We remain so today . . . we were the last group to grow up under the formidable discipline of the nineteenth century whose effect, however much we resent it, cannot be entirely eradicated from our systems. [We were taught that] abnegation and hard work would give us security and peace.[16]

Bryher went on to say that the only thing left which they could believe in after the war was art: 'We were very young . . . war had made the momentary our concern. We laughed at everybody and no idea was sacred.'

For Sylvia, the sense of loss and loneliness must have been equally acute: many of the young men she had known at Harrow had been killed in the trenches, and she believed this had broken her father's heart and caused his early death. And yet, the modern and the momentary seems not to have been a focus for her: perhaps partly because of her ten years' grounding in early church music, she never pursued the new and experimental in her writing. Hers was, above all, a supremely-crafted traditional art.

Despite the disruption and change brought about by the war, Sylvia's life soon settled into a busy and productive pattern. Perhaps this was partly to do with the fact that unlike Bryher and many other English upper-class writers, Sylvia did not have any money of her own, at least no 'real money', as Bloomsbury considered it – that is, unearned income. She had only herself to rely upon.

In the company of the young men from Harrow and other friends, and with her one close woman friend, Bea Howe, Sylvia cooked excellent suppers, drank the innumerable cups of black coffee, smoked the countless Gauloises that would be her hallmark to the end of her life, and in the long midnight rambles and street-mooching around unknown London she found sights and scenes to provoke her imagination. She began to write to amuse herself, and was soon writing in earnest.

Encouraged by her father, she had already tried her hand with an article published in 1916,[17] on her experiences as a relief munitions worker in a factory, for which she was paid sixteen guineas. In the long evenings in London she wrote poems, a novel, and a play which she sent to Theodore Powys, to whom she was introduced in Dorset in early 1922 by her friend the sculptor Stephen 'Tommy' Tomlin, to whom she was very attached. (He did not return her feelings.) The poems were the first to be published, but it was the novel *Lolly Willowes or*

1.5 Sylvia during the London years, following the success of *Lolly Willowes* (Howard Coster, National Portrait Gallery)

Loving Huntsman, which was to make her name. When she could, she escaped from London for long walks, first of all to Essex, and later, from 1923 on, again and again to Dorset.

Valentine came to London when she was seventeen, in 1923. Her father had just died of cancer, but Ruth Ackland was determined her daughter should enjoy a gay London season nevertheless. They threw themselves into 'a riot of dances and parties'; the experience was one of living in a 'strange desperation of enjoyment'.[18] Since she was a child, Valentine had feverishly scribbled poems whenever she could: in Paris as a 15-year-old, 'after the manner of Verlaine'. She was involved in her first passionate friendship with a young woman, which caused her father to disown her right in the midst of the hectic London season. She continued to write amidst all the socialising, the balls, dining-out and cocktail parties, by which the aspiring upper-classes marry off their daughters:

> I wrote into the night, I wrote all day; I wrote in buses and in the lavatory; I wrote in the cloakrooms of restaurants, of hotels where I had gone out to dance.[19]

Every time she read a poem, by Keats, or Shakespeare, Raleigh or Wyatt, she experienced 'a deep and shaking ecstasy'.
The paths of the two women may have crossed when Valentine returned from some late night party or café session to her parents' house in fashionable Brook Street, for not far away in Bayswater, Sylvia was pursuing her hard-working, thrifty independent life. As Sylvia walked to the British Museum, to the free warmth of the manuscript room, or sat in tea-shops, and hunted for bargains amongst the fruit at greengrocers' stalls, or weighed the price of a one-shilling egg, which might turn out to be bad, against other expenses, Valentine was perhaps leaving the Savoy, in her 'bare-backed, sleeveless bright green evening dress',[20] with her monocle screwed into her eye. Since leaving school she had been leading a fairly wild life in London, posing as a model for well-known artists such as Augustus John and Eric Gill, for she was tall and striking in appearance, with a fine bone structure. She also became involved in her first serious relationship with a woman, Bo Foster, named only as 'X' in *For Sylvia: An Honest Account*, who was to remain a friend for the rest of her life. A Tory political speaker and quite a wealthy woman, Bo introduced

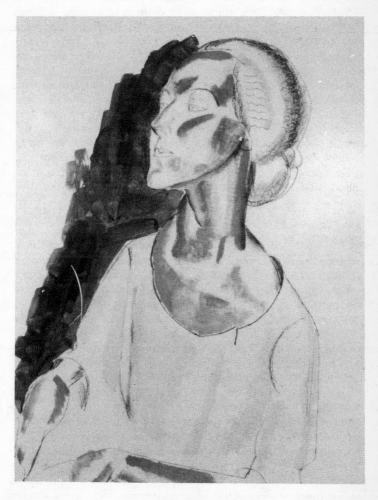

1.6 Sylvia, from a watercolour by Frank Dobson

Valentine to moderate poetry and to modern art, and brought the desperately shy young woman into a world of sophisticated social and artistic contacts where she longed to shine. In return, Valentine took Bo back to Winterton, where she was warmly welcomed, and their relationship lasted until Valentine fell in love with Sylvia.

But in her social life Valentine found herself crippled by shyness, which was to afflict her for the rest of her life; to try and cope with it she started to drink, and soon came to depend upon it. As she said in her autobiography, 'London was extremely gay and it was fashionable to commit extravagances and follies.'[21] She wished to live recklessly and extravagantly, and to make an impact, and from the time she was seventeen she had learned that if she drank she was the more readily able to do this.

Valentine took pleasure in flouting 'Society', as much by what she wore and did as by being another woman's lover, which at one point she describes as affording her 'exactly the same degree of pleasure that I felt when I wore a daringly-low-cut dress, or first wore trousers and walked in Mecklenburgh Square'.[22] But in some things she acted conventionally – her 'flouting' was, apart from her lesbianism, a matter of the more superficial conventions. Her sister Joan, eight years older than her, had already married, and told her that if she wanted to escape from their mother, then she must at least marry: 'once that was done . . . things would get better. Even if I did not love my husband . . . I should be free from Home.'[23] Otherwise she would be 'one of those miserable, dowdy daughters, travelling from place to place, unhappy, cheated, oppressed'. Valentine, who was already engaged to a young man she hardly knew, promptly decided she must be married the next day.

Her fiancé, Richard Turpin, was reluctant, but agreed to obtain a special licence. He at once caught a train to Ilfracombe to tell his mother, and Valentine and her mother followed: 'I got the route from the AA and my mother got a hamper of food from Fortnum and Mason; we got into the little open Wolseley car . . . and started for Ilfracombe.'[24]

Richard's mother did not approve and he tried to back out: Valentine, however, was determined to be married. The matter was complicated because they were both in the process of being received into the Catholic Church (under Bo's influence

Valentine had started to take instruction, and she had then converted Richard), and the church had not yet given permission for the marriage. Valentine got her way with Richard: the Registry Office ceremony took place in Westminster the next day, after they had driven back from Devon through the night.

The religious ceremony, which took place eight days later in Westminster Cathedral, was a grand affair: characteristically, Valentine's main concern was with the impact she made. She wore a 'very handsome jewel' which Bo lent her – and insisted she wore – and a 'nun-like coif' for a head-dress with her white wedding-dress. After the ceremony she had her hair 'Eton-cropped':

> it made me look extremely boyish . . . I was very tall and thin
> at that time . . . (almost six foot and weighing just under
> eight stone) . . . When I changed into my 'going away' outfit,
> I chose not to wear a hat, and I was gratified by the sensation
> I caused when I came down into the large salon.[25]

Unsurprisingly, the marriage was not a success; Valentine was erotically and emotionally deeply involved with Bo, and Richard was inexperienced with women, unsure of himself and confused about his own sexuality. The marriage was never consummated, although Valentine endured a gruesome interlude in which, following the instruction of her Catholic confessor, she went into a nursing home to have her hymen stretched: 'Richard was told he must deflower me, or else he would inhibit himself and do himself a nervous injury.'[26]

Meanwhile, Bo and Valentine were maintaining their passionate though covert relationship. Bo was committed to this closet existence by her need to support her parents (she lived with them) and equally, no doubt, to sustain her credibility as a Tory Party speaker. Valentine was turning more and more to drink to enable her to endure her life. It was with Bo that she had first learned the power of alcohol to give release from the self-consciousness and timidity that plagued her: 'When I was a little drunk . . . I became amusing and beguiling . . . I became *integrated*, together in myself, and possessed myself.'[27]

After the operation was over, a friend of Bo's (named R. in the autobiography and whom Valentine described as 'one of the near-stage people; the people who knew People'[28]) suggested to Valentine that she go down to Dorset to recuperate, and stay with her in a small cottage in East Chaldon, the village where T. F. Powys lived. Shaky, but content, Valentine set off with R. for Wool, which is the nearest station to East Chaldon. They travelled in a third-class carriage, Valentine reported, and she had bought, at R.'s suggestion, a pair of men's flannel trouser to wear, from the Army and Navy Stores: 'R. had said that we could wear these clothes down in Dorset, and the idea amused me.'[29] (From then on until she was middle-aged she wore trousers.)

Besides their suitcases, Valentine took a box of books, a portable gramophone and some records – the Siegfried Idyll, some lieder and dance tunes. A new phase in her life was about to open.

Valentine's autobiography tells a curious tale, and presents a picture of a young woman for whom everything was lived at a pitch of great intensity: it is as if she were endowed with one layer of skin too few. Everything made her suffer, or respond ecstatically. And yet there is a curious passivity about the personality she presents, as if all the dramas happened *to* her, and she had no control over any of the events she relates. The photographs and snapshots of the time tell a similar story. A still, fixed pose: long languid limbs in fine, full-cut shirts and trousers, leather belts and boots, neckties and cigarette holders. It is a glamorous, seductive image, at once posed and frozen. An image from a world of hidden identities, of masks and disguises, a still from a world of 1920s café society of gossip, rotating lovers, assumed lightness of heart and the travail of faithlessness. Valentine at this time seems to have flitted in and out of a society which was the slightly less cosmopolitan equivalent to the world of Natalie Barney and Romaine Brooks in Paris.

She gives little detail of this life, except to say that she got 'into a set . . . which was dominated by Dorothy Warren; it touched the Augustus John–Nina Hamnett set and a theatrical set too, as well as the border lines of some others. It was far above my financial capacity . . . I could only maintain any sort of standing there by being a little drunk all the time.'[30] Judging by Nina Hamnett's autobiography, Valentine was not the only one to be perpetually 'sozzled'.[31] Valentine took a flat in Bloomsbury and there, as she put it,

> I lay with many people. . . . I was naturally more inclined to love women than men; I found deep pleasure, true pleasure and complete satisfaction from making love with women, and less complete pleasure, but still good pleasure, from being made love to by men.[32]

Curiously, the next sentence almost contradicts that last phrase, saying she did not 'ever really and completely make love with men' (the kind of language that reminds one of the adolescent niceties of distinction about sexual practice). By contrast, the account of love-making with women is affirmative and proud. When Valentine was writing her autobiography at the age of forty-three, this was the image of herself as a lover she claimed. Both fulfilment and achievement are present in the description: 'With women I was released and happy, and I gave happiness and pleasure; and I did not need any kind of help from drink to make me feel competent and secure in making love.'[33]

But for most social situations, she did need the support of drink, to become a bit 'tipsy' or 'fuddled', and by the late 1920s she believed that she had become a 'dipsomaniac.'

Dorset offered an escape from the pressure of London and Valentine returned there more and more frequently. It did not stop her drinking but it gave her a more settled pattern. When she drank she would go to the village pub, The Sailor's Return, immortalised in David Garnett's story of that name; she would drink a tankard of brown ale, smoke a pipe of twist tobacco ('with considerable difficulty') and take a little measure of spirits: a reassuring routine, if an unconventional one for the times. Hardly a life of debauchery.

It was a routine that restored her to health and contentment, and the company of the Powys family close by was congenial and encouraging for an aspiring poet. Many other writers were drawn to Chaldon by the magnet of that extraordinary family. Later, Valentine was to be scathing about the intellectuals who came down to the country and then stayed to live the simple life, forgetting that she too had come down to Dorset to escape the racket of London, and stayed under the benign influence of Theodore Powys and his family.

More immediately, Valentine had come to recover after the operation which was to allow Richard to do his Catholic duty: instead of this, she became pregnant by another man in one of her many affairs in London. She was delighted: 'I wanted a daughter; it never occurred to me seriously that it might be a son.'[34] Unfortunately, she slipped down a bank at Chaldon and miscarried, but while she was pregnant she did achieve another ambition – to gain her divorce from Richard. The annulment of their marriage was at last secured from the Church (he was still a practising Catholic), after examination by doctors and 'all the attendant business of bell, book and candle'.[35]

Meanwhile Valentine was living for a large part of the time in Chaldon, mainly on biscuits and Bovril by her account, with sausages and lard-cake for treats. Her income consisted of an allowance of £300 a year from her mother, which she found very little to live on, but which seems to compare favourably with Sylvia's £160 after rent when she started her life in London. (Meanwhile the *average* wage was less than £200 p.a., and nearly three-quarters of the population lived on less than £4 per week.) Valentine spent her time reading widely, seeing the Powys family every day, borrowing books from them, and reading everything from Voltaire and Rousseau to the new American authors, to David Garnett and Sylvia Townsend Warner. At the same time she was writing voraciously. Later, it was to Sylvia that she was to turn for help and critical feedback on the apprentice poems.

Valentine stayed on in Chaldon, in the tiny terraced cottage just below the church, sometimes on her own, sometimes with Bo. She became close friends with the Powyses, and nearly became involved with one of their two sons, both of whom were in love with her. The other writers and artists who lived nearby included Llewellyn Powys and his wife, the writer Alyse Gregory, who were important friends and influences, the novelist and poet Philippa Powys, known as Katie, who also joined the Communist Party later on, and Betty Muntz, a sculptor, who made many drawings of Valentine. Other friends and acquaintances came to stay in East Chaldon too; there was a considerable artistic community.

1.7 Sylvia at Beth-Car, the Powys' home in East Chaldon, 1929

In such circumstances it was inevitable that Valentine and Sylvia should get to know each other well, for they shared a common love for Theodore and Violet Powys, who lived at Beth-Car, an ungainly redbrick villa on the hillside towards the next hamlet of West Chaldon. East Chaldon is a tiny village, its cottages grouped around the green: at one end lies the pub, at the other the church, and in the middle the village store and post office. The writers and intellectuals who stayed there made up a fairly tight-knit group, of which Theodore Powys was the pivot.

Sylvia's *New Yorker* editor, William Maxwell, gives this description of Sylvia's first encounter with Valentine in 1926:

> She kept hearing of a young woman in the village who lived alone and exchanged books with Theodore. . . . She wore trousers, which were not commonly found on young women at that period. Not in Dorset, anyway. And she wrote poetry. [The wearing of trousers seems to have been more remarkable than the writing of poetry.] The meeting was not a success. She felt afterwards that she had seemed aggressively witty and over-talkative, and she noticed that the younger woman was avoiding her.[36]

However, if Valentine's shyness and Sylvia's verbal fireworks made their first meeting somewhat constrained, within three years they had got to know each other quite well. Sylvia, when she saw a cottage she wanted to buy as a retreat from London, suggested to Valentine that she might live there and look after it for her. Valentine's account in her autobiography was that Sylvia acted on an impulse of concern for her: 'I had shown her some poems of mine; very weakly and bad ones, and she had seen good in them, or perhaps seen good in me, and become friendly to me.'[37]

There were already many things that they shared: a common delight in books, and writing poetry, for Sylvia then was as much a poet as she was a novelist, having had two books of poetry published, and three novels. They also shared their love for the Powyses — and especially Violet — and a common sense of humour and zest in deflating pretension and humbug. Many of Sylvia and Valentine's shared moments of laughter and relief in the early stages of their acquaintance occurred when escaping from the pretensions of some of the Chaldon visitors.

1.8 Valentine, the hectic years: Winterton, 1926

1.9 Valentine with her gun, Winterton, 1928

1.10 Valentine with some village boys, Winterton

There was, it seems, so much social life amongst the artistic community that Sylvia and Valentine, soon after they met, were considering how one might evade unwelcome visitors. It might be done, they concluded, in a cottage they had seen, if one were to apply judicious partitioning, a thick stair-carpet and a pair of felt slippers at the ready, as at the door of a mosque. (I would have thought one would need a second staircase, for foolproof evasion.) One such visitor might have been Alyse Gregory who had an earnest (American) cast of mind and liked to engage in Serious Conversations About Modern Art.

Their equally strong attachment to Violet Powys derived from a common recognition of – and exasperated delight in – her husband's eccentricities. They both felt she was sorely tried indeed by the whole Powys clan; there were ten of them altogether, of whom five lived around East Chaldon. To both Sylvia and Valentine, Theodore himself was an exceptional person. Valentine was very much in awe of him. When Theodore said of her husband that he thought Richard was: ' "a very nice young man but not the sort of young man who would get on very well with our country manners", that dissolved, instantly . . . all ties between Richard and me. God had spoken. I cheerfully obeyed.' Valentine had, she said, what they knew as 'Powys mania' very badly; 'everything all of them said was wise and beautiful and true'.[38]

Sylvia and Theodore had been exchanging manuscripts for some time, and she did a great deal to promote his work, recognising *Mr Tasker's Gods* (1924) – T. F. Powys's greatest novel – as a work of genius and persuading David Garnett to take it to Chatto. But she was not overawed by him, and was gratified when he was worsted in conversation, for he was apt to make disputatious and oracular pronouncements. Once he proclaimed he was a Communist, but when one of the other guests said so was he, to Sylvia's delight Theodore was silenced. He also made a fearsome opponent in their games of cricket: she reported that before commencing to bowl he would let rip an almighty roar of WAH! which effectively discountenanced all but the most stout-hearted opponents.

Their conversations about religion must have been curious: Theodore's creative imagination was moulded upon the substance of the Old Testament, the realities of sex, death and a gloomy, avenging patriarchal God. He read the lessons in

Chaldon Church on Sundays in a deep, booming voice, and indeed looked rather like one of the old patriarchs. Sylvia and Tommy Tomlin attended church on her first visit to the village in March 1922, for which occasion Theodore searched for an appropriate passage in the Scriptures about a young lady coming down from London, musing 'Perhaps I may find you in the Apocrypha.'[39]

Sylvia, despite, or perhaps because of, being taught her lessons from the Bible by her mother, was not impressed by the Good Book and used to say that religion was left out of her. She once asked her mother if all Christians were so unpleasant as her Nanny, to which her mother replied scrupulously that not all were. And her view of St Paul's animadversions against women was that he must only have known women church-workers. However, God evidently came into her exchanges with Theo, for in one letter to her he wrote: 'Did the face of God peep up over the high hill . . . if we talk about Him – or Her as you wish it to be – I hope he won't listen.'[40] Perhaps one of her objections to Christianity (or indeed any other formalised religion) was its extraordinary insistence on ascribing the male gender to the Supreme Being; perhaps she was teasing.

When Valentine and Sylvia were both in Chaldon they saw each other quite frequently. They exchanged manuscripts of their work and books, and Sylvia went quite often to Valentine's cottage. In 1930 Sylvia found a cottage in Chaldon and decided to buy it. From then on she and Valentine remained in close touch.

Sylvia was at that time relatively well-off from her earnings. In 1929, Virginia Woolf had recommended that a young woman beginning a career as a writer needed £500 a year and a room of her own: by this reckoning Sylvia was doing quite well. As an author she had made as much as £700 in a single year, the larger part from sales in America where *Lolly Willowes* had been chosen in 1926 as the first book of a new book-of-the-month club. A large part of the money came from royalties, from America and England; and as well as the novels, her books of poems *The Espalier* (1925) and *Time Importuned* (1928) sold well. Nonetheless, buying the cottage stretched her resources – even to equip it cost money and there was none to spare for improvements and alterations. Even so, Sylvia was aware that the change in her financial situation had altered other aspects of her life too.

In response to her suggestion to Valentine that she might occupy the cottage if it were acquired, Sylvia recorded that she received a 'very pretty' letter which was 'too grateful'. She felt that it was the increase in her financial means which altered people's behaviour towards her, so that she felt as if she were the Royal Family. She had only to wag her finger and people were attentive and pleased. But she reflected that it was not that people were mercenary; it was only that they were human beings and so must butter their parsnips.[41]

These fairly hard-nosed reflections show that Sylvia entertained no romantic feelings for Valentine at this point. Indeed, she was busy pursuing an affair with a male lover, and worrying whether she might be pregnant: 'I was incommoded by having to bring on the curse with alternate doses of gin and castor oil. However ... it was an excuse to sit in the backyard.'[42] (The drastic folk-remedy seems to have worked.)

The cottage that Sylvia had set her heart on was a plain, squat building, with a sloping salt-box roof and a large, overgrown garden, approximately one third of an acre in size. It stood opposite The Sailor's Return, and was, the agent advised her, 'a small, undesirable property in an out-of-the-way place with no attractions whatsoever'.[43] I don't suppose one would get an agent to say that of any property today. His recommendation, and the valuation of £65, clinched her mind. By June she heard the cottage was hers for £90. Valentine was kept informed of developments.

The sitting-room was small, with an uneven stone-flagged floor, upstairs half a crooked staircase led to two tiny bedrooms, divided by a thin partition. There was one tap in the small, dark kitchen, giving a trickle of cold water from the rain butt; the main water supply was a well up the street, and the privy was up a long path at the end of the garden. Although it was solidly built, it was a typical rural labourer's cottage, with all the usual disadvantages of lack of sanitation, electricity and mains water, cramped living conditions, little light and less privacy that agricultural labourers had to put up with.[44]

An American friend, Jean Starr Untermeyer described the cottage as:

One of the least promising of dwelling-places. Near the road

1.11 Chaldon Green, East Chaldon. Miss Green's cottage lies out of the picture, on the northern edge of the village (picture taken looking west)

squatted a small boxy structure of yellow stucco, a story and
a half high, with a single chimney pot . . . no thatch . . . no
climbing roses, no leaded casements, none of the country
endearments associated in the literary mind with rural
England.[45]

Which was precisely why Sylvia liked it.

In winter, a cold damp wind blew across the valley, and the
inn sign opposite creaked incessantly in accompaniment; even
so, Jean Untermeyer grew fond of 'Miss Green's cottage', as it
was always known, 'which looked as if it should have been
occupied by the tiniest of witches'.[46] During her stay there in
1934 she also became quite attached to Chaldon's friendly and,
she felt, law-abiding community, even if it did make a deal of
clattering late at night, weaving to and fro from The Sailor's
Return.

In between visits to Chaldon to inspect Miss Green, and
escapes to the country with her lover, Sylvia was back in
London, writing furiously to pay Barker's of Kensington's bill
for all the items Miss Green needed, and working on her long
poem in blank verse about Rebecca, a village woman who had
an overriding passion for gin. Sometimes Valentine drove her
back from Chaldon to London, and visited her while she was
there. She would drive Sylvia to the shops, and gave her a
number of small presents. One Sylvia particularly liked was a
cross-stitch acrostic of Christ in a maple frame, for she loved
embroidery and sewed beautifully herself. (Valentine's Roman
Catholic name was Scholastica, which delighted Sylvia.)

At this time an incident occurred which they both recorded:
it marks the first suggestion of something more complicated
between them than friendship. After one journey, Valentine
went up to Sylvia's flat for a drink. Sylvia went to clear the
wine-glass away after she left, and cut her hand on it. Perturbed
by the incident, she phoned Valentine to find out if she was
alright. Valentine said she was, but had suddenly felt quite
queer.[47] The deeper currents between them momentarily
surfaced here, but it was to be several more months before they
recognised the true nature of their feelings for one another.

Meanwhile, Sylvia remained in London, worrying about
where the money was to come from for Miss Green, for her
earnings varied widely from year to year. (In a letter of 1932

she noted that her biennial Chatto cheque came to £4 3s. 5d.)
She was still composing and was busy 'sewing' a motet. She
thought the Church had lost a great religious poet in her, but
since she was not religious, she had lost a great deal of fun in
the Church, so the loss was even.[48] And to keep the raven at her
door, she knew she would have to, as she said, 'recapture the
Lolly manner, and be light and satirical, and talk of ladies and
gentlemen'.[49] When she tried to do it, she found it so easy that
she 'blushed like a Bennett'.[50] She also considered turning out
her cupboards and selling off manuscripts to raise money, her
anxiety heightened by the price of curtains and the need to
equip Miss Green properly.

Valentine, meanwhile, stayed in lodgings in Chaldon with Bo
and went over each day to Miss Green's to dig the garden:
one of Sylvia's first decisions had been to ordain a potato patch
along the east border. In October Sylvia moved in. Valentine
described how she went down on 4 October, 'with a few
oddments of furniture, and found her there, with a duck
cooking and one large dubious-looking horse-mushroom which
she had picked on the Five Marys that afternoon'.[51] (The Five
Marys is a nearby hill at the end of the lane, with five great
tumuli, which were said to have existed long before the
Romans.)

What followed was to change both women's lives. Much
later, Sylvia and Valentine each gave their versions of this early
October night, Valentine in her autobiography and Sylvia in a
letter to Valentine of 1953. For Sylvia was the product of a
particularly intense moment in Valentine's life. She wrote it
during the crisis in the summer of 1949, when she was poised
between her love for Sylvia, with whom by then she had been
living for 19 years, and the ache of her newer love for Elizabeth
Wade White, an American woman. (She met Elizabeth through
Sylvia in 1936 and they had been lovers for ten years.) It is a
strange account: part literary document, part confessional, part
eulogy of, and plea to, Sylvia, without whom she knew herself
to be lost.

This is Valentine's account of their first week together at
Miss Green's cottage:

> After about a week, during which I had felt shy and tried to
> behave as if I were not, while we were talking through the

partition between our narrow bedrooms I said sadly 'I
sometimes think I am utterly unloved.' And Sylvia thought
she heard heart-break melancholy in my voice, and with that
passionate immediacy of succour, which matches through all
her character . . . she sprang up and came through the
connecting door and fell on her knees by my bed and took
me in her arms.[52]

Sylvia's account was written in a letter to Valentine, which
seems never to have been sent, dated 1953. In it, she also
stresses Valentine's sadness. She felt an overwhelming need to
succour Valentine because she was sad, and described her in
terms reminiscent of the Unicorn as a creature lovely,
mysterious, grieving, alone. It was an impulsive act in Sylvia's
account too, for without considering whether she could
comfort Valentine she ran into her bedroom, and it was not
until she lay in Valentine's arms that she knew that what she
had craved and what she had found was love.

From these two accounts one draws an impression of the
counter-balancing qualities and needs that drew each woman to
each – as Bea Howe, Sylvia's lifelong friend said in her
Foreword to Valentine's autobiography: 'They each had
something to give the other . . . which they alone could give,
and isn't this the base, the keystone, for all enduring human
relationships?'[53]

CHAPTER 2

THE PARTNERSHIP – EARLY YEARS

CHALDON, TO FRANKFORT MANOR, TO CHALDON, TO FROME VAUCHURCH

The love that Sylvia and Valentine discovered on that early October night was to bind them together for the rest of their lives. From 1930, when they pledged to love each other and began their partnership, to 1933, they lived at Miss Green's cottage, Chaldon Herring, or East Chaldon as it is more commonly known. Here the garden was gradually tamed, and many poems written, some of which were later to appear in their joint collection, *Whether a Dove or a Seagull* (1934). Sylvia was writing short stories (one of her finest collections, *The Salutation*, appeared in 1932), and had begun work on her long novel on revolutionary France of 1848. By 1933 she and Valentine were beginning to feel restless and they moved 'for an experiment in larger living' to a seventeenth-century manor house in Valentine's home landscape of Norfolk. Sylvia described it as a 'mouldering grange' and gave a precise description of its curiosities: 'It has a Dutch gable, a drive, two asparagus beds and a trap for visitors – [inside] they are tossed straight into an intact Edwardian long hall, complete with carved oak staircase and c.1900 beams.'[1] Valentine's description was more poetic:

> It was the loveliest small manor house I have ever seen, and our bedrooms had a powder closet, and long low windows with roses all about them; and shoe-rose poppies, tall and romantically pink, growing up to look in at the sitting-room window.[2]

Further descriptions of it appear in the introductory story to

2.1 Frankfort Manor today, from across the lawns

2.2 The façade of Frankfort Manor

another of Sylvia's books, *The Cats Cradle Book*.[3] This gives a detailed and intensely felt evocation of the place; in one of her letters Sylvia expressed the pain she felt on having to leave when they had hoped to settle there: 'The only house I can never be dislodged from was our lovely Frankfort Manor, where we lived for two years and then were forced to be sensible about. I can still turn its door-handles and remember where the squeak came in the passage.'[4]

Sylvia had let Miss Green's cottage when they went to Frankfort Manor to a farmworker, Jim Pitman, and his wife May: clearly Valentine and she were not intending to return, for she would never have given Jim notice to quit. When the experiment of living at Frankfort Manor did not work out, they returned to Chaldon to an even rougher, if slightly more spacious cottage, outside the village in the hamlet of West Chaldon.

Today the house is mellow and golden, the gardens unkempt. You approach it down a curving drive, sheltered by tall chestnut trees, across a lawn. (The trees, said Sylvia, took some mastering.) It is long and low and finely proportioned in shape, with curious twisted chimneys and a fine framed door. It was a large house for just two women and three cats; the grounds, too, are big, about three acres, Valentine estimated. The contrast with Miss Green's cottage could not be more striking, and for a time they must have luxuriated in the sense of spaciousness.

It is an isolated spot: there are no other houses nearby, and the village of Sloley, of which it is part, has a church but no pub or shops. Their life there was quite solitary, apart from, of course, duty visits over to Hill House, Winterton, to see Mrs Ackland. Winterton was rather too close for comfort. Few strangers came to call – and fewer still who offered any real companionship. (The Norfolk people who Sylvia and Valentine respected were the village people, and especially the fishing people, not the 'county' set, for whom neither of them had much time.) They both accomplished a great deal of work: Sylvia was writing her massive novel, *Summer Will Show*, which was published nearly two years after they left Frankfort Manor, and Valentine was working hard at her poems.

For Valentine neither working hard nor being settled with Sylvia in Norfolk, nor, indeed, being out of reach of temptation as far as the pub was concerned, made any difference to her

2.3 Valentine in the doorway of Frankfort Manor, 1933

2.4 Sylvia with one of the kittens at Frankfort Manor

2.5 Sylvia sewing in the hall at Frankfort Manor

drinking problem. At first she was intensely happy at Frankfort Manor, and by her account it was a golden time for both of them. At last she had the opportunity – and the space – for the kind of vigorous outdoor life she loved; Sylvia sighed:

> She has only one request: for more rats to shoot with her rifle. I could almost wish for more rats too, since today, failing other targets, she must needs put three bullets through a fine sleek swelling jargonelle pear, hanging harmlessly on the south wall.[5]

But still, in the evenings, as Valentine worked at her poems, she failed to conquer her demon:

> In my room, with books all round me and working hard at poetry every evening for hours on end, I still fought a constant, and a constantly lost, battle against that accursed habit. After a while I kept a bottle of whisky in my cupboard there, as well as a bottle in the dining-room cupboard.'[6]

Gradually, she became disillusioned with herself and with their life, and yearned for a simpler 'cottage life' again. The size of the house and grounds presented problems too: they could not manage all the work themselves, and had to hire a servant, besides being exhausted with the labour of the garden. They found some of the outdoor work, like managing the pump which was their only source of water, too hard, so they had to hire a man to do the work for them. There was also the pressure of Valentine's mother living so close, and, perhaps the last straw, a murrain that killed off their beloved cats. Sylvia, too, was homesick for Chaldon; possibly it had been Valentine's restlessness and despair about drinking that had precipitated the move to Frankfort in the first place. (However, Sylvia had not bought Miss Green's cottage with the intention of living there permanently, let alone two people making their home there, and it was extremely cramped.)

Their reasons for leaving Frankfort Manor were partly financial but also a combination of a number of other factors – and for Valentine the chief one was the belief that she could only vanquish her demon, drink, if once more she undertook a 'drastic change of place and circumstance'. The clinching blow was that they had been sued in a libel case, and were fairly certain they would lose the action, as indeed they did; the upshot was likely to be costly, too costly to enable them to maintain Frankfort Manor.

What happened was that a number of people in East Chaldon had become concerned at the management of a home in the village for training mentally defective girls, and Llewellyn Powys had circulated a petition against the matron which Sylvia and Valentine had signed, amongst thirty-nine other people. The girls were believed to be treated barbarically and were often to be heard sobbing; tales of how unhappy they were, and how they were treated, abounded. Frequently they ran away, but were only brought back and returned to the home.

Sylvia and Valentine, along with Llewellyn and James Cobb, a local farmer, were the only ones to be sued. Sylvia and Valentine were fined £100 and costs (which, in Llewellyn's case, came to around £570): a large expense on their joint incomes of perhaps £700 a year at this time. The case made a great splash in the *Dorset Evening Echo*, for by this time Llewellyn was ill with TB and had to be wheeled into the courtroom on a stretcher, it was reported; he described an equally dramatic if less terminal mode of transport: 'I am to be carried over the downs in an armchair placed in a dogcart like some . . . Buddha for the populace to bawl after and the seagulls to molest.'[7] (There were no tarred roads to Chydyock where Llewellyn and Alyse Gregory lived.)

By 1935 Sylvia and Valentine were back in Chaldon. They found a larger but fairly primitive stone-built cottage, known simply as 24 West Chaldon, out on the bare hillside called High Chaldon in the hamlet beyond the Powyses' home, Beth-Car. In the winter the ground became a quagmire: the cart-track which passed the house was impassable unless Sylvia threw the morning ashes on it. However, the goat they brought from Frankfort, Victoria Ambrosia, liked her surroundings, and Sylvia wrote that Valentine and she were very happy in their new home. Valentine thought their inaccessible situation would guard her against temptation: 'There . . . right out on the bare side of the hill, it will be difficult to get drink: it will be solitary and sombre and stern.'[8]

It was at 24 West Chaldon that their political involvement in the Communist Party and left-wing causes in general really began. They were to remain there until 1937, when they moved

2.6 Valentine aged 29, West Chaldon

2.7 Valentine at West Chaldon

to a larger house in Lower Frome Vauchurch on the edge of the river Frome, below Maiden Newton. It was intended to be a temporary move but they remained at Frome Vauchurch for the rest of their lives.

WRITING: THE EARLY 1930s

Valentine's first published book was her joint collection of poems with Sylvia, *Whether a Dove or a Seagull*, which appeared in 1934. It is an impressive and interesting collection, a rare example of two poets communicating through their art, although there are also quite strong pieces which stand independent of one another. The *London Mercury*, reviewing it in 1934, found that it was: 'extraordinarily difficult to decide [who are the respective authors of these verses]. There seems to be a strong sense of unity binding together the individual minds . . . an intermingling of identities and imaginations.'[9]

The book was presented without the poems being attributed, and only the curious who hunted up the key at the end of the book would be able to decipher – from the list of page numbers beneath each poet's initials – whose poems were whose. In the Preface, Sylvia and Valentine said that this method of presentation was offered as an experiment, and as a protest against 'the frame of mind which judges a poem by looking to see who wrote it'. They also hoped that the element of contrast from their separate authorship would enhance the readers' pleasure, and afford 'some of the freshness of anonymity'.

In editing Sylvia's *Collected Poems* (1982) Claire Harman excluded the poems from *Whether A Dove or a Seagull*, on the grounds that that book existed on its own terms. The book has never been reprinted and its republication is long overdue. Harman describes it as 'a large and wandering book in which the reader soon loses sight of the grand design';[10] however, there seems to be no evidence that the authors did have any grand design in mind. There are 109 poems in the collection, roughly half by each poet.

The book is important, not because it does have any grand design but because it reveals the interaction and growth of feeling between two writers. It sketches another small part of the history of women's literary and creative partnerships: that they did not repeat the experiment does not detract from the significance of the book. The poems themselves were not written in collaboration: rather the reverse. They represent voice speaking to voice in antiphonal dialogue, each voice separate, distinct, clear-toned. As such they grew out of a shared and mutually creative life together. The project of the book, however, the selection and arrangement of the poems was a collaborative process.

Whether a Dove or a Seagull offers an exciting precedent for women poets to recover, and for that reason, and for the high quality of individual poems, it is high time it was republished. While women poets may often lie together within the promiscuity of anthology covers, there is rarely any creative exchange within this closeness; there is juxtaposition but little fruitful dialogue. In this book, however, the voices of the two women speak to, slide past, touch upon, and explore the shifting growth of feeling in their relationship. In a remarkable sequence of lyrics, Valentine, in what were for her some of her earliest poems that she was willing to stand by, explored aspects of her love for Sylvia. Sylvia, too, wrote more directly from her feelings in some of these than in any other of her published poems.

Later on Valentine was to look back critically on some of this work, as she struggled to engage her craft as a poet with her beliefs as a Communist. A year after the book appeared she wrote to their friend and comrade, Julius Lipton, that the poems were:

> written as my first efforts . . . while I was under the influence
> of first happiness which could not but evoke a profound
> anticipation of terror to come – war, destruction. . . . I had in
> fact, only isolation . . . this made for a solitary mood . . . but
> it was indeed the only truthful mood to portray.[11]

But if the poems are apprentice-work, they are nonetheless remarkable in their freshness of feeling and their direct, clear evocation of complex mental states, and momentary physical realities. The voice of the love lyrics modulates as it mediates between the tough but fragile, because evanescent, moments of heightened existence that go to make up the poet's awareness, between pain and rapture. At one moment this voice presents an almost prosaic, melancholy clarity, recording and setting the scene in such a way that, almost imperceptibly, elements shift.

Another poem shows her quality of rapt attention to creation – 'Why does the bird rap on our window?'[12] She describes it as 'A small bird, hard-beaked and yellow-breasted . . . a small tidy bird . . . rapping authoritatively on the glass', and in the last stanza speculates on the nature of the bird's impatient summons, 'Rapping as sharply as an angry heart.' It is a powerfully appropriate and disturbing image, which recalls Emily Brontë in its violent yoking of the human and natural worlds. Brontë is the poet who first comes to mind in some of the best of these poems, but in her sequence of love lyrics Valentine inhabits the persona of the lover in a passionate, direct and at once elusive manner that is freed from the constriction/construction of the female self. The poetic voice moves between the open eroticism of:

> The eyes of body, being blindfold by night,
> Refer to the eyes of mind. . . .
>
> Thus and by these ordered ways
> I come at you – Hand deft and delicate
> To trace the suavely laid and intricate
> Route of your body's maze
>
> . . . seize with more than sight
> Your moonlit meadows and your shadowed night[13]

and the pleadingly casual inflection of:

> Don't go out alone on a night like this,
> I can't bear that you should go.
> The wind winds and curls across the crouching snow . . .[14]

The poems move between the enigmatic imagery of 'Whether a dove or a seagull lighted there' and the beautiful, calm resolution of 'Beneath this roof tree':

> And those words you said
> Drew toweringly
> The leaved green to spread
> Quietly and blessedly
> Above our bed.[15]

Perhaps here is the bonus of a lesbian identity for a woman poet, in that it may be a means to freeing the self into a range of possible modes of address in the love-poem. For Valentine, there seems to have been no need to have recourse to mythology in her writing, no use of masks or any other disguises, in contrast to her life.[16] The openness of that engagement with her 'subject' does not imply simplicity of feeling. Only the inattentive reader will be lulled into the belief that her writing is straightforward. Neither Sylvia nor Valentine were affected by the currents of modernism which swept around the literary world in the twenties and thirties, but Valentine's achievement in this sequence is to render dramatically, from one lyric to the next, the shifting states of the lover's being.

In almost all the poems, her voice is the active one: she is both the wooer and the speaker. She brings about, participates in, recoils from, broods over, the moments of their encounters, the anticipations and the partings. As protagonist, the 'I' of the poems, pleads, persuades, cajoles, sympathises, laments, celebrates, utters her longing, diminishes distance and recreates it; unites her to the beloved and in imagination destroys her unity, suffering the hand of time. This little world is indeed her everywhere – but in the fluctuating of her will and active, desiring self against the buffets of the world beyond, the reader is reminded how little, how fragile are these intimate worlds and intimate selves on which we so deeply depend, how cradled and impressed on by that larger social and material world.

It was to that larger world that Valentine, while a Communist Party member, came to owe her allegiance, and to which she assiduously devoted her craft over the next half decade.

It is interesting to compare the treatment of erotic love and desire by other bisexual and lesbian poets. For H.D., for example – a far greater poet than Valentine, and one thoroughly immersed in contemporary European modernism, love was always an imminent haunting to be structured in myth and spoken through the forms of the gods and goddesses, concealed by palimpsest. By contrast, Valentine's reading, formed to a large extent by her friendship with Bo who introduced her to the (English) 'moderns' – to Huxley and Eliot and Lawrence and Powys – and later by the resources of

Theodore Powys' and Sylvia's libraries, left her content to employ traditional modes of address and imagery. She read an immensity of poetry, she said in her autobiography, and various new American authors, but apparently did not feel the need to experiment aesthetically. *Whether a Dove* gives ample testimony of her gifts within the range of the traditional love lyric:

> Is the hawk as tender
> To the belly of its prey –
> White belly wet with dew –
> As I am to you,
> In the same way,
> My slender?[17]

For Sylvia, the early thirties were a productive if not particularly financially rewarding time. While Valentine worked at poetry Sylvia was involved in a number of writing projects. Occasionally she produced reviews or literary profiles for periodicals, such as a piece on Pope for *The New Statesman*. One of her short stories, 'Stay Corydon', was chosen for the 'Best Short Stories' of 1930. A collection of three stories was published by Furnival Press with a forward by T. F. Powys, and a larger collection by Chatto & Windus, *The Salutation*, in 1932.

The Salutation contained some older pieces, such as 'Elinor Barley', the tale of a condemned wife who murdered her idle, drunken lout of a husband, in which Sylvia was continuing the exploration of narrative form which she had begun in her third novel *The True Heart* (1929). The title piece is a sustained novella of an elderly Mexican widow of an Englishman and her relationship with an equally elderly English wanderer who turns up on her ranch in Mexico. Through this situation, Sylvia makes a poignant study of loneliness and disappointment. It is a marvellously realised and evocative piece, and, as with *Mr Fortune's Maggot* the exotic scenery is delicately and convincingly created. The heat, the dust, the slow passing of time in which the dogs barking or the coming of the afternoon cup of chocolate at the end of the siesta are notable events, the emptiness, all are protagonists in the drama: against the sense of slow time and space the human characters appear small, at the wrong end of the telescope.

The other project which preoccupied Sylvia for many months was writing what she called her 'truthful pastoral in the jog-trot English couplet'. *Opus 7*, as it came to be called, was an attempt to 'do for this date what Crabbe had done for his'. It was the realism, and the unerring humour, wit and compassion of Crabbe's judgment that she admired. The main character of this long poem, set in the time of the Napoleonic wars, is a poor old village woman, Rebecca, who discovers that she has a gift: she is green-fingered and the flowers she raises in her cottage garden begin to attract attention – customers come to her garden to buy her posies. But there is nothing sentimental about this portrait. All the money Rebecca gets from her flowers she devotes with ardour and single-minded dedication to her one passion in life: gin. The poem recreates both the hardship – and meanness – of village life, the sensuous beauty of the flowers, and the detailed experience of intoxication. Rebecca is no mere toper: she is a high priestess of the art of drinking, of every stage of preparation, guardianship, conservation, presentation – a hieratic sequence in which consumption plays only a minor, final part.

Opus 7 was published in 1931 by Dolphin Books, a Chatto venture which included amongst their other titles books by Aldous Huxley, Richard Aldington, T. F. Powys, Samuel Beckett and Norman Douglas. Sylvia's reputation as an important modern writer was established by this time, as a poet equally as a novelist and short-story writer.

She was featured in 1931 in a book called *Writers at Work* by Louise Morgan, also published by Dolphin Books. The book is chiefly interesting for the accounts Sylvia gives of her likes and dislikes at this time (an even more categoric list appeared much later in answer to a request for information on her likes and dislikes: likes were listed as: 'Cats – Owls – Purcell – Eccentrics'; dislikes as 'Irish Stew – Hygiene – Exterminators of wild animals and wild flowers – People who cut down trees'[18]). For example, the gramophone is 'a useful little instrument like a potato-peeler'. The wireless, on the other hand, is a 'cheat', 'so damned God-like'.

Sylvia did not often go to the theatre or to see films, but she liked painting and architecture. She also particularly enjoyed what she called 'ordinary people – the kind you meet in the street and see in buses'. (During the abdication crisis in 1936 she commented in a letter that she wished she were in London and could hear what people were saying about it all on the buses.) She loved people like her London 'char', as she called her, Mrs Keates, for whom she had a great respect, and late in her life, Mrs Cleall, another Londoner, who helped take care of her when she was old, and who was a refreshing source of humour and stories.

Of the characters in her fiction, Sylvia said that you could look them all up in Bradshaw, 'where you find all the very slow country trains that stop at every junction. Ordinary people and the adventures of the everyday are much the most interesting.' This response may have been prompted by a wish to put her heroine, Lolly Willowes, into perspective, for Sylvia was rather dogged by her reputation as a creator of witches. A life of Mrs Beeton, on the other hand, would, she thought, be enthralling.

The list of authors she admired is eclectic. It includes Hopkins and Crabbe amongst the poets, and T.F. Powys (who was to her the most important writer of the time), Lawrence, Hemingway and Richardson amongst the novelists. Sylvia read and re-read *Clarissa* many times. The difference between writing fiction and writing poetry, she maintained, is that when you are writing prose you see how much you can get out of a subject, whereas when you are writing poetry you see how far you can get into it: a lucid distinction. The two require quite different techniques, and have to be written at different times. Whatever she was writing, she said it was probably true that she wrote as a composer still – 'I must get the shape first, before the actions or words', a view of her craft that she was to hold to all her life.

Sylvia's poetry in the early thirties consisted most importantly of *Opus 7*, and the poems she contributed to *Whether A Dove or a Seagull*. These were the last collections of poems she was to publish for over twenty years.

There are some stepping-points in *Whether a Dove*, some junctures between her own voice and Valentine's, where she experimented with a simplicity and directness of address that was new in her work. For example:

> 'I, so wary of traps
> So skilful to outwit
> Springes and pitfalls set
> Am caught now, perhaps.'[19]

Late in life she was to say, 'Wit has been my enemy'; less frequently than in some of the short stories, but still occasionally, the bravura display of her poetic and musical craft makes one long for a little less skill, a little more heart.

In *Whether a Dove or a Seagull*, once again one can see how steeped Sylvia was in the traditional English pastoral and lyric tradition. Amongst several possible examples, the long poem about Granny Moxon, a Chaldon character reputed to be a witch and highly esteemed by both Valentine and Sylvia (and whose death was one of the factors which detached them from East Chaldon in 1933 when they moved to Frankfort Manor), draws upon the Wordsworth of *Lyrical Ballads*, of 'Resolution and Independence' and 'Michael'. For example, at one point she compares the old woman digging her garden to the thorn trees:

> . . . at one
> With them seemed she, wrathful and resolute,
> As though her root
> Went deep as theirs into the ground and thence
> Sucked like a harsh sap the will to be . . . [20]

Another example, 'Swift at Moor-Park', reveals her ability to project herself into other times, places and characters. In poetry the act of self-dispossession she makes is the more complete because the language itself is shaped by it, which does not happen in her 'historical' novels: in prose the mode of writing remains contemporary, however distant the time:

> Whole-summer-long, the summer day
> In a dull dusk consumes away.
> Time looks these full-grown trees among . . .
> Time is too heavy for the young.
>
> . . .
>
> There go the fools, the vile, the dead!
> While I these gout-foot alleys tread,
> Where all day long my fancies twirl
> Between green fruit and a green girl.[21]

In the poems which speak directly to the lover, which are part of a continuing dialogue between the two lovers, the poetic technique is subdued to a great urgency of purpose:

> You can come to me if you choose
> But I to you
> Cannot, nor would, draw near –
> You'll need to use
> All of your root-steel strength to get you through.[22]

Besides the poems, many of which were published in literary reviews and periodicals, Sylvia completed the first draft of *Summer Will Show* during the early 1930s; she had started writing the long novel about the Paris Revolution of 1848, and the experiences of an English heiress caught up in it, in 1932.[23] There were also other short stories, some of which were collected in a volume called *More Joy in Heaven*, published again by Chatto, in 1935.

For the first three years of their partnership, Sylvia and Valentine were absorbed in their lives together. Each worked hard at her own sphere of writing, and it was clearly a stimulating and exciting time for both women, despite Valentine's anxieties. However, even while they were living out the idyll of Frankfort Manor, the changing forces in Europe were beginning to affect writers like themselves. To sketch in the background here very briefly, the Fascists had been in power in Italy under Mussolini since 1926. In January 1933, Hitler seized power as Chancellor of Germany, his party having previously won a majority in the July 1932 elections. The repressions and pogroms, the burning of books and destruction of civil liberties that led to the concentration camps, had begun. By Autumn 1933, British writers were so concerned at the spread of Fascist ideas at home and in Europe that they were setting up a group (the first of many) called 'Writers Against Fascism and for Collective Security'. This was Storm Jameson's initiative, and amongst the other well-known writers she enlisted were Lord David Cecil, Rose Macaulay, and Rebecca West.

Soon writers could no longer ignore what was happening across the Channel. Already there was a remarkable contrast in feeling amongst intellectuals and writers to that which had prevailed after the First World War, and the contrast for those who remembered (as Sylvia did) the halcyon pre-war days was even more marked: 'We were', wrote Storm Jameson, 'in the position of never having known anything about war, and so never having feared, indeed fearing nothing.'[24]

Moreover, hunger and unemployment were growing at home. Within a year the lives of Sylvia and Valentine were to change radically.

JOINING THE STRUGGLE: DORSET AND THE COMMUNIST PARTY

From the evidence of their early lives, neither Sylvia nor Valentine would seem to have been obvious candidates for membership of the Communist Party. There was no tradition of political involvement in either of their families. There is nothing in Valentine's autobiography that indicates any concern with social and political issues: the fact that Bo was a Tory party speaker was apparently as incidental to Valentine as her own canvassing for that Party. (Valentine had taken up canvassing, she said, because she had nothing to do for a few months. It was an appropriate occupation for someone of her class and background. At the time, she was planning to leave England for Java, to marry a young man she had not seen since she was a child.)

Sylvia had rather more experience of political realities. Her experience in a factory as a relief munitions worker during the war, stamping out metal cases for shells, had given her first-hand experiences of work-place conditions. At the same time it fuelled her indignation against them, and gave her a sharp sense of fellow-feeling with the work-force, as her 1916 article makes clear. She was also involved in helping to organise a scheme to help house Belgian refugees, about which she wrote humorously later on for the *New Yorker*. One account tells of how she scandalised the good burghers of Harrow by bringing home a rowdy docker's family, who thieved the milk from the doorsteps; more seriously, she deplored the awful cattle-market atmosphere, in which 'nice' looking families were easily adopted, while the less socially appealing were left to the bottom of the pile.

Writing later about the munitions factory, Sylvia pointed out that the scheme under which she went to work was:

a 'dilution' scheme, devised to avoid the payment of overtime to the regular workers. I am ashamed of an ignorance that made me a blackleg: on the other hand I am glad to have worked, even for a little time, in a factory. The conditions were bad, there was an incessant shortage of small tools, there was no canteen, and the sanitation was an outrage. . . . Women of the leisured class [had] a rapid training and then worked at weekends in order to relieve the regular hands. . . . The leaflet of information . . . said, 'Low-heeled shoes are advisable and evening dress is not necessary.'[25]

The article she had originally written about the scheme for *Blackwoods Magazine* in 1916 was sharp-eyed, though less politically aware. She was paid sixteen guineas for it. In the 1939 article Sylvia pointed to the disparity between this fee and the workers' wages: the eight-hour shift in the factory paid six shillings, including the bonus. (She also described how in 1916 a newspaper had asked her for a further article to expand upon the poor conditions of the munitions workers, saying they were sure they need not offer her payment since it was to help to improve the workers' lot. She retorted it would not better the condition of the workers to write commissioned articles for nothing: 'They saw the force of this and paid.')

Hard-headedness about money, and her realisation that as an upper-class woman she was 'presumably subsidized but unpayable', were to remain central features of her outlook as a writer for the rest of her life: they provide an illuminating pointer towards one basis of her Marxism. For example, she wrote to Arnold Rattenbury in 1944 complaining, 'I wish more writers would remember to put in the circumstances of their economics. It might help to dissipate this notion that we sing like birds and pick up a few worms.'[26] Not for the first time, a bourgeois woman discovered that she need not be useless and dependent on others for her bread if she could wield a pen.

For both Sylvia and Valentine, the path towards political involvement was one which wound its way forward with the developing events in Britain and Europe through the thirties: but most particularly, it was the lengthening shadow cast by events in Germany that came to dominate their consciousnesses.

In *The Theory and Practice of Socialism*, published by

Gollancz and the Left Book Club in 1936, John Strachey had written:

> Ever-increasing numbers of relatively well-circumstanced men and women are now finding themselves impelled to examine the basis of contemporary society. . . . They cannot lead lives which yield them no mental or physical satisfaction in the existing world. Over us all . . . there now hangs the prospect of war.[27]

For Sylvia and Valentine, the process of examination seems to have begun in 1933, with the trumped-up charges of the Reichstag Fire Trial in Germany, and the subsequent imprisonment of the Bulgarian Communist, Georgi Dimitrov, and the German Communist leader, Ernst Thaelmann. A copy of Dimitrov's *Letters*[28] remained in their library at Frome Vauchurch, and when Sylvia was interviewed in 1981, she recalled the impression he had made on her, and the factors that had most influenced her politically at that time:

> What influenced me . . . and almost all the people of my generation more than anything was the Reichstag Fire Trial. Extraordinary courage and enterprise and *poise* of Dimitrov. And that was very well-reported in *The Times* and made me interested in contemporary politics. And that of course made me immediately interested in the doings of the Black Shirts (sic) and *that's* how I came to meet the people in *Left Review* and eventually to do some writing.'[29]

The Reichstag Fire Trial which first caught Sylvia's attention lasted throughout 1933. Of the men who were charged with setting fire to the Reichstag, both Dimitrov and Thaelmann were eventually acquitted of a trumped-up charge and freed in 1934, after considerable international pressure (including intervention on Dimitrov's behalf by Amabel Williams Ellis, one of the founding editors of *Left Review*.)

Meanwhile, the Fascists in Britain were claiming a membership of 20,000 in Sir Oswald Mosley's Blackshirt army. In June 1934 they staged a huge rally at Olympia, and the stewards brutally attacked any critics or people they suspected of being unsympathetic. Although many people were appalled by their behaviour (Virginia Woolf later wrote in the *Daily Worker* that the events at Olympia and the Jarrow March were the decisive factors in persuading very many people of the need for a Popular Front in Britain), the government refused to ban the Fascist marches and meetings. The Labour Party executive denounced any opposition to the Fascists on the grounds that it gave them the publicity they sought; a familiar argument. Labour Party members were prohibited from co-operating with demonstrations led by Communists or Independent Labour Party activists, while the police actively protected the Fascists, and attacked the left-wing opposition. It became quite clear that the only real resistance to Fascism in Britain would have to come from the revolutionary, as opposed to the constitutional, left. The combined fears of Fascism and of the Hitler–Mussolini pact signed in 1934 spurred many people to join the Peace Pledge Union, and to sign the nationwide petition that a clergyman, Dick Shepherd, launched in October of that year.

Meanwhile, there was another shadow darkening Britain: unemployment, which had stood at 1.6 million in 1932, was still rising. The Ramsay MacDonald Government had no solutions, except to attack unemployed assistance via the hated means tests. The Fascists were able to make political capital out of the situation, playing upon people's fears of being out of work and the Government's failure to react. By January 1935 the Government had introduced a punitive act to deal with the unemployed. The Public Assistance Boards were centralised, payments were slashed to two shillings per week – well below starvation rate – labour camps for unemployed men were set up and so-called 'industrial schools' created for the jobless under-18-year-olds.

It was against this background of increasing despair and hopelessness in the political situation at home and in Europe that Sylvia and Valentine took the decision to join the Communist Party, some time between late 1934 and early 1935. It was, said Sylvia later, the only party that appeared to be doing anything.

One of the first hallmarks of their new commitment was the scrapbook they compiled from early 1935, documenting the struggles and tragedies of the time.[30] They had always read the newspapers widely; now they made an almost daily record of cuttings about the issues of the moment from a wide range of newspapers. Many of these deal with tragedies arising from families being out of work: broken marriages, drunkenness, wife-beating, petty crimes, suicides; many of them deal with the brutalities and spread of Fascism. The battered red cloth-bound book, with its red and black lettered index, scrupulously filed in Valentine's small, cramped handwriting, shows entries ranging from the Army, Agriculture, Armaments, Air Force and Atheism to Water, Wages and Women. Most of the early entries are by Valentine, and agricultural problems and local issues predominate. Later on, many are headed in Sylvia's handwriting, and an extra index in her writing gives as many as twenty-four entries for Children, with others for Spain and Portugal.

A typical page has cuttings about Jewish-Christian fighting in Rumania, a man sent to gaol for caricaturing Hitler in Poland, the setting-up of a legislative council for Palestine, the details of the anti-Jewish laws in Germany which deprived Jewish people of their citizenship and all their rights, orders for armaments in Abyssinia placed with a British armaments firm, the banning of British newspapers in Italy, the establishment of Fascism in Lithuania. 'Lighter' entries include one about Stalin greeting the women 'shock-workers' from the collective farms: 'Women of Russia we have set you on your feet and freed you from the bondage of husband and father. Today you work and honour yourselves as workers, for today you work for yourselves, free and independent.' (This piece of news was almost certainly a perfectly serious entry.) Another is about a law introduced in France to prevent a French woman in the Diplomatic Corps from ever becoming, heaven forfend, ambassador (one presumptuous female had risen in its ranks meteorically until The Law awoke). The next page has items with headings such as 'Weeping Mother on Murder Charge', 'Widow's Plight', 'No Desire to Love', all pointing up the human tragedies behind unemployment and starvation.

The newspaper cuttings also show the other side of the coin, the continuing lifestyle of the rich, which ensured that Fascism was left alone by the British Government, mindful of the interests of the class which the Government represented. On page 100 of the scrapbook, for example, there are two items from the *Daily Express*, 'The King is Richer than His Father', and 'Robes for Coronation Will Cost £160,000'. ('Robes cost £85 each; coronets a mere £18. Those coronets have set a pretty problem for young peeresses. They are made to fix in coiled-up hair. Bobbed or shingled hair will not keep them in place.') These, and an item on surtax, are juxtaposed with a *News of the World* 'special' on the ages of the unemployed (43 per cent under 35), another on 'Life on 3/2 a week. . . . Expert says 4/- a week is inadequate' ('there are nearly 5,000,000 in this country who can only spend 4/- a week each on food'), and two more items: 'Hero in a Pauper's Grave', 'Deserted the Army to Help his Family'.

For the scrapbook, Valentine and Sylvia had combed papers from the right-wing, left-wing and local Press, but about events in Germany by 1936 a notable silence had fallen over all but the left-wing Press. This contrasted sharply with the early reporting of events there by *The Times*, which Sylvia had found so informative. The 'sinister silence', which Leonard Woolf recalls in his autobiography,[31] was no accident: the British Establishment did not want people to know the facts as they got worse, and to draw the inevitable, and with hindsight, correct conclusions. One example of that silence was when Charles Morgan, then drama critic of *The Times*, tried to alert his readers to the dangerous atmosphere he had found at Oberammagau: the paper did not publish his review. Only the *News Chronicle*, the *Daily Herald*, the *Daily Worker* and *Reynolds News*, (with the *New Statesman* and *Time and Tide* amongst the periodicals) continued to report in any detail what was happening in Germany – and what the German and Italian troops were doing in Spain between 1936 and 1939.

As historians have since revealed, a large section of the British aristocracy, industry and the Establishment, including the Foreign Office and the Bank of England, colluded with Fascism in silence, primarily because of their fear of the Soviet Union. But, of course, for all those on the Left – not just members of the Communist Party – the Soviet Union represented the only force for progress, a shining light in a violent and darkening world. They did not see the mirror processes of authoritarianism at work in their Utopia, and when they were awakened to the political reality of that country's emergence from barbarism, they felt themselves the more betrayed. Sylvia, however, was one of those who never did feel betrayed. She wrote, for example, in her autobiographical article for *The Countryman*, that the gains the Soviet Union had made in agriculture were gains for the British worker too:

I have realised that the essential thing in gardens is the soil, and that the soil from which these people grow [i.e., her neighbours], the conditions which deform their lives, are more than Britain and the decay of British agriculture.[32]

Prominent in the library at Frome Vauchurch were the foreign novels in translation, particularly Russian novels, that told of such new and hopeful developments; novels that Valentine would meticulously grade and lend out to these same neighbours, who had, said Sylvia, more knowledge of what went on in other countries than they had in their own. At the same time, Valentine and Sylvia took periodicals like *Russia in Construction*, which showed through photographic images the processes of technological transformation in that country with the flair and excitement of an Eisenstein. And Valentine procured enough source material from the Russian Trade Delegation to write three articles on Russian Agriculture, which were published by the Communist Party's agit-prop, or publicity, department. (According to Sylvia the department seems to have performed the task with all too familiar incompetence. She wrote complaining about this privately to other comrades. Unfortunately, the articles have vanished without trace.)

From early 1935 until they left for the United States in spring 1939, when Sylvia was to attend a conference of writers in New York, Sylvia and Valentine were involved as Communist Party members in the practical day-to-day struggle for an alternative to those 'conditions which deform [people's] lives', an alternative to the unjust and arbitrary workings of capitalism. At that time, although it numbered only about 7,000 card-carrying members, the influence of the Communist Party of Great Britain (CPGB) was growing rapidly. (From 2,500 members in 1930, it rose to 17,500 by the outbreak of the war, and by a massive leap to 56,000 at the time of the German invasion of the Soviet Union in 1941.) Since the days of the isolationist policy of the late 1920s, when the Communist Party had seen trade union movements and labour parties only as examples of how the people were misled by reformists (the days of what was called 'social fascism'), the CPGB had already moved towards a policy of co-operation and of seeking to work within the broad labour movement. It was, in effect, already pursuing a policy of the Popular or People's Front for two to three years before this policy was formally approved by the Comintern in Moscow, at the Seventh Congress of July 1935.

Although working with the Communists was impossible for many of the liberal intelligentsia, for others like Amabel Williams Ellis it was essential. To still others, the path 'Forward From Liberalism',[33] led directly to membership of the CPGB. For some of them, like Cecil Day Lewis, their membership came as an almost religious experience, as he describes in his autobiography *Buried Day*, and as an escape from the intolerable burden of selfhood. Perhaps it did have something of this quality for Valentine, who was at heart deeply religious, but for Sylvia, once her sense of injustice had been aroused it seems more likely that she implacably pursued the arguments to their logical conclusion. Comrades who knew them both in Dorset in the late 1930s, where they were the leading Party members in the area, turned to Sylvia for guidance and saw her as the natural leader. Valentine was always quiet and reserved, but Sylvia would talk to, and argue with, anyone.

For Sylvia, as for Margot Heinemann, another middle-class recruit, the Party (as it was, and still is, always called by members) was the obvious place to be if one wished to change conditions and to fight Fascism. For Margot Heinemann, it was the experience of the hunger marchers who came through Cambridge in 1934 when she was a student, and of visiting the South Wales coalfield during the strike and seeing the conditions there, that drove her into the Communist Party. 'We came in because we were activists. . . . The Party was fighting Fascism: no one else was. The Party was fighting unemployment: no one else was.'[34]

Sylvia wrote in 1939: 'I still amass a solid fury at the conditions [my neighbours] have to endure'[35] – and many of her pieces of political journalism and letters to national newspapers at this time were ones in which she wielded her 'pen as a sword'.[36] Such considerations must surely have lain behind the decision to join the most class-conscious and best-organised section of the workers. In Sylvia's novel *Summer Will Show* (1936), the heroine Sophia rejects, quickly and decisively, the romantic posturings of the revolutionaries who gather round her friend Minna in the Paris revolution of 1848. Sophia is moved by the obdurate analysis of the Communists alone, their calm appraisal of the realities of the political situation and their resolute preparedness to act. There seems to be more than a little of her creator in Sophia.

There is little doubt that the united international force of Communism, and the growing power of the Soviet Union in particular, were important contributory factors in Sylvia and Valentine's decisions to join the Party. Until André Gide delivered his critical account of the Soviet Union at the Madrid writers' conference in July 1937, to the consternation of Communists and sympathisers in many countries, the dissenting voices on the Left were few compared with those who, like the Webbs or Amabel Williams Ellis, had been there and had come away impressed. (Even after the war, J. B. Priestley visiting Moscow for a performance of a play of his, gave the Muscovites the ultimate accolade of being as good as Yorkshiremen.) And despite Gide, and voices like his that were increasingly beginning to be heard, many people outside the Soviet Union thought that the famous Treason Trials of 1936–7 were bringing enemies of the State to book. (This belief was fed by the experience of Trotskyism and Anarchism in Spain, but also, of course, by the belief that the ends justified the means where what was seen as 'objectively counter-revolutionary activity' was concerned.)

The Communist Party, although possessing significant strength in the British trade unions and having powerful allies in the developed Communist parties of Europe as well as in the growing might of the Soviet Union, nevertheless possessed little direct power in Britain, and practically none electorally. It exerted its influence through the policy of the Popular Front, or as historians now call it, the People's Front, for the Popular Front never became truly 'popular' in Britain as it did in Spain and France, where Popular Front Governments were elected. Most of the activities with which Sylvia and Valentine were associated in the 1930s through the CP were in progressive movements, such as the Dorset Peace Council; or they were involved with trying to improve the conditions of the labourers locally, in what today would be called by the Communist Party the 'broad-democratic alliance', and by its opponents, 'Communist-infiltrated' groups or Communist-fronts.

THE STRUGGLE IN DORSET

There were many different kinds of work which were directed towards building as broad a base as possible to win support for the hearts and minds of the people in the fight against Fascism and for socialism. This involved Party members working in a variety of organisations and in their neighbourhoods: militancy began at the parish pump. It is apparent from their letters of the time to comrades and friends that Valentine and Sylvia entered with zest into all the work. The first time that Jim Fyrth and his brother Patrick remember meeting Sylvia, for example, she and Valentine were selling the *Daily Worker* outside the huge Peace Rally that was being held in the ancient amphitheatre at Dorchester, at which Vera Brittain, George Lansbury and the Revd Dick Shepherd spoke. Vera Brittain recorded in her autobiography that she was so nervous at the illustrious company and the huge audience she became quite tongue-tied.[37]

Very few examples of the letters describing their political activities in the thirties found their way into William Maxwell's selection of Sylvia's letters. This is the more surprising since Sylvia did not ever turn her back on those years of hectic activity and commitment. She remained a left-wing supporter to the end of her life, unlike some of her male literary comrades and fellow-travellers, who sought later in their memoirs not merely to exonerate themselves from their youthful political aberrations but also to abuse their past alliances. In a letter of 1970 to Arnold Rattenbury, Sylvia wrote: 'This house has the accumulation of 39 years of Valentine's wide range of interests. Today I found a handhorn which says Cuckoo. We used it to vex plain-clothes policemen in the dear thirties.'[38]

Political life in Dorset itself had a surprisingly wide and varied face. One of the most enjoyable snooks Sylvia and Valentine cocked at the face of Toryism and the Church (the entrenched powers of the English countryside then as now), was to organise village hops. Valentine wrote to Julius Lipton:

We found the Jubilee[39] such a success here. . . . Sylvia and I went about spreading dislike of the parson and got him boycotted by the people. . . . Tom Wintringham[40] was here for the party we got going. . . . Now the village is determined

2.8 Sylvia and Valentine with Julius Lipton

to run its own pleasures, without any interference from the gentry, and there's to be another party after the harvest is in, and more during the winter. AND NO INTERFERENCE will be tolerated.

Consider what a great, earth-shaking affair to these people who have never, within memory, done anything by themselves, for themselves.[41]

Deference and fear held the agricultural workers in check, as much as low wages, long hours and isolation. Not only isolation from other villages and towns, but isolation within communities, particularly between men and women. Writing again to Julius and Queenie Lipton, Sylvia explained in detail how they organised their social occasions:

Our essential is that we have a band. . . . We spend no money whatsoever on decorating the room, which is hideous. And we strew two or three packets of soapflakes on the wooden boards, for a dancing surface. Food is penny glasses of lemonade, twopenny cakes and sandwiches. . . . Children come too. It is a shame for mothers who would like to dance to have to stop at home with the children, and we have infants of five and six dancing till midnight and none the worse for it next day. We wear our ordinary day clothes of course, and are very hot and happy.

But I do strongly stress the importance of a band. Wireless is so unadaptable.'[42]

No creches then of course, and the social focus of village life, which again has not changed, was The Sailor's Return, which was largely the men's preserve – with notable exceptions, such as the village character, old Granny Moxon. Sometimes they would discuss politics but mostly the evenings passed in singing, talking and drinking; the women did not share in the life of the pub.

Villagers today do not recall there being a great deal of discontent in the thirties, although life was hard. They were used to it. It took the sensibilities and the eye of an outsider to register the appalling conditions of their cottages, the exploitation of their long hours of labour, the scandal of the low wages, and the lack of any decent health care or transport to school for the children and so forth. All these things the Chaldon people put up with, though they might grumble about the 'buggyness' or running damp in a cottage. Talking of those times today, they seem almost to relish them, to take pride in what they endured, now that their lives are undeniably better in many respects.

Relatively, however, their position has not changed; and in a couple of ways has worsened. There are no longer cottages to rent in the village, and local people cannot possibly afford to buy cottages that sell at inflated prices as snug retreats for Londoners and other metropolitan visitors. Secondly, even the old van transport that used to run in the thirties no longer exists to connect Chaldon to the outside world. If you haven't a car you must whistle for it, or beg a lift from a neighbour, unless you can walk the three odd miles to the main road.

One possible explanation of the lack of discontent in villages like Chaldon, apart from the deeply rooted traditions of deference based in such a static society (the only changes an agricultural worker was likely to experience was if he changed his job, was sacked or left for some other reason), is that life was *not* so bad in the country in the thirties in southern England as it was, for example, in South Wales or the industrial North East.

Although more farms were being put down to grass and cereal crops, with a consequent loss of jobs associated with stock (Sylvia's letter of December 1984 to Llewellyn Powys reports an 'improving' type of farmer who had just moved into the village: 'We shall put it all down to grass', [the farmer's wife] said grandly. I thought of the whispering barley on the way to Chydyock, and of the silent men working in those fields.'[43]), there was still a variety of work available – hedging, ditching, labouring, or working as a cowman or shepherd. And although wages were low and food not particularly plentiful, vegetables could be grown.

Rabbits were another main supplement to their diets, of which Dorset's chalky escarpments and deep valleys possess – depending on your point of view – a paradisal or pestilential richness. Valentine, who was a very good shot, took pride in getting rabbits for their guests' suppers, and later on, fish from the River Frome. And Georgy Goat's van, which did the twice weekly run to Dorchester (some six miles distant) on its solid tyres, jolted and banged up the steep hill over the rough flint lane to the main road, loaded up to the gunwales with rabbits as well as all the other produce and goods for sale and exchange. (This same Georgy Goat, on being caught for overcrowding the van – which was loaded up on the roof and tailboard as well as being jam-packed inside – could not read or write and had a sturdy contempt for numbering. The magistrate asked him how many he was carrying, to which he replied 'Oh, a tidy few, m'lord, a tidy few.'[44])

Even today, Sylvia and Valentine are remembered in the village for their political views – although they are equally remembered for their possession of a green MG car. The car was Valentine's pride and joy, and an object of great rarity and interest in the village. The kind of memories of the two women which endure include the lending out of books (which was one of Valentine's pet schemes); expeditions with them to May Day demonstrations in London; poster-sticking against the Fascists; taking people to meetings; and that same little green MG ferrying people to vote at elections. Jim Pitman, Sylvia's tenant at Miss Green's, remembered going to London in the MG for a demonstration, and what a grand outing it had been. He said it was great fun, but there were such a lot of people that although he went three times to London in those years, he had never been back since.

On the way back from London, Valentine would say, 'Do you think it's about time we stopped, Jim?', as they neared a pub, and he would say 'Oh yes Miss', and they would go in and have a drink. (He clearly did not think that Valentine was an alcoholic, if indeed that is the right word for her condition.) They would stop off at several pubs, each time the party becoming more and more high-spirited; but it seems that, even so, class divisions did not altogether disappear.

Another villager, the carpenter, went to attend one of the Fascists' meetings in Bournemouth with them. Valentine wrote to Julius about this occasion:

[It] was an unpleasant experience . . . a very long, tedious, profoundly silly speech to listen to into the bargain. No wonder they have to beat people up to make them stay. He came back in a daze. He is, or was, an old-fashioned Fabian-

cum-Labour Party [man]. I have an idea he has dyed his
colours a bit deeper now.[45]

The villager who recalled their extreme left-wing views –
'well almost Communist'– thought that Sylvia and Valentine
had been recruiting for the International Brigade, for Spain. He
remembers their lending him books about Spain; perhaps he
was the same lad of whom Sylvia wrote that he had been
coming to see them: 'absolutely twitching with excitement to
learn. In a town I could pour him straight into the YCL, as it is
I just have to rely on the milk of the word. But he is lapping
it.'[46] Such forthrightness in pursuit of spreading the word and
gaining recruits for the Party was entirely characteristic of
Sylvia at this time, a side of her character which many of her
friends seem to have preferred to overlook, or perhaps did not
know existed. One friend who shared her views and was
unsurprised by her ruthlessness in pursuit of her ideals, Arnold
Rattenbury, wrote of her that: 'However bewitched her pen,
however bewitching, she lived wholly in an unambiguous world
where the only duty lies in taking sides. The books as well as
the author are always partisan.'[47]

When a young Party member from Bridport, Jim Fyrth,[48]
was still at University, he was worried about the reports of the
treason trials in Moscow. He wrote to Sylvia to ask her her
view. She sent him a long, extremely detailed reply, giving her
reasons for believing that the trials were genuine. He was
convinced.

No doubt it was this hard-headed quality which made her an
invaluable member of inner-Party literary discussions, as the
letters requesting her presence at meetings to and from Edgell
Rickword (convenor of the Party literary group and editor of
Left Review) testify. She was, for example, involved in some
delicate inner-party negotiations over what to do about the
problem of Stephen Spender: the Party had gained a good deal
of useful publicity when Spender decided to join, and when he
became disillusioned within a short time, members were
concerned about the adverse publicity if he left. Sylvia favoured
expelling him first – and regretted that during his membership
he had not written anything of value. She was concerned, she
said, lest they were giving the wrong advice to their young
writers: this was an issue of far greater importance than the
fate of Spender.

Another way in which Sylvia and Valentine pursued the goal of a Popular Front was the book-lending scheme which Valentine initiated in the village, which probably grew out of day-to-day discussions with their neighbours. This began as loaning out books such as J. L. and Barbara Hammond's *The Town Labourer* and Engels' *The Condition of the Working Class in England*. Sylvia commented upon the number of proletarian novels about foreign countries their neighbours had read too – far more than about their own. For this reason she welcomed the publication of John Summerfield's novel *May Day* (1936), 'a circus with a message' as she described it, which, since it dealt with socialist consciousness in Britain, might be useful and relevant in East Chaldon:

> For lending down here (and that is not a bad standard of literary criticism, after all, though it may sound rather parochial) a certain sectarian stiffening is all to the good. . . . We have found that very objective books . . . don't remain in the memory much more than a circus.[49]

This comment again reveals a clear and unashamed didactic purpose. The intellectuals, who, Valentine said, were not much more use to the villagers than bringing them their dirty washing so they could earn a few pence and loaning out books to them, were in this case anxious to educate them as well. Tactfully and gradually; but still to educate them.

From lending out their own books, Valentine went on to devise a scheme she hoped would be introduced by the Communist Party throughout the country: library slips, which graded different types of books with the purpose of introducing and by degrees winning over the reader to socialism. There was a difference in this scheme from the Left Book Club, of which they were of course both members, and founder-members of its writers' and readers' group. In Valentine's scheme, which seems not to have got off the ground despite the backing of the agit-prop department, non-political books were to be in the majority, and the scheme was to include 'ordinary shockers and/or highbrow novels'.[50] In other words, it was aimed at a much broader mass audience.

Something of the character of the breathless non-stop activity of those years comes across in this letter from Sylvia to Julius:

We have had a great deal of wind and weather, and visitors;

2.9 Sylvia with Towser at West Chaldon, 1937

Milly came here while the slander about Tom (Wintringham) being killed . . . was being investigated; then we had that nice creature Kit Dooley, to nurse up after a long doing of bronchitis. And we have gone on collecting for Spain, and I have spoken on Spain. . . .

And on Friday, as a reward for all these rustic diggings and delvings, we shall sit proudly on a Unity platform while Cripps[51] speaks for the local Labour Party. This is really nice isn't it? . . .

I can't actually trace our own handywork in this satisfactory state of things; but i am sure we must be something to do with it, for all that! Perhaps my breathings of Unity to the poor old dot and go one Peace Council.[52, 53]

This letter is characteristic both in its verve and tireless enthusiasm, its open-eyed and humorous but tough-minded commitment to the cause of being a Communist, and the day-to-day business of living and working as a Communist. In one sense it speaks of and to its time; but in another it is also familiar. Being a Communist in the 1970s was not so very different.

To catalogue the full extent of their activities as party activists might suggest some dry and harrassed politician's life, crammed to the full with dates, appointments, meetings, obligations. But the reality, from the testimony of letters and the few friends who recall that time, was quite different. The hallmark of their accounts of the shared political life is a full-blooded, vigorous, often malicious, sometimes surprised or delighted, but constantly alert enjoyment. One last example: anyone involved in politics knows the sinking feeling of being roped in to help at the fund-raising bazaar, but even this had compensations when it was the *Daily Worker* bazaar:

I sold a book to a child called David Coram, he was twelve years old and much enjoying Paine's *Age of Reason*. It is lovely to see a young intellect freely enjoying itself, not kept back in educational and social swaddling bands.[54]

Meanwhile both Sylvia and Valentine were using their intellects to further the advance of socialism, and the cause of Republican Spain. Activism in the CPGB meant dedicating their skills as writers, as well as selling books at a Party bazaar.

CHAPTER 3

WRITERS IN ARMS

From the time they became involved in the Communist Party, Sylvia and Valentine were both using their pens in the cause of their beliefs. The papers for which they wrote ranged from the liberal, left-of-centre *Time and Tide, New Statesman* and *News Chronicle,* to *Woman Today,* paper of the broad-based 'World Women's Committee Against Fascism and War', *The Countryman,* a non-political monthly of country topics (which included some highly political pieces by Sylvia), *Country Standard* (a CP monthly), the *Daily Worker,* the Party newspaper, and the Left periodicals *Left News,* an offshoot of Gollancz's Left Book Club, and *Left Review.* Of these, by far the most important was *Left Review,* which ran from October 1934 to May 1938, and could justly claim by the time of its demise that 'its history has been a gradually mounting graph of influence. . . .'[1]

It was through their involvement in *Left Review* that they became close to the Party, for many of the liveliest intellectuals, such as Edgell Rickword, Tom Wintringham and Montague Slater were grouped around it.

The concern of writers about the events in Germany had been growing since the early thirties and particularly since Hitler seized power in 1933. As well as the group 'Writers Against Fascism and for Collective Security', a British Section of the Writers International was formed in 1934, and that year also saw the founding of the National Council for Civil Liberties. This was set up in a concerted move by writers and academics to throw out an authoritarian and dangerous 'Sedition Bill', proposed by Ramsay MacDonald's Government, which would have effectually made outright propaganda and freedom of speech impossible. The council had the support of such eminent people as E. M. Forster, and the bill was defeated.

Left Review was launched within a context of broad, developing concern amongst writers about the growth of Fascistic and extreme right-wing ideas. The first editors were Montague Slater and Tom Wintringham, both Party members, and Amabel Williams Ellis, who was not a member. The list of contributors to the first issue included Louis Aragon, translated by Nancy Cunard (who became a close friend of Sylvia and Valentine's), J. B. Priestley ('the great white whale' as Sylvia called him), Siegfried Sassoon, George Bernard Shaw, Hugh MacDiarmid, Edgell Rickword, Pearl Binder and A. L. Lloyd. Priestley wrote:

> The *Left Review* has my support and sympathy if it can persuade even a few people that the horrible atmosphere we live in today is really our own creation, that we can, if we wish to, awake from this thickening nightmare of armaments and war.[2]

Women writers who contributed to *Left Review* besides Amabel Williams-Ellis and Pearl Binder included Storm Jameson, Naomi Mitchison, Winifred Holtby, Nancy Cunard, Vera Kay and Christina Stead, as well as Sylvia and Valentine. Naomi Mitchison's article 'The Reluctant Feminists', was one of the few feminist pieces to appear in the *Left Review*'s four years of publication (Lady Rhondda's *Time and Tide*, by contrast, over its much longer period of publication, drew upon a large number of women writers). Mitchison's article looked at the economics and politics of feminism:

> Capitalism (can) no longer afford itself the pleasant amusement of a class of un-owned women. . . . The Fascist and Nazi movements, reducing women to complete subjection . . . [have] had the effect of shoving a number of intelligent but . . . politics-shy women into the field of political action. It has also led them to consider the economics of feminism as a part of the general economics of possessors and possessed.[3]

Given the significance of the way in which Fascism treated women (a subject which Sylvia herself touched upon in a short review in *Left News*, a forewarning of how more brutally it was to treat other subject peoples), *Left Review*'s chauvinist bias looks more than usually myopic. Not only did it fail to deal with the situation of women in Nazi Germany, it also failed to pay serious attention to the specific problems women faced in bringing up their families on assistance-level incomes, with husbands out of work, poor housing, and children suffering from malnutrition. As with the CPGB, women's problems were masked in the global struggle of the British working class. For both Sylvia and Valentine, problems such as these that women faced were very much in the forefront of their minds, although neither of them took a specifically feminist perspective upon women's role in society. While they recognised the exploitation of the working class, like other Communists of the time, they did not see women as the exploited class in relation to men.

Sylvia's first contribution to *Left Review*, a poem, 'In this Midwinter', appeared in the January 1935 issue. It is a Marxist carol, for a 'co-heir of earth, comrade'. The vision of the new-born child reverses the usual religious point of view. The infant is 'Tougher than God or beast', 'Not lamb nor Lenin' but 'co-heir of earth, comrade' to whose 'Plight we darkling our lantern's friendly assurance'. It is a determinedly unemotional and tough-speaking lyric. The poem savagely dismantles the traditional associations of Christmas, through a combination of knotted diction and contemporary reference that makes for awkward reading:

> . . . not a saviour possibly.
> No godling, God not even in turncoat mufti of doubt.
> Man having rationalized destruction inalienably
> Needs God no further.

The next poem Sylvia contributed, 'Red Front',[4] contemplates the horror of war through the example of France: associations of the revolution, but also of later conflict, run through the banally rhythmic blood-thirsty chorus ('Comrade, are you grim enough,/Taut to fighting-trim enough-/Hark! – to march with us today /On the tall Bastille of Nay?)' The chorus is interset in more reflective and narrative passages, but at no point does the reader feel any personal engagement in the language. It remains a choric, dramatic, piece but not a particularly successful example.

Neither this poem, nor some others of Valentine's in *Left*

Review, show Sylvia and Valentine at their best. The insistence on the message, and the search for a 'hard' contemporary style rarely blend with their individual poetic gifts. It was a problem Valentine was to wrestle with for some time in the thirties. For example, her first contribution to *Left Review*, 'Communist Poem 1935',[5] combines an uneasy blend of rhetorical invocation and clichéd image in an attempt to deal with the ravages of de-industrialisation and unemployment:

> What must we do, in a country lost already,
> Where already the mills stop, already the factories
> Wither inside themselves, kernels smalling in nutshells,
> ('Fewer hands – fewer hands') and all the ploughed lands
> Put down to grass, to bungalows, to graveyards already.

However, *Left Review* was more than a place for publishing occasional poems or articles, it was also a focus for writers' political discussions, for thrashing out policy and promoting new initiatives, in much the same way that the Left Book Club groups and *Left News* were to do some eighteen months later. For Sylvia and Valentine, it provided a means of connection with other left-wing writers, many of whom (such as Wintringham, Julius and Queenie Lipton, Edgell Rickword and his wife Johnnie, and Nancy Cunard) were to become close friends. The veteran Communist writer Jack Lindsay, who was also living in the remote West Country during the thirties, said that for people like him *Left Review* was a lifeline. It kept people in touch with vital information and debate and reassured them that there was a vanguard movement to which they belonged.[6]

Sylvia and Valentine were involved in quite mundane and regular work for *Left Review* which, particularly for Valentine at this early stage of her career as a writer, must have given an important sense of audience. In May 1935 Valentine complained bitterly to Julius Lipton that they had been 'struggling through some really filthy poems sent on for criticism. One promising but ten rotten.' The worst of it was that all the poems came from Oxbridge, or Chelsea or Bloomsbury and were by: 'time-servers, toadies . . . desperately imitating Auden and Day Lewis with the exception (entertaining) of an appalling woman who tries to out-Sitwell Edith'.[7]

She went on to complain about *Left Review*'s habit of dividing sheep from goats in its search for authentic 'worker-writers' (Proletkult ideas had affected the Left in England too), which she described as a:

> phrase . . . better fitted for a Conservative Parish Paper then for a really Left Review. If we want a classless society, we mustn't start off by making a new class before we've even abolished the old ones!

Both Sylvia and Valentine took their turn at reviewing books. Sylvia contributed a scathing review of a Soviet concert in which she described her own favourite instrument, the piano, as inescapably bourgeois:

> The piano is a bourgeois instrument. Whether it be sought to proletarise it by the strumming-in-excelsis methods of Mepurnov and Polovinkin, or to purify it by following those invaluable counsels of high-class simplicity, Stravinksy's Cinq Doigts . . . it stays in the parlour. . . . An audience anxious to applaud anything from the USSR gave itself away by applauding too vigorously what was most reminiscent of the dear old music of capitalistic Russia.[8]

Sylvia could be more than a little sanctimonious when on her 'high horse' – the counterpart, perhaps, of that later quality of smugness that mars some of the letters and later stories.

Sylvia also set and judged one of the writers' competitions which were a regular feature of the *Left Review* since its inception. Amabel Williams Ellis had thought of the idea after attending a workers' press conference in New York: she was struck by the common and damning admission that the Left groups could not get out a paper the workers actually wanted to read. The subject of this particular competition was criticism. In her report Sylvia wrote that:

> Criticism is an important element in Left-Wing progress. . . . A literary critique is not merely concerned with literature. As literature is concerned with living, its criticism must have a life interest also, must express an outlook on behaviour and social conditions.[9]

As criticism for the left-wing critic must be incontrovertibly linked to the social conditions, so also, she pointed out with asperity, was it: 'supposed to be the expression of a mature opinion. There is no need for it to wear swaddle.'

Setting the competition, she had stated that: 'the first condition of good criticism is complete frankness in stating [one's] impressions... the critic must actively relive the writer's experience as his own, and then criticise [his own] involuntary comments.'[10] And she quoted Dimitrov that '"literature must serve the great revolutionary ideal of millions of workers." It is in the application [of that standard of judgement] that questions arise.'[11]

The same forthright expression of her viewpoint characterises Sylvia's contributions to other periodicals, whether she was writing about literature, music, the diet of the poor, Fascism, events in Spain or agriculture. In a review of *New Writing*, the magazine edited by John Lehmann, she notes approvingly that the writers in that magazine have extricated themselves: 'from the slough of Art for Art's sake, [and] have gone back to the better foundation of Art for Man's sake, to a time when people wrote to express their convictions rather than their feelings'.[12]

She praises those stories that come from: 'that admirable tradition of a straightforward story with good sense and good feeling behind it – an underlying morality, in fact, a serious outlook upon mankind'.[13]

Sylvia's concern with morality was deeply serious, but her criticism was always seasoned with wit and style. None the less, it expresses a concentrated fury which seldom fails to hit the target head-on. For example, in *The Countryman*, whose more usual fare concerned the nesting habits of bats and the ancient art of dry-stone-walling, she wrote an article about a Government Nutrition Committee pamphlet, which had purported to show how people living on low wages might adequately feed themselves. Her article is entitled 'Recommendations to Starvation'.[14] She quotes some of the recipes for a family of *five* persons given in the pamphlet:

Sausages in Batter:
½lb sausages. Skin the sausages & roll them in 12 portions.
Cornish pie:
About 2-4oz cold meat, 1lb potatoes, ½lb flour, 2 onions, 4oz lard . . .

Sylvia comments acidly:

These five persons are not, as one might suppose, maniacs

thinning. They are a family on the dole. . . .

There is only one good thing to be said in favour of this bad book. It is as good a giveaway as one can wish of a vile state of things. Science, medical and domestic, all the jargon and apparatus of a cookery book, coloured plates and pious preface, spell but one word. Malnutrition. Or in plainer English, Not Enough to Eat.

As someone who loved to cook, and cared a lot about food, Sylvia was made intensely angry by the hypocrisy and meanness of a government that pretended families could live on four shillings a week for all their meals. This was the subject of one of a number of letters she wrote about social issues to national newspapers. Amongst others there were ones protesting about the treatment of children; calling for international peace; and, of course, for support for the elected government of Spain and the abandonment of the British non-intervention policy.

In another article in *The Countryman*, she makes plain her anger at the conditions of the agricultural workers. Her view embraces every aspect of their exploitation. What has come to interest her after living for nearly a decade in the country, she says, is: 'The average amount of unpaid overtime filched from the labourer . . . the average weekly mileage covered by the labourer's wife who fetches all her water from the well and carries all her slops to the ditch.'[15] The article continues through a long catalogue of pointed questions about the labourers' conditions, concluding with the 'average number of sleepers per bedroom and rats per sleeper'.

For Valentine, even more than Sylvia, her political writing centred around Dorset and the lives of the agricultural workers. She wrote a series of three articles called 'Country Dealings' for *Left Review* based on her first-hand knowledge of Chaldon and of the villages in Norfolk, as a result of which she was commissioned by Martin Lawrence to do a book on the agricultural workers' lives.

The subject was extremely topical, for many rural areas (Dorset amongst them) were depressed and forgotten areas. The book, *Country Conditions*, was published in 1936; it was the only book of hers to be published during her lifetime, apart from *Whether a Dove or a Seagull*.

At its best, Valentine's political journalism has a flavour of crisp directness and concentration. Her articles are vivid with the immediacy of the experience she describes, for example in 'Country Dealings',[16] her account of the cottages – which, as one agricultural labourer said, were only fit for a 'red jacket' (i.e., to be burned down):

> Yesterday I went over a row of three thatched cottages . . . .
> In one of these cottages, I remembered, had lived . . . a family of six children, mother, father, and mother's brother. I went into that cottage and up the stairs. 'Look out', called a workman urgently, 'Thik house be all buggy all up walls'.[17]

Describing Sloley in Norfolk, Valentine commented that it was far enough from the sea for the soil to be rich and the people slow and poor (unlike Winterton-on-Sea, where she grew up, where fishing and smuggling had made the people hardy and independent). The only people who were certainly not poor were the 'county' people, who, 'in other respects . . . differed nothing from the labourers except possibly in their really scandalous ignorance'.[18] There was no shop in the village, no tarred roads, and no electric light, for the landowner would not allow the electricity poles to be erected on his land. This same landowner refused to mend the roof of one of the farm cottages, which leaked onto the tenant's bed. When the tenant asked the farmer if he could persuade the landowner to repair the roof, the farmer advised him to go and see the lady of the Manor about it:

> He did, and came away again, and the roof went on leaking, and the labourer and his family went away at the end of the quarter. There is another family there now, and the roof is still leaking. I suppose they have put up their bed in a different place.[19]

Letters of this time show an equal spirit and disgust at the conditions Valentine observed; they are passionately partisan, breathing confidence and humour and a complete absorption in what she is writing about, though with less of the telling understatement which was a hallmark of her best journalism. For example, in one of her letters to Julius Lipton, Valentine wrote a telling account of the confrontation she and Sylvia witnessed when they went over to Trelewis, South Wales, during the miners' sit-in of 1935:[20]

The people are magnificent, and the women are as ferocious

as tigers, or more so! . . . there were at least 500 police visible, and many more concealed behind trees and bushes when the time came to take the scabs home. But the miners got the best of it. The battle was fought out on a steep mountain-side, and the stout policemen felt the steep ascent much more hardly than the lean miners!

But the whole village was in a state of martial law – No one allowed to go out in the street and even the women and children shoved indoors if they so much as stood on the doorstep – Four policemen walked together always. They were scared out of their lives.[21]

It was on this occasion that a policeman entrusted them with instructions to fetch up the waiting ranks of police hidden in buses, when the miners were getting the better of the day, clearly misreading their appearances. They assented civilly, and walked on past.

Valentine did not find writing prose easy. She lamented to Julius in the early stages of writing *Country Conditions*, that she was not sure if she would ever get the hang of it, and asked plaintively whether he thought it would come with practice. Sylvia said of her that her mind had not the 'novelist's plod', and Valentine seems to have found the 'plod' involved in a non-fiction book equally irksome. None the less, the book was a success in its left-wing market. It was commended for its informativeness and clarity: the *Daily Worker* praised the 'quietness and simplicity' of her writing, and said that she had not sacrificed 'comprehensiveness to concreteness'.[22] More euphoniously, the *Left Review* critic noted that she had 'persuaded a large number of labourers and their wives to speak for themselves, and has recorded their actual words without varnish. This is a telling method of writing.'[23]

Despite the social investigative work of the great nineteenth-century pioneers such as Mayhew and Booth, little work of this kind was being done in the early thirties. Valentine's reporting can be seen as an early part of the interest in how working people lived which came to its peak with the work of Mass-Observation.

The flavour of the places, the times and the people come across very vividly in *Country Conditions*. The criticisms that were made of the book centred on the lack of any proposed solution to the rural workers' problems: but the Communist Party had not yet formulated a coherent rural policy. Politically it was far behind in its attitude to the countryside compared to the town; just as Valentine pointed out in her book, the rural workers' living standards lagged behind those of their urban counterparts. What *Country Conditions* provided was a handbook setting out all the disadvantages the agricultural worker suffered, in work, housing, transport, education, health, wages and social life. Valentine argued that conditions had not changed since the Industrial Revolution (a source of satisfaction only to town visitors): privies were still emptied into the garden, water was drawn from wells, and only two houses in the village (East Chaldon) had electric light. She examined the workings of landlord-tenant, farmer-labourer relations, and the insidious control of the workers through deference and fear of victimisation. She looked at the effect of the slump on the countryside and the landowners' only solution, which was to: 'Cut down expenses, dismiss one or two employees, sell the extra hunter . . . put the burden on the workers and carry on as usual.'[24]

In these circumstances, she argued, agricultural workers were ready prey for the Fascists' arguments.

An important part of the book looked at the position of women in the agricultural community. Everything in a village depends on the woman, since her husband is out all daylight hours at his work, sometimes having tramped miles to get to it; she has to make do and arrange everything when the family arrive in their new home. They will have had no choice in where they are coming to, since cottage and village come with the job, and no chance to inspect their new home beforehand. The wife must solve all the problems of the move for the whole family, at once and without help. She must work out how to fit the furniture; where the shop is, who delivers, and who can be trusted not to overcharge; how to fit all the family into the cottage; how to deal with a stinking drainage ditch; how to get the children to school; where the water supply is. It was no wonder, Valentine concluded, that the women were quicker to reason, more advanced in their thinking, and more embittered than the men.

In the third of her 'Country Dealings' articles, Valentine had scornfully berated the town-bred intellectuals who came to live amongst the villagers for their pie-in-the-sky ideas about how the country people lived, and their selfishness, perhaps getting her own back on some of the Dorset intelligentsia from whom she and Sylvia fled:

> They have an idea that the land-worker is ideally situated, that he has unmatched opportunities for studying Nature, that he has, because of this constant contact with the mother, sublimated his needs and desires, and that they themselves can achieve contentment and all-wisdom by copying the labourer's way of life.
> So they take the best houses and spend their days in the open air.[25]

In *Country Conditions* she showed conclusively what the harsh realities of that way of life really were.

CAMPAIGNING WRITERS

There were many different organisations in which Valentine and Sylvia were active as writers and threading in and out of them all were concerns for peace, opposition to Fascism, and support for Republican Spain. Sylvia was Secretary of the Dorset Peace Council, which organised broad-based activities like the big peace meeting in the amphitheatre at Dorchester at which Vera Brittain spoke, and a peace-march through Bridport that was so un-sectarian every group was represented except the British Legion and the Conservative Party. Six hundred people, out of a town of 6000, took part. Sylvia, who was advertised as 'the novelist', made a speech that was little different from one a Christian Socialist might have made. The *Dorset Daily Echo* reported her speech fully.

She described the children as the banners of the crusade, and deplored the fact that, twenty-two years after the beginning of the last war,

> countries were still in arms and even worse, in hate. . . . Wherever they looked there was mistrust, lies, hatred, hypocrisy; every denial of the Christian spirit. . . . One generation had been wrecked. Another had grown up – like another harvest field. They did not want another wicked harvest when the crop was ruined.

In a fine flow of rhetoric she pleaded that 'behind armaments, statesmen and militarists were men, women and children who did not want war. Behind every army was a country of people who did not want it and under every soldier's tunic there was a heart that would prefer peace.' She concluded with a plea to love our neighbours 'who are even now being slowly driven to become our enemies'.[26]

Occasions such as these had a far-reaching impact in spreading the ideas of pacifism and Popular Front unity locally, and were the more important in an area as backward as Dorset where most of the local MPs had extreme right-wing sympathies. (One Dorset MP even sent £100 to Mussolini, congratulating him on the invasion of Abyssinia.) Such reports give an insight too, into what Sylvia called a 'Whale of a Job'. She and Valentine wrote letters by the hour for the Peace Council; and although Sylvia later described it as a 'poor old dot-and-go' affair, it undoubtedly brought together in a concern for peace many widely disparate groupings and people with very different political consciousnesses.

This kind of broad-based work, organised around a programme of minimum demands, was also at the heart of the success of the huge aid-Spain network of 1936–39; but there were other kinds of Popular Front groupings which Valentine and Sylvia were active in as writers. One of these was the Left Book Club, which had been founded in 1936 by the publisher Victor Gollancz, with the assistance of Harold Laski and John Strachey, as a means of reaching a mass audience with left-wing books, which other publishers and distributors alike said would not sell. Through a cheap subscription system the Club offered a book a month to its members, together with 'Left Book Club Specials'; it soon took off and within three years had nearly 57,000 members each buying a book every month. It also organised meetings, conferences, rambles, summer-schools, and set up groups of readers in different work-groups; for example there was a printers' group, a musicians' group, an accountants' group, and so on, as well as locally-based groups around the country, often with their own bulletins for members to keep in touch with each other. In 1937 a Writers' and Readers' group was set up, of which Sylvia and Valentine were advertised as being founder members.[27]

By the end of the decade there were more than 1000 of these groups, and the spread of left-wing ideas and the development of resistance to Fascism throughout the period owed a great deal to the success of the Book Club and the groups. The Club could not be described as a Party front, but it did work enthusiastically with Communists: its activities were more openly anti-capitalist than those of some of the broad-front organisations which the Party, discreetly or otherwise, controlled.

Gollancz's proclaimed position was that the Left Book Club did not have a policy of the Popular Front but that 'the very existence of the Club tends towards a Popular Front'. Certainly there existed a dialectical relationship between the Left Book Club, *Left Review*, and the ventures of popular and left-wing publishing such as Penguin Books, founded in the mid-thirties to make good books cheaply available in paperback, and later on, the Party-orientated magazines *Poetry and the People* and *Our Time* which succeeded *Left Review*.

In Dorset, local groups were in existence at Wareham, Poole and Lyme Regis, and Sylvia spoke at a meeting on refugees in Portsmouth in 1939. She also contributed articles and letters to the organ of the Club, originally called *Left Book News*, later *Left News*. Writing in the latter, Sylvia made it clear more than once that there was only one political choice to be made: 'The choice for all who think and feel is already between Fascism and socialism.' Hitler had stated in *Mein Kampf* that the individual personality has no right to liberty and dignity ('this dogma . . . can mean nothing but destruction'): but it was no use knowing only the theory of Fascism: 'we must, if we are to understand it properly and combat it properly, understand the Practice of Fascism also'. People must pass this knowledge on: 'it should be part of the duty of every Left Book Club member to *lend* his books as well as read them'.[28]

What Valentine and Sylvia's feelings were about this constant string of Popular Front activities is hard to gauge: anyone who has spent a few years in the unending round of flyposting, organising, writing, petitioning, lobbying, will know how tiring and mechanical such activities can become. But the letters to their comrades of this time show no jadedness. In one letter, Sylvia, about to address a meeting of the British Medical Association, pleads with their friend Queenie Lipton to try and get away from her work at the *Daily Worker* and come to stay a week earlier if she can – 'Our house is getting more and more filled up, very soon I shall have a notice painted saying, This way to the Olde Communiste's Reste.'[29]

One welcome antidote to continuous politicking was working in the garden: Valentine reported that even teasing would not make Sylvia ashamed of the state of her knees, and that Victoria Ambrosia, the goat, preferred lettuces and Valentine's carefully-reared young carrots to her trousers. (They both responded deeply to the country, 'very noisy at this time of year', Valentine told Julius in another letter; 'birds and beasts all round the place, all singing and bellowing and bleating'.[30]) Being on good terms with the local farmer and a retired Army gent, she was allowed to go out with her gun and try to keep down the rabbits: 'I spend an hour or so a day, sitting in the shelter of a hill-side, in a badger-hole, with a little rifle.' She could not, she said, 'get hardened to the act of killing', but admitted to loving shooting, while she hated rabbits 'for the land's sake'.[31] She also liked the food they provided.

Discussions with the friends who came to the 'Olde Communiste's Reste' provided another source of relaxation: when Tom Wintringham was coming to stay, Valentine determined to get to the bottom of the question as to what dialectical poetry really was; she asked Julius if he thought he knew – 'I don't',[32] she admitted simply. It was a matter of some concern to her, for when she was not gardening, shooting, organising, or writing her political articles, Valentine was still toiling away trying to write revolutionary poetry – not propaganda but 'true and unmistakeable poems, coming straight from the mind of the movement'.[33] In order to do this she felt a whole new technique would have to be mastered. She was uncertain

whether to carry on along the lines that poetry has gone . . . trusting that . . . the difficulty of reading a 'new' style will wear off. . . . Or whether to make a partial return to the old, simpler forms. . . . Blake is a perfect example of what I mean by a partial return. . . . But we need something really *hard* . . . definite and deliberately reasonable, as well as having the quality of poetry – being well-devised and musical.[34]

Meanwhile, Sylvia's reputation as a writer had resulted in her being elected to the august position of an executive committee member of the International Association of Writers for the Defence of Culture. This was set up in 1935, at the end of the First International Congress of Writers held in the appropriately named Salle de la Mutualité in Paris. The IAWDC aimed to be a more partisan and effectual international force than PEN. The British delegation to the Congress included Amabel Williams Ellis, E. M. Forster, Aldous Huxley, Pearl Binder and Christina Stead. (Also present were three other women writers, all associated with the Left, Winifred Holtby, Storm Jameson and Naomi Mitchison.) The association was made up of thirty-eight participating countries with their members organised into national sections. The British section was called the 'Association of Writers for Intellectual Liberty', liberty being, as many commentators pointed out, the particular watchword of the English. ('In the early thirties the concept of freedom', wrote Julian Symons in his cynical account *The Thirties: A Dream Revolved*, 'appeared an absolute good.'[35]) Sylvia was elected to the Executive Committeee in 1936. Internationally established writers, such as André Gide, Thomas Mann and Maxim Gorky headed the Central Bureau of the International Association, which linked all the separate national constituents.

For Sylvia the work involved the usual round of organising meetings, attending meetings in London, speaking, and a good deal of manoeuvring in the delicate business of trying to bring the group more firmly into the progressive struggle, while not alienating those writers whose interest was less political. Discussing the composition of the executive of AWFIL with Edgell Rickword in 1938, for example, she weighed up the proposed election of an anti-Communist, John Brophy, with some misgivings:

> on the whole, though with the liveliest anticipations of schisms and rumpusses, I am for asking him on; and *then seeing that he has a lot to do*; if kept constantly occupied and on the move he may be all right. But Satan will simply romp with his idle hands if they are left idle.
>
> I do hope that Compton Mackenzie's suggestion of a Scotch branch of the Writers Association will come off. If it does, then I shall consider our meeting a real success.[36]

The view that Communists working in these organisations put forward to try to win over other writers was that, as Cecil

Day Lewis put it: 'The writer needs peace to write in and therefore he must be prepared to work for that peace';[37] or, more positively, as Erwin Piscator, the great German theatre director, expressed it:

> The artist is a man who lives his life more intensely and vitally than other men – he must therefore take part in the struggle with more means at his disposal . . . he must stir up the energies of men on the side of liberty.[38]

One can catch something of this upsurge of enthusiasm and commitment amongst writers in a report that Christina Stead wrote for *Left Review* on the first Congress of IAWDC in Paris, which gives a distinctive impression of the ideas and heady atmosphere of the time. She pointed out that the European repression of writers had hammered it home to every writer that 'the armies of reaction are trampling into the very heart of his own country'.[39] The problem for writers outside the Soviet Union was that:

> If they are not persecuted nor in exile, they pant for a public. The giant circulations [of the USSR] suggest a way out. But they [i.e., the writers] have to switch from the macadam of bourgeois culture which is leading them obviously into a morass, to a new clay road, hardly rollered. . . . The younger writers, trembling and eloquent with their will to survive and create, have to give up their poetic solitudes and soft self-probings to study worldly subjects, enter the political arena, take lessons from workmen and use their pen as a scalpel for lifting up the living tissues, cutting through the morbid tissues of the social anatomy.[40]

Her metaphors have a flavour of Zola, but the point about the writer moving beyond the absolutism of subjectivity and examining the tissue of society is one that Valentine and Sylvia, like many other writers of the Left, seriously attempted to engage with, with differing degrees of success.

In some respects, Christina Stead's attitudes were strait-laced: writing of the audience of two and a half thousand workmen, students and writers at the Congress, she notes with satisfaction that: 'The hall was not full of half-feminine masculine revolutionaries and half-masculine feminine rebels. They were neat, had no postures and poses. The air was clean and pure intellectually.'[41] It would be interesting to know how, if they had met, Valentine and Christina Stead would have viewed each other. Valentine would surely have qualified amongst the category of despised, impure 'half-masculine feminine rebels', with her long lean boyish good looks, cropped hair, well-cut trousers, ties and shirts, her guns, fishing-rods, passion for cars and handiness with tools.

One meeting that Sylvia organised for the AWFIL was: 'In Defence of Freedom – Writers Declare Against Fascism' held at the Queen's Hall, London on 8 June 1938. At this meeting, as so often with the Spanish meetings, the net was clearly being cast as widely as possible so as not to offend anyone and to catch the most liberal sympathisers. The programme of the meeting is prefaced by three epigraphs on freedom, from Cowper, Swift and Byron; it also quotes Milton, Morris, Keats and Mussolini. There is a message from the League of American Writers (the American section of IAWDC), and a moving letter from the Czech writers from the heart of their resistance to German occupation. The programme lists writers who had been exiled, imprisoned or killed under Fascism – some thirty names from Germany, Spain and Italy – together with a list of authors whose works had been publicly burned in Germany, including Gide, Proust, Freud, Helen Keller, H. G. Wells, Heine, Lessing and Rousseau. In a section called 'Fascism at Work', the organisers pointed out that: 'The ceremonial burning of books symbolises the Fascist hatred and fear of the intelligence . . . how much of our English literature Fascism would have to destroy if it were to blot out the thought and love of freedom.'[42]

In their statement 'On Fascism', the Executive Committee called on all members of the liberal professions actively to oppose Fascism. Their main function, as they saw it, was to warn people in Britain and Europe of the danger it constituted – the more necessary since so much of the Press was silent on the issue, and the government abetted it through its policy of so-called non-intervention in Spain.

The whole meeting was clearly an impassioned cry for liberty, but offered little in the way of analysis of the root causes of Fascism. Sylvia wrote afterwards to Rickword that she was glad he was 'fairly satisfied with the Meeting', but she regretted the 'elderly windbags': 'it was too much of a good thing to have Desmond McCarthy as well as Walpole each taking up a valuable eight minutes. It is much more important to have *les jeunes*. For instance, Prokosch, who is a coming name, would have counted for much more.'[43]

In the campaigns of support for the Spanish Government, many of these same problems, of course, arose, for the Communist Party, and its allies were aiming to draw in the widest degree of popular support and were therefore tiptoeing in many instances to avoid alienating centre-of-the-road opinion. Inevitably this approach created its own tensions and problems, but none the less the degree of popular mobilisation that the Party and left-wing sympathisers drew upon in the Aid-Spain committees constituted, despite its failure to shift Government policy, one of the few genuinely successful chapters in British Left political history.[44]

SPAIN: WRITERS TAKE SIDES

Valentine and Sylvia were involved in the Spanish war from the very beginning. Valentine could not wait to get out to Spain and become involved in the action: she always regretted she had no opportunity to use her marksmanship.

On 12 September 1936 an article had appeared in the *Daily Worker* and the *News Chronicle* by Nancy Cunard, who had been in Spain. It contained a report on the Medical Mission to Spain already established on the Aragon front: the war was two months old. (In July, four generals, Franco, Mola, Quepo deLLano Sanjurjo and Goded had risen against the Government of Manuel Azana which had been in office barely four months.) In her report, Nancy Cunard made an impassioned appeal to the papers' readership:

> As one who has personally seen the heroic courage of the people's anti-fascist Militias, let me make this plea to the Press of working-class Britain and its readers. 'Send the loyalist forces active material aid.'[45]

Within two days Valentine had written to both papers proposing a scheme to raise immediately forty-nine first-aid volunteers (she wished to be the fiftieth), self-funded and with their own transport, to go out and supplement the medical staff. The volunteers should have anti-typhoid injections and be in good health, be able to meet their own expenses, and have £50: she also suggested that 'Volunteers who can offer a car as well as themselves are naturally most welcome! I have a small fast 2-seater which I would take over.'[46] She warned that the cars would probably not return intact.

Her own arrangements for departure had already been made, she said, and took about a week: however, the letter she wrote to the Communist Party headquarters asking for official clearance for her scheme clearly met with a frosty reply; hardly surprising in view of the proposal's Bulldog Drummond romantic adventurism. She explained to Julius:

> I think this scheme would speed-up the Medical Aid
> Committee and also furnish some sort of reply to General
> O'Duffy's army of 2000! . . . It would serve as a gesture
> towards the United Front too . . . since we can't counter
> O'Duffy's 2000, it seems to me that 50 is a reasonable
> number.[47]

(O'Duffy was a Fascist Irishman who organised volunteers for the Spanish rebels.)

She claimed that her scheme was in no way intended to cut across Spanish Medical Aid, and those with professional qualifications should join the medical units. However the Medical Aid Committee does not appear to have been much impressed by her proposal, and shortly she and Sylvia made their way to Spain, without the MG, on their own.

They had managed to attach themselves to an ambulance unit in Barcelona, through the offices of a man by the name of O'Donnell; neither the Party nor the Spanish Medical Aid Committee in London sanctioned their departure. (There is a distinct air of apology in Valentine's letters and reports to Party headquarters and to the committee on their return. She also sent detailed information about the need for ambulances and a report on conditions out there.) Despite their unconventional route to Spain, Sylvia and Valentine were issued with official passes in Barcelona attaching them to the 'Primera Unidad Sanitaria Britanica' and the 'Primera Ambulancia Inglesa en Espana'. Sylvia described what they did during their three week stay as an 'office-boy sort of job',[48] while from Valentine's reports to Party HQ in King St, and recollections of friends at the time, it seems that she may have been driving too.

The visit made a profound impression upon both of them, and in Sylvia's case sowed the seeds of a love-affair with Spain that was to last all her life, even though once Franco had gained control of Spain, she vowed she would never go back as long as he lived. (She kept her word.) Barcelona in the early days of the war was a city of revolutionary Utopian character that swept away all resistance. Sylvia was enchanted: she wrote to Elizabeth Wade White:

> I don't think I have ever met so many congenial people in the whole of my life, liking overlept any little bounds of language. . . . Barcelona, by the time we saw it, was I suppose the nearest thing I shall ever see to the early days of USSR . . . the very first days, when everything was proceeding on the impulse of that first leap into life. . . . They (i.e., the Republicans) sit in the mansions and the offices of the great (which they keep in the tenderest order, I saw one where they were preserving the original aviary, and another was a kind guardian to a flock of goldfish). . . .
> A people naturally intellectual, and with a long standard of culture, have thrown off the taskmasters who enforced ignorance on them.[49]

Her natural respect for the people themselves, and distaste for institutions, shines through this account, which ends with her delight in the political philosophy of anarchism, which she was to maintain to the end of her life. (She maintained that the Spanish themselves were nearly all anarchists, not Communists as the papers called them – as indeed at that stage in Spain they were.)

> You cannot imagine, after this mealy-mouthed country, the pleasure of seeing an office with a large painted sign, Organisation for the Persecution of Fascists. Anarchists, of course. That beautiful directness is typical of anarchism, a most engaging type of thought, though I do not want to be an anarchist myself. The world is not yet worthy of it, but it ought to be the political theory of heaven.[50]

Most of Sylvia and Valentine's work for Spain was amongst the innumerable Aid-Spain committees at home in England, but the two visits that they made to Spain were crucial experiences for both of them in rousing their devotion to the country and its people. Valentine in particular was always longing to return; while in Barcelona, they had made friends with a woman called Ramona Siles Garcia, who was clearly an activist. In the early days of the war women did play a leading part in the militias and in organising the defence of the republic; however, Spanish machismo soon reasserted itself, with the growing control by the Spanish Communist Party, and women were sent back to more 'proper', supportive duties.

Within two months of returning from Barcelona Valentine had written to Ramona asking for work in Spain. Ramona's reply, in February 1937, was categoric: there was no work for Valentine there – the work they relied on her to do was in Britain. The most immediate necessity was to organise the evacuation of Spanish orphans.

The second of the two visits which Sylvia and Valentine made to Spain was in July 1937, to attend the Second Congress of IAWDC in Madrid, at the height of the bombing: not many English writers were prepared to go to Madrid under those conditions. They were, therefore, amongst the few British intellectuals who actually went out to Spain; and while many Communist men went out there to fight in the International Brigades, the number of Communist women who went was fairly small.

Most of the women who were there went out as nurses; a few, such as Nan Green, went to help on the secretarial and administrative side. Felicia Browne, the artist, was one Communist Party woman who was killed, right at the outset of the war. She was with a party of ten volunteers in a militia in August 1936 who went to blow up a rebel munitions train. They were outnumbered four to one by the Fascists and had to retreat, during which one of the party was wounded and had to be left. Felicia returned to help him and was killed. But for the most part, Party women remained at home to support the cause by organising the aid-committees, homes for the orphans, support meetings and so on.

The Communist Party, never at the forefront of change in sexual politics, did not look to its women members playing any more militant a role. Sue Bruley in her study of Feminism in the CPGB shows how rooted the Party were in a conservative view of women's role.[51] As Elsie Gollan said, as far as women activists in the Party were concerned, they thought of themselves not as women, but as Party members.[52] While there were examples of strong, active women leaders and speakers, Communists accepted that women's place was in the home. There was work, and there was women's work; women's work was what you did if you couldn't do work. However, the active contributions that were made by women in Spain are at last beginning to be discovered.[53]

Besides their activities as writers in the Spanish cause, which forms the last part of this chapter, Valentine and Sylvia were involved in a great many other campaigns. Sylvia was writing letters to other notables she knew, such as Naomi Mitchison, trying to obtain soap to send to Spain – the cause of the women who had nothing to wash their children or clothes with had moved her considerably: 'It is really a serious matter, this shortage, and entails much suffering on all classes. It is heart-rending to see the women patiently *rinsing* the children in that very hard water.'[54] The work that Ramona Garcia had singled out in her letter to Valentine, organising relief and homes for the Basque orphans, also preoccupied them. After the bombing of Guernica, more than 4000 children and teachers came over on the *Havana*, which docked at Southampton, and a huge operation was set up to disperse the refugees to places all over the country where committees had been set up in preparation to welcome them, and homes made ready.

In June 1937, the National Joint Committee for Spanish Relief, the umbrella organisation of all the Spanish Aid Committees, organised a large, prestigious meeting at the Royal Albert Hall in support of the refugees. The programme cover was designed by Picasso, who was one of the speakers at the meeting, and in all there were fifty-four distinguished names from the arts, politics and sciences supporting it, including Sylvia's. A sale of pictures was organised to raise funds, and a broadcast of Paul Robeson singing, played from Moscow. (Sylvia had greatly admired him when she saw him play Othello opposite Peggy Ashcroft's Desdemona, some years before.)

For Sylvia and Valentine political work during this time swung between Dorset and London. It is quite clear that neither Sylvia nor Valentine joined the CP because of Spain, but Spain was undoubtedly for them, as for all Communists and a great many left-of-centre people in the thirties, the test-case of their hopes, and between 1936 and 1938 it made up the heart of the struggle.

They were collecting for Spain; Sylvia was speaking for the 'fish-faced' League of Nations Union; they were trying to organise a showing of Ivor Montague's stirring film, *The Defence of Madrid*. This film, which received more than 6,000 showings up and down the country, showed the defence of Madrid by the Republicans against the far superior forces and weapons of the Fascists:

> either the film won't fit the cinema, or the hall can't be got on a weekday, or the principle enthusiast can't bring himself to break the Sabbath, or the man who would turn the handle has a dead aunt. Or something.[55]

Meanwhile, they were also organising a booksale for the AWFIL – 'the spare-room is heaped with books . . . I wish I could be sure of getting as many buyers.'[56] Sylvia was writing recipes for the Basque children, who were becoming constipated on wholesome English food; they organised a meeting in Dorchester Labour Hall at which Sylvia spoke on Spain and 'John Cowper Powys . . . on John Cowper Powys'[57] and there was a 'decency bit' thrown in about the Left Book Club. All of which was, and is, the inevitable lot of anyone struggling with the problems of rousing militancy in a sleepy backwater. The pace was hectic, and the momentum unremitting. In the middle of it, country life went on: Valentine killed a partridge with a ·22 rifle at 150 yards; friends came to stay; mushrooms were picked and despatched to a friend and comrade, Nan Green. Nan's husband had been killed fighting with the International Brigade. Having seen active service at the front in Spain, she returned to England 'merely changing the front and the weapons' (as she quoted the Brigaders saying in her memoir[58]) to raise food, money and medical supplies for Spain.

They entertained a leading Chinese Communist writer Professor Shelley Wang, who came to talk at the Dorchester Labour Hall and bemused his audience with revolutionary stories from China which he forgot to say were three thousand years old, 'we loved him very much but I'm afraid his Dorchester audience found him perplexing'.[59] He arrived to stay with his suitcase under one arm and its handle under the other 'like a talisman', Sylvia wrote, the case having given way under the weight of all his books.

Being a top Communist Party activist – they were regarded as the leading comrades in Wessex at this time – meant quite a lot of exhausting expeditions at short notice, juggling time-tables and being prepared to hare up to London when summoned at short notice to confer on some recent point of policy discussion. (In those days it could take six hours to get from Dorset to London.)

Three years after joining the Party, Sylvia was writing somewhat plaintively to Edgell Rickword.

> Just got back from London. To find you asking me to go there again. But I'm afraid I can't. Just now I'm waiting on Chalmers Mitchell[60] to say when he will be free for a Spain Sub-Committee meeting. . . . SSC had its first break into high society on Wednesday, we got the loan of Paul Lathom's house and butler, and invited a large throng of respectables to listen to Lorca read aloud and Rosita Bal play. It went off well, and got into the *Daily Telegraph*.[61]

The wooing of the middle and upper classes continued unabated, whether the cause was just anti-Fascist, or one of the many different Aid-Spain committees. (The Tory MP The Duchess of Atholl was one of those who was most vigorous in this work: the alignment over Spain crossed usual political and class boundaries.) Sylvia seems to have been responsible for one such committee, in support of Spanish intellectuals, for which collections were made at the big anti-fascist meeting of 1938 organised by AWFIL. A complete record of all the meetings of this kind at which one or other of them were present, or helped to organise, or which Sylvia spoke at, would be quite a lengthy document. She developed a flair for public speaking – and also discovered she had a formidable talent for heckling, which she greatly enjoyed. In the last throes of the war in late 1938 and early 1939 (after the International Brigaders had been sent home by the Spanish Government in a futile last-ditch attempt to persuade the foreign Fascist forces to withdraw), starvation was the immediate problem for the Spanish people. More and more, foreign support for the beleaguered Republic focused on the food-ships, and in England almost every trade union group was involved in collecting and sending food. Letters that passed between Valentine and Sylvia and one of their Spanish friends, Asunción, reveal how desperate the situation was. Late in 1938 she begs them to send her help for her two children – anything that they have and she can't get. She can't send them money, not until after the war, but hopes they will do her this favour, as she can't give her children what they need.

In January, sending them thanks for the parcels that did get through, Asunción enclosed the only presents she could offer them, a calendar with photographs of three of the great Republican hero/ines, La Pasionaria, the great orator, Prime Minister Negrin, and the Communist Party General Secretary José Diaz:

> You'll never appreciate how much your efforts mean in these critical moments that we are going through – since you will have received my letter I put the list of the contents of the parcel which you sent me which are all basic necessities which we can't get here because this fascist rabble who can't break us with armaments want to break us by hunger.[62]

None the less, she remained optimistic, for 'all the workers of the labour movement of the whole world are with us'. Despite the official opposition of the Labour Party hierarchy in Britain, and of Prime Minister Chamberlain, they were getting enough bread and milk through the labour movement to feed sixty-five thousand children. They were not giving up hope, Asuncioñ said,

> because on our Spanish soil liberty is being fought for and the future of all democratic countries – be sure that with our blood and your help there will come such good times when all the proletariat will enjoy liberty.[63]

It was to express their solidarity with sentiments such as these that Valentine and Sylvia also used their pens to contribute to the Spanish war effort.

WRITING FOR SPAIN

Valentine wrote poems and contributed journalism about Spain: both articles and reviews of some of the many books that were published about the Spanish conflict. Many of these pieces were published in *Left Review* but she also contributed to the American periodicals *New Masses* and *New Republic*, to the *London Mercury*, and others. One poem which captures the anger of the Left in Britain at the selective indifference of the Government and British Press, is 'Instructions from England, 1936'.[64]

> Note nothing of why or how, enquire
> no deeper than you need
> into what set these veins on fire,
> note simply that they bleed.

The Spanish conflict is seen as something perennial, about which no questions are asked; but the casual spectator notes 'churches burned and popes in pain'. Only s/he does not see the actual men who are dying. The poem is short (only two quatrains), laconic and barbed.

Valentine's journalism lacks Sylvia's wit and breadth of reference, but her accounts can be vivid and immediate. In the following piece she is describing the POUM, or Revolutionary Communists, in Barcelona, which comprised Trotskyists, Anarchists and others opposed to official Soviet Communism, and in particular were bitterly opposed to the Catalan Communist party or PSUC (to which Valentine and Sylvia were officially attached while in Spain):

> In Barcelona the POUM was the smallest, and noisiest of the three parties. They managed to put a convincingly Fascist appearance, with their cavalry, their arbitrary behaviour, their brightly decorated and noisy cars which raced up and down the Ramblas every evening. A noisy party . . . and fond of show, and rich, the people said. But no one who watched them would have said there was a war on. Carnival yes. War no.[65]

Her lack of sympathy with POUM is in striking contrast to Orwell's account in *Homage to Catalonia*; and nowhere in any of her or Sylvia's writings on Spain is there any attempt to engage with the problem of how the PSUC dealt with the POUM, of the leaders it killed, and the brutality of its suppression of that movement. For them, as for many British comrades today who were part of the Spanish struggle, the PSUC's actions *were* justified, for POUM's utopian non-authoritarian politics spelled certain death to the Republic, pitched against the military strength of the Fascist powers.

Sylvia wrote many short stories, sketches and accounts in these years, some of which have been recently reprinted. Both Valentine and Sylvia tried to get as much as they could written and printed about Spain wherever possible, to spread the word and counteract the official view put forward of the fighting as a matter that was solely of concern to Spaniards, and not to the rest of the world. (A view that was shared, incidentally, by Vera Brittain.)

In a piece written for the *New Statesman* (July 1937), Sylvia conveys the sense of poverty, heat and toil, the low, monotonous harsh life of the peasants, that was to form the core of the subject of her fifth novel *After the Death of Don Juan*, published towards the end of 1938:

> The reapers are too sunburned to look hot. Faces and bared arms are dark, shining with sweat they look like oiled wood. The men wear broad-brimmed straw hats, the women muffle their heads in thick kerchiefs, sometimes they have a white cloth bound over the mouth. This prevents the rasping straw dust from irritating the throat. The dust settles on faces and bared arms, the flies buzz. . . .
>
> Subdued to this rhythm, working on under the heavy sun, the corn-dust flying, the flies buzzing, the beat of the swollen vein, the ache in the loins . . . to those who reap it can this harvest of 1937 seem so very different from the harvests of other years?[66]

She answers this with a concluding anecdote of the Government lorry passing along the road to Madrid, and all the reapers, stiffly, awkwardly, with the sweat running off them, rising to salute and shout to *their* soldiers.

There were many different kinds of 'propaganda' pieces like this, which reveal Sylvia's deep empathy for the people and the country. A long piece for *Left Review* speaks openly of the contradictions as well as the euphoria in the early days of Barcelona, the ransacking of the nobles' houses for treasure, and careful storing away of the great artworks, the gutting of the churches. She describes seeing the men from a local revolutionary committee arrive with hammers to smash up a religious plaque:

> Seriously, without a vestige of either rage or contempt, they

smashed it to bits. Their expressions were exactly those of two conscientious decontaminating officers dealing with a bag of infected linen which had been discovered in a house which was supposed to be free of infection.[67]

Sylvia also wrote some fine poems as a result of her Spanish Civil War experiences, such as 'Benicasim', 'Waiting at Cerbere',[68] and translated a number of popular Spanish ballads, the Romanceros. The Romancero is a loosely structured ballad-form, which enables the poet to deal with public events, to make public pronouncements; it is rhetorical and celebratory, and many were composed for the Republican cause during the war. Spender, Tom Wintringham, and A. L. Lloyd were amongst other English poets who translated them.

The Romanceros deal with simple sentiments and simple images, heartening the soldiers; 'Encarnacion Jimenez', by Felix Paredes, is about the fate of a woman who washed the militiamen's clothes and was shot by the Fascists:

> Out of the foaming suds
> What love-tokens of clean linen
> you fetched for your brave lads!
> . . . [we] greet on your tattered carcass
> each springing gillyflower,
> each gout of blood blossoming
> under the metal shower.

In July 1937 Valentine and Sylvia went to Madrid for the Second Writers Congress of the IAWDC. The British Foreign Office ruled that the Congress was not a valid reason for visiting Spain and refused to grant visas to the delegates. Visas could be issued for business purposes, for journalism, or for humanitarian purposes, but not for culture, Sylvia was told.

The Congress, which included writers like Hemingway and Malraux, was a star-studded and, under the circumstances, well-attended affair. It was organised from Paris by the Chilean poet, Pablo Neruda, and reports vary of the number of delegates (between sixty and eighty) who attended, representing twenty-six countries. Few of the delegates were women. Sylvia and Valentine were the only women in the British delegation, which was to include W. H. Auden, John Strachey, Lascelles Abercrombie, John Sherwood, Montague Slater, John Lehmann and Frank Pitcairn, better known today as Claude Cockburn.[69] (In fact the official list was not correct. Auden did not go, John Strachey clearly stayed in London, and possibly Lehmann too, while Edgell Rickword was one of the party.)

Valentine wrote to Edgell Rickword on their return of the difficulties they had encountered trying to let the Party, and Strachey in particular, know of their departure, for the visit was arranged at the last minute. The whole episode is quite revealing, for officially Strachey was never a Party member:

> We arrived to find John Strachey very angry with us and having reported us rather precipitately to 16. [i.e., 16 King St, Party headquarters.] Failure to let him know about leaving – but we tried as hard as possible.[70]

She went on to complain she had spent an hour telephoning him at his club, while Sylvia had taken a taxi to the *Daily Worker* to look for him – and both John Lehmann and Amabel Williams Ellis had joined in the search.

Whatever the ins and outs, one person who certainly was on the delegation, and with whom Sylvia and Valentine did not see eye to eye, was Stephen Spender. Sylvia's account of their Madrid visit in a letter to Steven Clark, a friend they had met in Barcelona the year before, stresses that this visit was 'infinitely happier than Barcelona. It was like Barcelona with a great many Asuncións[71] and no O'Donnels[72] and Feas.'[73] Sylvia went on to say how they had Stephen Spender with them, and he was 'a kind of O'Donnel in the flesh, an irritating idealist, always hatching a wounded feeling'. However, this was clearly a minor irritant compared with the delight of being with the Spanish people: 'I find myself deeply at home with the Spanish, I cleave to their particular variety of practicalness.' She gave as an example the driver of their car who, when they had a puncture and the spare tyre turned out to be useless, 'wasting no time in useless acrimony or lamentation, went off, gathered a large handful of walnuts, hammered them open with a stone, and fed us as we sat by the roadside.'[74]

The Spanish people vied with each other to entertain the delegation wherever they went, and to receive them hospitably, to lay on banquets and take them on tours of inspection in death-defying motor cavalcades, whose driving left Valentine breathless with admiration. The pace, and the contrast between this VIP treatment and the realities of war which they were experiencing at first hand, clearly left some of the group with taut nerves. The reports of the time, however, concentrated upon the Congress and what was happening in Spain, without opening up all the inner dissensions. Some particularly sharp divides occurred over the question of the Soviet Union, from which André Gide had just published a highly critical report. The congress was split into two camps; Sylvia and Valentine, of course, supported the Soviet Union.

Stephen Spender gave an account of the delegation which appeared many years later in his autobiography.[75] An unpleasant and cynical piece, amongst its disillusioned descriptions of the Congress and the celebrations, there is a vitriolic personal attack on Sylvia and Valentine, thinly disguised as a 'Communist lady novelist' and her friend, a 'lady poet'. (At the time, Spender was making something of a nuisance of himself in Spain in his anxiety to obtain the release from the International Brigade of his ex-lover, T. R. Hyndman, who had joined up in a fit of pique.) Spender compared Sylvia to:

> a vicar's wife presiding over a tea-party given on a vicarage lawn as large as the whole of Republican Spain. Her extensory smiling mouth and her secretly superior eyes under her shovel hat made her graciously forbidding. She insisted . . . on calling everyone comrade.[76]

He painted a picture of Sylvia manipulating the delegation to do what *she* wanted to do, and related a conversation purported to have taken place between Valentine and Sylvia, which seems to have come straight out of *Vile Bodies*.

Spender's heterosexism and homophobia in his description of the part Valentine and Sylvia played in Spain are representative of the exclusive 'male club' quality which dominated the set of privileged left-wing intellectuals from Oxbridge to which the 'MacSpaunders' belonged. Reporting Sylvia as saying 'what is so nice is that we didn't see or hear a single act of violence on the Republican side',[77] and a fictitious conversation between the two women, narcissistically gushing to each other in self-satisfaction and self-approval at what they have endured, Spender confirms the exclusivity of the tough, 'realistic' male world in which political struggles take place. Women, by implication, simply don't belong there.

The Communist Party itself was not without its own

heterosexism. As a woman, if you had no family then you had no sex and could do any work the Party asked you to. As independent women, who did not occupy a place in society through their attachment to any men, and as lesbians, Sylvia and Valentine did not quite fit anywhere. This, one must conclude, can only have had serious implications for their work, its reception and treatment by the largely male literary establishment.

It seems more than likely Sylvia's independence as a woman did affect her success as a writer. (She thought her Communism had.) Although she had good and loyal friends who were men, such as David Garnett, and Ian Parsons at Chatto, Oliver Warner and many others, she never concealed her primary attachment to Valentine. It was left to the mealy-mouthedness of later times to describe them as 'companions'. However, in 1939, in *Poems for Spain* which he edited with John Lehmann, Stephen Spender could still write appreciatively of Sylvia and include work of hers, despite the experience of the delegation which had clearly provoked each of them.

In his most recent anthology of Spanish Civil War writing in Britain, Valentine Cunningham implicitly underlines the exclusive, male picture of the period.[78] Attempting to insert women (missing from the earlier anthology in any focused way) into his picture of the war, Cunningham relies quite heavily on Sylvia and Valentine's example. He makes a roll-call of honour, La Pasionaria, Felicia Browne, Simone Weil, Nan Green, Sylvia Townsend Warner, but admits that for the most part women's role in the war was the traditional, supportive one: – organising, waiting for news, raising money and supplies, mourning.

Indeed, the Spanish war *was* a macho affair, for British writers and supporters at home as much as for those primarily involved in Spain. Women's position in the Republic, which was promoting education and literacy and which had instigated divorce and abortion and freed women from the oppression of the church, was profoundly better than it had been, but the actual fighting, after the early days, was man's work.[79] For women to engage in that struggle, they had to remain within the boundaries of their gender roles, and the Communist Party maintained a conservative view on those boundaries. Felicia Browne was unique amongst foreign women supporters of the republic in dying as a militia-woman on active service.

On their return from the Congress Valentine and Sylvia both wrote accounts of their experiences. Valentine's, published in the *Daily Worker*, is an exuberant paeon of praise to the Republic. (She wrote it 'under orders' hastily on return, and was not pleased with it.) Sylvia's, for Lady Rhondda's *Time and Tide*, is a rather more measured piece.

What struck Valentine most forcibly was the hospitality and welcome afforded to them as intellectuals, the greeting they received, 'Viva Los Intelectuales'; everywhere the Spanish people were carrying on their lives with grace and chivalry, despite the intensive Fascist aerial bombardment. All the people they met showed hospitality and culture in the way they lived. At the Congress, soldiers and youths took part as well as the foreign delegates; everywhere the foreigners were treated with honour, with handshakes and embraces. They were fed and given the best accommodation, no matter how poor the people, they were fêted, treated to concerts, banquets, receptions. Even in the smallest villages, the 'extraordinary, the unbelievable greeting, from even the smallest group of peasants, the most isolated villages: "viva los intelectuales"'. These incidents showed, Valentine said, that Spain is the 'real future of culture – and by contrast, we know where is barbarism and gross intellectual darkness.'[80]

Sylvia's piece, 'What the Soldier said' for *Time and Tide* focusses on the implications for Spanish democracy of the contribution by one Spanish solider-delegate at the Congress, and upon the question of the place of culture in the Spanish struggle. The soldier's speech makes it plain that 'We will fetch peace and culture at the point of a bayonet for the sake of our own happiness and that of our children.'[81] It expressed, Sylvia said, a 'more solid appreciation than yearning, an intention to have and to hold. And what the soldier said to us was borne out by a hundred speeches we heard in Spain.'[82] She celebrated the traditional culture and style of the common people, the painting of an inn sign, the arrangement of fruit on a stall, the making of a recipe, preserved in the face of massive poverty and illiteracy, and she detailed some of the Government's achievements in the field of culture. At the same time Sylvia praised their readiness to show hospitality to the foreign delegates in the midst of war, but added: 'From Barcelona to Valencia, from Valencia to Madrid, we had no doubt that this hospitality of the Goverment of Spain was the hospitality of the people of Spain also.'[83] She too, welcomed the cry, 'Viva los intelectuales', which greeted them: 'We learned to hear ourselves spoken of as *los intelectuales* without dreading words usually so dubious in good intent, without feeling the usual embarrassment and defiant shrinking.'[84]

The contrast with Britain, where cultural purposes were not a valid reason for granting a visa, could not have been more striking. And as Cunningham and others have pointed out, the experience of Spain provided a welcome change for Communist intellectuals only too used to feeling cut off from the people in Britain by their class.[85] In Spain they were welcomed by the people 'not as curiosities, not even as possible propagandists, but as representatives of something they valued and under-stood'.[86]

AUTHORS TAKE SIDES ON THE SPANISH WAR

In June 1937, the *Left Review* had published a sixpenny pamphlet entitled *Authors Take Sides on the Spanish War*. The idea had originally been Nancy Cunard's and she indefatigably set out to write to all the famous writers she knew to ask them which side they stood for. The sponsors of the pamphlet included Auden, Spender, Louis Aragon, Pablo Neruda and Heinrich Mann. Characteristically, Nancy's role in the now-famous questionnaire[87] has since been overlooked, as indeed has the extent of her work for Spain. Who actually did the editorial work, sorting the entries into one hundred and twenty-seven for the Spanish Government, sixteen 'Neutral?', and a handful of supporters for Franco, is not clear. Some replies were not printed: the Introduction left little doubt that the authors were determined to show where writers' sympathies lay, and where they should lie:

> It is clear to many of us throughout the whole world that now, as certainly never before, we are determined or compelled, to take sides. The equivocal attitude, the Ivory Tower, the paradoxical, the ironic detachment, will no longer do. . . . Today, the struggle is in Spain. Tomorrow it may be in other countries – our own. . . . This is the question we are asking you:

*Are you for, or against, the legal Government and the People
of Republican Spain?*
Are you for, or against, Franco and Fascism?
For it is impossible any longer to take no side.
Writers and Poets, we wish to print your answers. We wish
the world to know what you, writers and poets, who are
among the most sensitive instruments of a nation, feel.[88]

Amongst the other women supporters of the Republic were
Pearl Binder, Margaret Cole, Storm Jameson, Rosamund
Lehmann, Rose Macaulay, Ethel Mannin, Naomi Mitchison,
Willa Muir, Christina Stead, Helen Waddell, Rebecca West,
Antonia White and Amabel Williams Ellis. Ruby M. Ayres,
Vera Brittain and Vita Sackville West were grouped amongst
the Neutrals, Vera Brittain from a pacifist point of view, and
Vita Sackville West because she loathed Communism as much
as Fascism, and thought the questionnaire hypocritcal since it
stressed the 'legal' Government of Spain – the implication of
which would be one should support Hitler or Mussolini
equally.

The sole supporter of Franco was one Eleanor Smith, who
claimed 'Naturally, I am a warm adherent of General Franco's,
being, like all of us, a humanitarian.' She regretted the
'destruction of so many beautiful objects, and the massacre of
so many innocent persons' – in that order – and claimed to pity
the 'ignorant red masses – subsidized by Russia.'[89] But 'Russia'
did not save the Spanish Republic, and by March 1939
Franco's rout of the loyalist forces was complete. The struggle
in Spain was over, the struggle in the rest of Europe was about
to begin.

Sylvia wrote in *The Countryman*, 'These are days that strain
the heart.'[90] Characteristically, she added that strain was better
than fatty degeneration.

Within two months she and Valentine had left for the United
States, where Sylvia was to attend a writers' congress called to
consider the loss of democracy in Europe. Their lives were
about to change radically.

CHAPTER 4

SYLVIA: THE NOVELS OF THE 1930s

THE TWENTIES' NOVELS: LINKS AND PREFIGURATIONS

Writing a review of Stephen Spender and John Lehmann's anthology *Poems for Spain* in *Life and Letters Today*, Sylvia said that those who went out to fight in Spain, unlike those who had, in Owen's famous words, 'died like cattle' in the senseless slaughter of the First World War, died as individuals, and as 'self-willed individuals at that.... They presented their lives . . . they did not offer up their opinions or their intellects.'[1] It is a statement that applies equally to the way she and Valentine lived their lives during these years.

The meaning of the individual's part in the national struggle was to be something which preoccupied her through her two major 1930s novels, and in *Summer Will Show* (1936) the situation of her heroine, Sophia Willougby, prefigures something of the Spanish predicament for British volunteers: Sophia also finds herself caught up in a struggle not her own, in the Paris Revolution of 1948. Only she has not gone there for a cause but to find her husband, and it is through the mechanism of personal relationships that she becomes involved in the political struggle, and finally becomes involved with Communism.

Summer Will Show is in other ways the mediating novel between Sylvia's first three novels and her major work of the late thirties and forties: it *is* about personal relationships, and about individuals. But it is also a novel about place, about country, and about politics. And the movement in the three major novels progresses from engagement with the individual in place and time to a broader canvas, to an attempt to engage whole social forces, and the social dynamic in which the individual plays only a small part. The progress of the novels marks, up till *The Flint Anchor*, where Sylvia returns to the human heart for her theme, a gradual withdrawal from character as an explanation of social change, or indeed as a sufficient explanation of how people behave. The balance shifts between people and landscape, but it is not just landscape as aesthetic or geography, but the socio-economic and political landscape too.

There was no point in Sylvia's writing career at which she specifically set out to write a political novel. As her interest in social and political reality began to predominate in her life, it surfaced in her work to shape two major and very different novels of the thirties. She had won her readership over by the skill and good humour of her story-telling, and by the lightness and elegance of her prose, and, despite her scorn for her 'light-hearted Lolly Willowes manner', she remained, as she commented, a 'bourgeois stylist'[2] to the end of her life, to the great delight of her readers. Sylvia was eminently pleased to discover that this quality in her writing (it was her own derisory label) disarmed the critics, for despite the outspoken subject-matter of *Summer Will Show*, as far as the reviewers were concerned she had, she reported, kept her 'pinafore still quite presentable'.[3]

In her first novel, *Lolly Willowes* (1926), she had pointed up the oppressive stupidity of the English bourgeois family in its exploitation of unmarried women. Lolly, tired of being taken for granted in the stifling dullness of her brother's family home in London, claims her independence by taking lodgings in a small village in the Chilterns, which turns out to be the heart of a coven of witches and warlocks. Lolly comes to accept the 'profoundly indifferent ownership'[4] of the devil, which she finds a great deal less tiresome than the obtrusive ownership of mortal men. Sylvia won herself a considerable notoriety with her spinster-heroine turned witch, and a wide readership on both sides of the Atlantic.

One of the main themes in *Summer Will Show*, the position of women in society and the forces ranged against their independence, shows through in this first novel. When Lolly announces to her brother Henry that she is going to live in the village of Great Mop, he does not believe she can be serious. When he realises she is, his reaction is that it is impossible for her to do any such thing: 'I cannot allow this. You are my sister. I consider you my charge. I must ask you, once for all to drop this idea. It is not sensible. Or suitable.'[5] Lolly replies that she is forty-seven, and if she is not old enough to know what is sensible and suitable at that age, she never will be. It is not impracticable for 'Nothing is impracticable for a single, middle-aged woman with an income of her own.'[6]

However, it turns out that her income is not what it was: Henry has halved it by speculating in the Ethiopian Development Syndicate, without, of course, telling her. Her anger at this discovery enables her to demand the remains of her inheritance and to sweep away all other opposition. The year is 1921 and, of course, had she not been single, middle-aged and middle-class, she might have whistled for her lodgings in Great Mop.

Towards the end of the novel, Lolly is telling the Devil about women's subjection in society. He proves to be a good listener. Imaginatively, through Lolly's impassioned speech, the novel encompasses hundreds of years of the drabness of women's lives, as wives, mothers, housekeepers, servants, primers-of-the-household-economy and keepers-of-everything-running-smoothly. Sylvia links together women's social subjection and their exclusion from speech, their corralling together into the world of their own 'silly conversation'. The women are the 'wives and sisters of respectable men, chapel members, and blacksmiths, and small farmers and Puritans';[7] and when the men talk, of politics, cock-fighting or mathematics, they listen. But:

> It is we witches who count. . . . Women have such vivid imaginations, and lead such dull lives. Their pleasure in life is so soon over; they are so dependant upon others, and their dependance so soon becomes a nuisance. . . .
> When I think of witches, I seem to see all over England, all over Europe, women living and growing old, as common as blackberries, and as unregarded . . . child-rearing, house-keeping, hanging washed dish-cloths on currant bushes . . . all the time being thrust further down into dullness. . . . Nothing for them except subjection and plaiting their hair. . . . If they could be passive and unnoticed, it wouldn't matter. But they must be active, and still not noticed. Doing,

doing, doing, till mere habit scolds at them like a housewife, and rouses them up – when they might sit in their doorways and think – to be doing still![8]

Women's knowledge and experience are not valued in themselves by Lolly; it is their exclusion from the world of men's speech and the necessity to be always cooking potatoes and servicing that she objects to. And the figure to whom she pours out her resentment is a male figure: to the devil she imparts the secrets of women's oppression, the meaning of female experience from a woman's point of view.

Her insight that women are dangerous, incalculable, extraordinary – which all women know in their hearts – is rendered in the context of the institution of a 'white' witchcraft that has no power to harm or destroy. It exists alongside society, but does not challenge it. Women become witches:

> to show our scorn of pretending life's a safe business, to satisfy our passion for adventure. . . . to have a life of one's own, not an existence doled out to you by others, charitable refuse of their thoughts, so many ounces of stale bread of life a day.[9]

If witchcraft is a metaphor for the power of change in our lives, Sylvia does not allow it to disturb the cool narrative texture of her novel, or the light surface of her prose: there are clear limits to what Lolly's witchcraft entails, and where it can lead. Sylvia was quite clear that she was writing to entertain. Before anyone else, she entertained herself in her writing. Of course the recognition about claiming one's life as one's own, not to have it doled out to you by someone else or by society's fiat, is at the heart of feminism – of second-wave as much as first-wave feminism. It is about claiming back power: and perhaps one should not underestimate the subversive potential of Lolly Willowes, who showed no need of marrying, who reclaimed her name (she became Laura again in place of 'Aunt Lolly' once she had escaped the family) and acted on her vision of independence with sturdy and unrelenting promptness.

Maybe Lolly is not such an unprogressive model, of how to disencumber oneself of family meshes, even today; although in this novel Sylvia had not yet confronted the question of the true (economic) cost of independence for a woman as she would do in *Summer Will Show*, and in particular, the far greater cost of independence for a married woman, even if she were childless. Meanwhile, the reading public loved Lolly, and Sylvia's success as a novelist seemed launched.

In her next novel, *Mr Fortune's Maggot* (1927), she makes an implicit criticism of the Anglican Church's pretensions to colonise souls, through the character of a simple-hearted and ineffectual missionary in the Polynesian Islands, Timothy Fortune. Her 'fatally sodomitic' missionary, as she described him to David Garnett, makes only one convert, a young boy whom he deeply loves. Lueli, the boy, remains wild and untouched at heart, and Mr Fortune has to admit his mission a failure. David Garnett was moved to tears by it.

The novel is a delightful and moving tale, full of Sylvia's characteristic relish for details of material life, most of it obtained from a volume of letters by a woman missionary which she happened upon in the Westbourne Grove branch of Paddington Public Library: Mr Fortune's equipment; how the islanders live; the leisurely, sybaritic existence; the climate; vegetation; the volcano's eruption. The whole book breathes a Utopia far from Western Puritanism and guilt, both of which Sylvia loathed, and has a strong sense of the redemptive power of love in Timothy Fortune's feeling for Lueli.

Love is also the redemptive motif of *The True Heart* (1929), which retells the tale of Cupid and Psyche set in the cold world of Victorian charity in Essex. As well as experimenting with narrative form, as she later explained, the novel had what she called a 'love-interest': it tracks the love-story of Sukey Bond, an ordinary servant-girl who is an orphan, and the half-witted son of a vicar, Eric Seaborn, and Sukey's determined effort to rescue him for herself and overcome class barriers. It is set in a marvellously evoked world of the bleak marshes, and a heartless Victorian hypocrisy and class pride as cold and bleak as they.

Each one of these first three novels has harsh things to say about the complacency, arrogance, hypocrisy and exploitation of the bourgeoisie and its institutions, especially the Church, for which Sylvia had a finely-tuned contempt bordering on loathing; but they are barbs buried beneath a light façade. It was not the social criticism which attracted her readers if they even noticed it, camouflaged in the dexterous narrative. For

example, one American review of *The True Heart* avowed that
the novel was a:

> whimsical, an ironic, a touching, a quietly beautiful story
> enriched by prose of the first order . . . the story once again
> of a servant girl . . . a very quiet Victorian story . . . full of
> hidden charm, humane mirth and unforced pathos.[10]

Reviews of the first two novels also stressed Sylvia's delicate
precision of phrasing and engaging fantasy, which said,
according to the reviewer, 'so many wise things about the
human adventure'.[11] One of her more perceptive early reviews
of *The True Heart* was by the American novelist Katherine
Anne Porter, which appeared in the *New York Herald Tribune*.
She was not lulled by the apparent simplicity of the book's
surface into believing it was merely whimsical; she described it
as fantasy, but in the sense of being:

> a deliberate effort to separate the reader for a moment from
> his ordinary mood of objectivity and set him down in a
> world of symbolic truths. . . . The whole book, in spite of a
> few living characters, a few credibly breathing animals . . . is
> like the changing landscape of a dream where figures move
> on some ageless errand.[12]

This separation of the reader from the 'ordinary mood', a
quality of suspension of disbelief such as we experience in
poetry and verse drama, is a hallmark of Sylvia's prose. The
language itself works to exert subtle transformations and to
people our minds with a new reality. This, to reverse the
dictum Leavis made upon Hardy,[13] is the fruit of being a poet,
of working her poetic apprenticeship with her first two volumes
of verse at the same time that she was creating the early novels.

SUMMER WILL SHOW

> This salt of reality, this acknowledgement, even in make-
> believe, of the actual nature of things and beings.'[14]

Above all, the imaginary worlds of Sylvia's novels are
notable for their quality of superadded reality, the tang of
things tasted, smelt, handled, known in their quiddity and in
their essence. Character is set within this dense texture of
material reality like a fly in amber: in *Summer Will Show* it is

character realised from within; in *After the Death of Don Juan* it is character presented externally, as 'humour', or type, a development that was to be carried further in her 1940s novel *The Corner That Held Them*.

Sylvia's ability to recreate a world, whether of Great Mop in the Buckinghamshire beechwoods, a Polynesian island, the Essex marshes, or Paris in the 1840s, gives solid reality to the middle-period novels. There is a persistent tenacity and inventiveness in the realisation of their landscapes, whether of the chalk hills of Dorset, the narrow streets of working-class Paris or the harsh bony terrain of Southern Spain, which renders them at once both familiar and surprising. Part of the reason for the sense of conviction she achieves, of familiarity, may be that her characters and settings haunted her so long before she began to write.

Summer Will Show first began to haunt her in her 'gaunt flat over the furrier in the Bayswater Rd'[15] in 1920 or 1921; at that time she was involved in the Tudor Church Music project, when the character of Sophia Willoughby appeared to her – 'an early Victorian young lady of means with a secret passion for pugilism; she attended prize-fights dressed as a man and kept a punching-ball under lock and key in her dressing-room'.[16] Sylvia knew her name immediately, and that she had smooth fair hair, was tall, reserved and very ladylike. (In some respects, not unlike Valentine.) The next character to appear was Minna – 'telling about the Pogrom in a Paris drawing-room and Lamartine leaning against the doorway'.[17] Many years later, in 1932 or 1933, she was in Paris with Valentine 'and in the Rue Mouffetard, outside a grocer's shop, I found that I wanted to write a novel about 1848. And Sophia and Minna started up and rushed into it.'[18]

The novel took four years to write, while, as she noted on the fly-leaf of Valentine's copy, they moved from Chaldon to Paris to Frankfort Manor and back to Chaldon again; she finished it at Lavenham where she went away to be alone and 'dispatch' it: it was a long work, 400 pages. The first 100 pages develop the character of Sophia Willougby in the setting of her Dorset estate, the fine country house of Blandamer, which has belonged to her parents and where she grew up. She is virtually estranged from her husband Frederick, who lives a profligate life in Paris in the company of a Jewish entertainer called

Minna Lemuel. Sophia's life centres around her two children and her estate, and she is well-enough satisfied with it, for an absent husband is really the best of all worlds, preventing any necessity of marrying, and allowing her as much freedom as a woman can possess, through her married status, without the interference of a flesh-and-blood partner. Until, that is, her children fall ill and die of smallpox. She becomes a woman trapped by her gender and her class whose sole reason for existence has been stripped from her. The only sphere in which she can think to assert herself is to go hunting.

Meanwhile, the doctor has sent for her husband: one male to another, taking charge and organising her life. The doctor's wife is appalled at her husband interfering with Mrs Willoughby and intercepts his letter, declaring that such a one as Mrs Willoughby has no need of Mr Willoughby. But Sophia's sense of decorum is offended by this unlooked-for assistance: she might in effect discard her husband, as indeed, given his behaviour she had; she might feel herself in every way his equal, if not his superior, and indeed she did; but it was quite a different matter for anyone in Society to put such things into words – 'Such things could be done, but not said.' Class and gender mesh, to prevent any overt challenge to the existing order: many things can be tacitly tolerated provided they are not named. As indeed, at another level, a similar process of 'not-naming' is at work in this novel; for the relationship that develops between the two main characters, Sophia Willoughby and Minna Lemuel, is never named as lesbian; many critics ignored the real nature of the friendship which is at the core of the novel.

To restore her position and her freedom in society, Sophia reluctantly comes to realise that she must have more children. There will be no escape for her from the 'sentence of death pronounced' that the young women 'Marry, bear children, and guide the house.' She considers having a child by the lime-kiln man, where she took her children to cure them of whooping cough, and from whom they contracted the fatal smallpox, but receives from him a bitter class rebuff. She tells him her children are dead and he retorts with a flat accusing anger listing some of the many reasons why children die – 'the smallpox, and the typhus, and the cholera . . . the low fever, and the quick consumption. And there's starvation. Plenty of things for children to die of.'[19] When she taxes him with his lack of pity he snarls back at her:

> I'm like the gentry, then. Like the parsons, and the justices, and the lords and ladies. Like that proud besom down to [sic] Blandamer. . . .
>   Plenty more children, they say, where the dead ones came from. If they die like cattle, the poor, they breed like cattle too. Plenty more children. That's what I say to you. Rich and poor can breed alike, I suppose.[20]

Angered but speechless, Sophia withdraws. The whole scene has a curiously theatrical air. The sense of staging continues when, to replace her children, Sophia goes to Paris to find Frederick. Up to this point in the novel, Sophia's independence, limited though it is, has been buttressed by her position as Lady of Blandamer House. Because she owns the estate, its workers, servants, dependants; because everything turns for her – the footmen's calves are clothed in unwrinkled white silk, the trees are felled and pollarded, the labourers toil in the bony dusty field – her true servitude is masked. And yet without her husband and her family, she cannot 'make her mark': it is only through them that she can act, for 'How should a woman satisfy her ambition except through a man?' The question reverberates throughout the next 300 pages, and the term 'woman's ambition' comes to mean in Paris something rather different from what she had understood by it in Dorset. If the first section of the novel sets forth the thesis of Sophia's need for liberation from the patriarchal family, the next section supplies the antithesis of her gradual recognition of her release through another woman, while the final section of the novel supplies the synthesis in which fulfilment comes in recognition and acceptance of political commitment.

What Sophia gains in Paris is not, in the usual sense, achievement of ambition: rather she goes through a gradual, inexorable process of stripping away what she did not know she wanted to lose – her respectability, her jewels, her fine clothes, her money – all the signs of exchange that signal her to be an upper class woman. With them go the habits of mind and body and of years of conditioning. Through her relationship with Frederick's mistress, Minna, she discovers love, poetry, excitement, risk, generosity, poverty, and happiness beyond her imagining. She also discovers suffering; what it is to be a member of a victimised and exiled group.

If the character of Minna Lemuel (raconteur and unscrupulous, bewitching, ageless hostess to a tatterdemalion mixture of bourgeois artists, poseurs, intellectuals and revolutionaries on the Left Bank in Paris) had been in the back of Sylvia's mind for many years, the early 1930s was the moment for that character to ripen. Minna's Jewishness and her suffering as an exile were an important part of Sylvia's theme. By looking unsentimentally into the past, Sylvia realised in the character of Minna a part of the nightmare that gripped her contemporaries.

Sophia's first sight of Minna is as she sits in her salon recounting the tale of her Lithuanian childhood and the Jewish pogrom to a packed audience. Sophia is enthralled; Sylvia gives the narrative – with its themes of freedom, persecution, struggle, national feeling, petty oppression and the irrepressibility of the human spirit – full weight within the novel. She also uses it implicitly to point up the curious alliance of motives and classes which heralded the 1848 Commune in Paris, and to suggest from the outset some of the inherent instabilities that would contribute to its eventual downfall. The narrative is interrupted by the outbreak of the fighting which heralded the days of the Paris Commune: the concierge announces that the 'people in the street are demanding the carriages for their barricade'.[21]

Through the medium of inserting Minna's tale into the novel, Sylvia realised the transition from the stable conventions of Dorset society to the revolutionary potential of Paris in 1848. The narrative exists perfect and entire within its own terms, set in counterpoint and tension to the discourse of the novel itself, always at the back of the reader's mind representing art's challenge to stable bourgeois societies. One of Sylvia's most perceptive critics, Eleanor Perenyi, said that this tale 'burned in her mind' long after the rest of the book had become dim.[22] The strange poetry and intensely felt immediacy of the narrator-as-child, recalling the remote, mysterious grandeur of forest, mountains and raging torrents, the fierceness of winter's grip – the stuff of folk-tales and fairy-tales and travellers' legends of distant lands – pitches the reader as well as the salon audience out of the world of bourgeois gentility, whether of a Left-Bank Paris salon or a Dorset country estate, and creates a world of unattached possibility.

As well as pointing up the political theme of freedom and the struggle of the people of Paris against the oppressive Bourbons, the narrative opens up a space of artistic freedom in which the two women can reach each other – a space which would otherwise be closed, positioned as they are each in relation to one man, as respectively wife and mistress to Frederick. (In her first encounter with Frederick in Minna's salon, Sophia is aghast to discover she is being used as 'his stalking horse' so that he can bait Minna – 'her wifely petticoats the shield whence he could attach his mistress'[23])

Art ignores, shoves aside social construction: it cannot transcend it, but it can make a temporary space in which transformation can occur. That is the measure of its revolutionary significance. Immediately, Minna's tale shocks Sophia out of her Dorset-bred preoccupations: she quickly forgets that she has come to Paris to be got with child by her husband, her assumptions obliterated at one blow by the intense curiosity Minna and her performance have aroused. She reflects as she stares at Minna:

> Are you the child who ran across the bloodied snow to kill the Christians? Are you the prophetess, the brooding priestess of Liberty, who spoke with such passion of the enfranchised river? Are you the woman so bitterly hated, my rival and overthrower?[24]
>
> Never in her life had she felt such curiosity or dreamed it possible. As though she had never opened her eyes before she stared at the averted head, the large eloquent hands, the thick, milk-coffee coloured throat that housed the siren voice. Her curiosity went beyond speculation, a thing not of the brain but in the blood. It burned in her like a furnace, with a steadfast compulsive heat that must presently catch Minna in its draught, hale her in, and devour her.[25]

Too tired to leave Minna's apartment, Sophia falls asleep on the couch. The metaphor of desire – the steady burning heat of her curiosity about Minna, and her siren voice – are transposed in sleep as she hears: 'Sleep, you must sleep, my beauty, my falcon' and feels hands stroking her, 'slowly, heavily, like the hands of sleep, stroking her hair and her brow'.[26] Throughout the next day that she spends in 'passionate amity' with her husband's mistress, she realises that she has crossed a boundary as surely as if she had renounced her position as a wife: 'She could go anywhere, do anything. . . . Hers was the liberty of the fallen woman now.'[27]

The first effect of that liberation is to enable Sophia to do precisely that which was so unthinkable in Dorset – to put her feelings, perceptions and experiences honestly into words. The effect is cathartic, but also traumatic:

> Talking to Minna she supposed that she must talk herself to death as others bleed to death; . . . .
>
> At intervals, in some strange non-apparent way, there was food before her, and more wine in the glass, the fire built up or a lighted lamp carried into the room. Sometimes a drum rattled somewhere through the echoing streets beating the *rappel*, or a burst of sudden voices rose from the barricade. And with some outlying part of her brain she recognised that a revolution was going on outside.[28]

At this stage, the revolution for Sophia is the Parisians' affair, an unreal show that is going on below Minna's balcony, from which she watches the life of the barricades in its quotidien domesticity, the men changing their trousers, washing themselves in buckets of water, the arrival of tin coffee-pots, bread and sausage in a 'paper chemise'. It is Minna's revolution, Minna who is standing unbonneted in the street drinking to it, giving her duelling pistols to it; but not her best pair. Indeed, Sophia is so little conscious of the reality of the revolution that she proposes to take Minna out to dinner, where they discuss Frederick over fillet-steak and Beaujolais: 'It had been an axiom of Papa's that under doubtful circumstances it was best to order Beaujolais.'[29] Even during a revolution the precepts of upper-class Dorset still hold sway. Sylvia's irony against the hapless but none the less dangerous husband is beautifully tempered in this exchange between wife and mistress:

> 'I have not had much opportunity to muse over Frederick's domesticity for the last three years', said Sophia.
> 'No. And for part of that time I had perhaps rather too much. So you see we must both be biassed.'
> 'Poor Frederick!'
> 'Poor Frederick! . . .
> However . . . our faulty appreciation would not trouble

him. Frederick completely despises all women. I think that is why he seems so dull and ineffectual.'[30]

Frederick asserts his revenge; to win back his wife, apparently out of pique and a sense of flouted convention, to which end he enlists the aid of Sophia's Great Aunt Leocadie, a formidable lady of Parisian Society. (The character Sylvia most enjoyed creating, 'so detestable and so estimable . . . the only person on her side of the fence who had enough stuffing to be set opposite Engels.'[31]) The ploy nearly works and a reconciliation is about to be effected when Sophia discovers that Minna is starving. She returns straight to Minna and gives her all the money she has. Minna promptly puts the money in a charity box, laughing that she has beggared Sophia. The effect of the gift, and of Minna's action, is to confirm the two women's delight in each other and fasten their affections ever more closely.

At the beginning of the third section of the novel, Minna placidly comments that Sophia has finally run away: 'I've encouraged a quantity of people to run away, but I have never seen anyone so decisively escaped as you.'[32]

Once Frederick has failed to divide the two women, he has in effect lost the battle for Sophia – although the real, because economic, basis of men's power over women continues to be demonstrated throughout the novel. To be free of that power means to lose all bourgeois comforts and status; there can be no compromise.

It is at this point that Frederick attempts to reassert his ownership by beggaring Sophia: he cuts off her bank credit and confiscates her gold and jewels – all of which he is entitled to do. (The Married Women's Property Act which allowed married women to retain independent control of their own property was not passed until 1870.) Sophia is left with 'what is left over from my ring . . . my clothes, for what they are worth. And my hair. I believe one can always sell one's hair. After that, unless I comply with Frederick's wishes, nothing.'[33] As Minna's friend, the Communist theoretician Ingelbrecht (based on Engels) comments, 'It is a lock-out.'

This showdown is the catalyst for the course that Sophia's life takes from now on: it becomes clear to her that she has joined herself to Minna and become an outcast – the shock of Frederick's abuse of the woman constantly named as his 'mistress' confirms the wife's position on 'the other side'. One effect of her new material position, stripped of any financial resources, is to make her a great deal more critical and sceptical of the revolutionaries for their ineffectuality: 'Whoever else might hope to survive a year of the republic its revolutionaries certainly could not.'[34]

There is both a shortage of work in the Commune and a shortage of food, and only the Communists appear to have a clear idea of what is happening or what to do about it. Sophia gains a grounding in the basics of material economy through talking to some of the demonstrators on a Communist march, which bears a banner with the demand 'Bread or Lead'. Minna is horrified: the Communists, she says are dangerous. Meanwhile, Sophia's only means of gaining a living is as a kind of pavement artist, singing Sunday School hymns to accompany a young man who makes speeches against the Church and plays the accordion. But she is aware that this is no way to live. If the revolutionaries persisted in this way, they would soon all be dead of starvation.

The need to get a living rapidly transforms Sophia's perceptions of life. The necessity to buy good food cheaply develops an unsuspected side of her nature and affords unsuspected pleasures:

> With her whole soul she walked from stall to stall,
> countering the wiles of those who sell with the wiles of those who purchase, pinching the flesh of chickens, turning over mackerel. . . . Her fine nostrils quivered above cheeses and sniffed into pickle-tubs and the defencelessly open bellies of long pale rabbits. . . .
> All round her were the kind of faces she liked to see; sharp clear glances, lips taut with cupidity, brows sharply furrowed with exact thought . . . she tasted the rapture of being first amongst peers.[35]

Now Sophia looks upon members of her own class as strangers, and day by day, her alignment with the 'mauvalis sujets', the outlaws of society, 'who live for their own way and by their own wits', frees her from the characteristics of her class, the whole set of false obligations imposed by 'Society', symbolised by the gloves which in that society one never removes. Shedding her gloves she sheds convention and prudence, and gains a sense of exhilarating happiness, the shabbier and hungrier she becomes.

The novel is free of both romanticism and sentimentality about poverty, however, for the shifts in Sophia's behaviour are noted exactly the lower down the social scale she sinks. At the same time, the novel conveys a sense of the absurd, spontaneous joy, the quite unmerited and unprepared-for delight, which springs up between two women in passionate sympathy of heart and mind. It is this, deriving clearly from the effusive joy of the relationship between herself and Valentine, which gives the book its dominant tone, a note as light and effervescent as 'a fountain . . . before unsuspected and now to play for ever, prancing upwards, glittering and uncorruptible'.[36]

In the last stage of Sophia's transformation, the unlikely *Bildungsroman* from heiress to humble revolutionary (when the final stage of the fighting breaks out on their street she loads guns on the barricade), it is impossible not to see something of Sylvia's own hard-headed attitude to political commitment. In the novel, she endows Sophia with similar qualities. When Ingelbrecht asks her what she would do with her peasants, she replies that one should not pity them. Then they will never get up. When a horse is down you beat it to get it up. He laughs appreciatively and says that her brains should be under a red bonnet. In the last days of the Commune, Minna and Sophia work for the Communists collecting old bell-pulls and other scrap lead for weapons, and Minna is content and happy to be thieving again: she approaches it as an art. At last, dedicated and united, they work together.

There is a sense of fusion of the all-too temporary possibility that the Commune represented, with the happiness and mutual self-discovery of the two women; the personal interwoven into the narrative of the progress of political events through those confused months in Paris in 1848. Both personal and political are overshadowed from the start by a sense of impending doom. It is a narrative that moves inevitably forward to the destruction of love and to the failure of the revolution. Personal fulfilment is doomed to the same thwarting as the political.

For the satisfactory artistic integration of the novel, politics and life must mirror each other: Minna's gratuitous death, stabbed on the barricades by Sophia's jealous nephew Caspar, may reflect the accidental and gratuitous outcome of so much political endeavour. And yet, aesthetically, there is something profoundly unsatisfying about this neat tying-up of the plot. It is not so much the *fact* of Minna's death but the manner of it, for the writing at this point in the novel sinks to bathos.

Caspar, placed by Frederick in the Garde Mobile, the most brutal and feared of the forces ranged against the Republicans, leaps over the barricade on which Sophia and Minna are fighting, and when Minna recognises him and calls out, 'her voice warm, inveterately hospitable', he stabs her through the breast with his bayonet, shouting 'Drab! . . . Jewess! this is the end of you.'[37] Sophia in blind fury shoots him through the mouth but is saved from execution because she is a woman, more particularly because she is a lady. Worst of all she is saved by a priest; Sophia rounds on him in fury:

> how many women are dead already, and how many more
> will be, with your consent and complaisance? Dead in
> besieged towns, and towns taken by storm. Dead in
> insurrections and massacres. Dead of starvation, dead of the
> cholera that follows starvation, dead in childbed, dead in the
> workhouse and the hospital for venereal diseases. You are
> not the man to boggle at the death of a woman.
>
> It seemed to her, and she was glad, that she had screamed
> this out like a virago of the streets.
>
> But with a bow he reasserted,
> 'I cannot consent to the death *of a lady*.'[38]

Dramatically these last scenes are of a high-pitched operatic nature, despite the power of Sophia's rhetoric. The solid reality of life on the barricades, of the quotidian life of Sophia and Minna together, is gone. Another kind of discourse has been inserted, and obtrudes.

At the close of the novel, Sophia is immersed in reading the pamphlets which Ingelbrecht has given her to distribute – another dangerous, practical job that she has undertaken to perform for the Communists. She opens one and begins to read: 'A spectre is haunting Europe – the spectre of Communism.'[39] It is the opening of the 1848 Communist Manifesto, and the novel ends with a fourteen line quotation from it. Sophia has moved beyond freedom and happiness, beyond personal love, into the sphere of dogged, unromantic commitment: 'She seated herself; and leaning her elbows on the table, and sinking her head in her hands, went on reading, obdurately attentive and by degrees absorbed.'[40] More alone than ever before, the next phase in her education is about to begin: freedom is not enough.

Whether the choice of ending was influenced by external, non-artistic reasons – whether Sylvia chose to end it with Sophia alone because she wished the emphasis to fall on dedication to her chosen politics (and she was writing the end at the height of her new-found political ardour); because Minna as Jewish victim must exemplify the doom of her race; because Minna as romantic revolutionary had to be swept aside for the forces of new Communist realism represented by Sophia – is immaterial to one's sense of the novel's achievement. What is material is the fault in the realisation of Minna's death, which suggests a more deep-seated uncertainty or unease. An artistic failing of this kind in the texture of even such a long novel as *Summer Will Show*, when it is the work of as sophisticated and skilled an artist as Sylvia, suggests some more deeply hidden contradiction.

It seems to Sophia that her happiness, 'blooming so late and so defiantly' is immortal, and it is characterised for her by one of Marvell's verses which she finds on a second-hand bookstall:

> My Love is of a birth as rare
> As 'tis for object strange and high,
> It was begotten by despair
> Upon impossibility.[41]

There are no obvious reasons that Sophia can see why she should love Minna; she stands for everything Sophia had been taught to shun in the world in which she grew up, 'policed by oughts', in which 'one's emotions were the expression of a bargaining between demand and supply, a sort of political economy'.[42] Minna offered but one flower, 'liberty. . . . One could love her for the only sufficient reason that one chose to.'[43] But liberty alone is not enough: Sophia must also pursue her own free path. She must become that which she has it within herself to be. The choices at some point come to be between love, artistic freedom and serious political engagement.

There is another layer to consider. Throughout the novel, the figure of the artist is represented in the character of Minna: even the eminently respectable and shrewd Great Aunt Leocadie tells Sophia that she is 'certainly an artist. . . . She tells fairy-stories and fables. It is something quite particular, a narrow talent, but perfectly cultivated.'[44] – words which Sylvia might have considered applying to herself.[45] The novel, written at the height of the creative encounter between herself and Valentine, when they were collaborating on *Whether a Dove or a Seagull* and entering into their political commitments together, draws upon aspects of her and Valentine's relationship. If, thematically, the destruction of the two women's love in the course of the revolution acts as a paradigm of the profound reach of political events in people's personal lives, it remains the case that at the point of rendering this destruction, Sylvia's artistic nerve failed.

The contrast between the flawless articulation of the events of the pogrom in Minna's tale and the tinny realism of the barricade scene is striking: removed by historical distance and controlled by the artifice of form Sylvia could handle such moments. Placed in the immediate, and attempting to resolve the complex emotion she has generated between her two women characters, the moment of dissolution is handled in a gestural manner. It is both perfunctory and loud.

It may be that this flaw indicates her inability to engage with the emotion of loss at this stage, or sheer tiredness (she said she finished the novel 'at a gallop'). Or it may be that there is another, unresolved sub-text concerning her own involvment in the problem of the artist's role in the revolution. If the death of Minna signifies the necessary sacrifice of the artist (as well as of personal love) in the course of the political struggle, the artistic failure here can be seen as prefiguring Sylvia's later withdrawal from overt political reality in her fiction. To shackle the artist was, for Sylvia, no solution: Minna alive was Minna free, amoral, unreliable, as Sophia at one point sadly realises, waywardly pursuing her own truth, as 'incorruptible and effervescent as a fountain'.[46] If, in *Summer Will Show*, Sylvia attempted to stifle the artist in order to free the dedicated revolutionary, her unconscious was unable to consent to such a move. The death of Minna remains a botch, an unsatisfactory imposition on the artistic unity of the novel. If here the choice did lie between the artist as heroine and the revolution, it was a choice she put behind her, for in her next two novels there were to be no heroines, nor heroes.

Most of the reviewers of *Summer Will Show* were impressed, although Peter Quennell thought it over-elaborate and the nicety of style sometimes a drawback.[47] Many of them commented on how apposite Sylvia's 1848 setting was to current events in Spain. The *Time and Tide* critic, for example, felt that, despite the general prejudice against historical novels, 'in the hands of such a gifted producer . . . they [the readers] will find that the world as it used to be provides not only a brilliant entertainment, but also an instructive commentary on the world as it is now.'[48]

But it was from the critics of the Left that Sylvia understandably received her most thoughtful and thought-provoking reaction. Ralph Wright, in his discussion of the novel in the *Daily Worker*, looked at the ways in which novelists on the Left were trying to reach their audiences and to communicate from a materialist and progressive standpoint. His view of *Summer Will Show* was that it was a work of: 'real history – the history not only of England but of Europe in the nineteenth century. It explains the . . . events of the revolution seen through those very English upper-middle-class ladylike eyes . . . almost a stroke of genius.'[49]

Wright barely notices the theme of Sophia and Minna's relationship, saying misleadingly, if with unintentional humour, that Minna and 'the English lady, united in a common hatred of the husband, become great friends'.[50]

The American neo-Communist publication *New Masses* and the left-radical *New Republic* both gave the novel warm reviews; Sylvia was delighted with this reception, and was further encouraged when, at one stage, there were plans for the Moscow-based *International Literature* to use it. *International Literature* was a prime focus for the discussion of writing sympathetic to the Soviet and Communist cause world-wide, and appeared in several European language editions, including German, French and English. In the 1930s, writers such as John Lehmann were publishing in the English-language edition: in 1936, for example, he contributed a survey of British poetry called 'Revolutionary Poetry'. But the magazine's prime purpose was to show off the new Soviet writing and theories, particularly a good deal of social realism.

But it was the review by Eleanor Clark in *New Republic* which may have influenced Sylvia's thinking as she worked on *After the Death of Don Juan*. Clark considered *Summer Will Show* to be a novel of conversion, but an individualist one. She pointed out that Sophia has no relationship to the people at any point, whether in Dorset or Paris; Sylvia is concerned with showing Sophia discovering her proper freedom, a freedom that takes her logically to act as the instrument of a group acting on behalf of the people, but still not to have any relationship with those people:

> For Sophia, the people are everywhere, and all, with their poverty and struggle, are for her benefit. This, if it were the end of the first chapter instead of the last, might be the story of a true conversion, in which collective activity became something more than the salvation of a private soul.[51]

Whether or not Sylvia took this criticism to heart, in *Don Juan* she attempts to portray exactly that – the collective response of the peasants of the village of Tenorio Viejo in a remote part of southern Spain, when confronted by the bungling, well-meaning projects for reform of their landlord, Don Saturno, and, finally, the outright Fascist repression of his son, Don Juan.

THE LESSONS OF COLLECTIVITY: CLASS AGAINST CLASS

Writing of *After the Death of Don Juan* to Nancy Cunard in 1945, Sylvia said it was:

> a parable, if you like the word, or an allegory or what you will, of the political chemistry of the Spanish War, with the Don Juan – more of Molière than of Mozart – developing as the Fascist of the piece.[52]

Sylvia felt this novel to be one of her most personal, 'though it appears to be quite impersonal because it's written with an arid degree of satire'.[53] The reasons why she saw it as personal are plainly stated in the interview she gave in 1975 and are to do with the strength of her feeling for Spain:

I wrote a few articles about life in wartime Spain and got them in where I could simply as propaganda. . . . By that time it was getting rather hard to get in any propaganda because the English authorities and respectables were clamping down on freelance journalists who had anything to say in favour of the Republic. I had a great deal to say . . . I've never seen people who I admired more. I never again saw a country I loved as much as I loved Spain. A most ungainly country to love, but it's extraordinarily beautiful.[54]

She loved it so much she wouldn't go back until the 'old brute' Franco was dead; when he finally died in 1975, she was too old. The experience of being in Spain affected her writing directly, and as a result she wrote *Don Juan*, 'which is definitely a political novel – at least perhaps I should say it's a political fable.'[55] She had already written a short fable for *Left Review* which bore reference to Spain: another 'The Bear' was a Christmas present to Edgell Rickword's first wife, Jonnie, in 1939.[56]

The form of the fable appealed to her: it was a form that she was to continue using throughout her life. Fable distances and depersonalises; it allows the artist to work from the impersonality of traditional form, detached from character, setting and superfluous incident. All the elements of story-telling are pared down in the fable to the essential. It exists as a form with one point, to deliver a message in an acceptable form; brevity is of its essence. In her eighties, Sylvia escaped the 'human heart' which, she said, she had grown weary of, and retreated to the Elfin kingdom, in which her fairy tales are another twist to the fabular form.

Sylvia had always been interested in form and was an adroit experimenter with it, whether in her poems or fiction. Fable allowed her a way of handling political themes, while taking character as given. In *Summer Will Show* she had taken the interweaving of individual and political development as far as she either could or wished to – and left her heroine, as Eleanor Clark pointed out, at the beginning of her struggle. In *After the Death of Don Juan*, she abandoned any attempt to ground action in character. Instead she focused on two opposing sets of interests and their allies, the peasants and the nobility, and in the clash of those interests and the interplay of particular types of character, realised the drama of the village of Tenorio Viejo.

The fantasy and fairy-tale elements of the earlier novels and stories remain visible throughout the whole of Sylvia's work, becoming subsumed by political purpose and transformed into fable in the middle period, and then in the late period suffering another transformation into the form of fairy-tale in *The Kingdoms of Elfin* (1977). Like the earlier work, this later one did have critical success, whereas, unsurprisingly, *Don Juan* did not. Sylvia's explanation of this failure was that the novel was published in 1938 in a small edition and was 'swamped in the circumstances of the time'.[57] It is difficult to get a clear picture of the publishing world of late 1938 early 1939; politically, of course, it was a very uncertain time, and the fact that a high proportion of thrillers and other escapist books were produced by, for example, Penguin Books in that year, suggest that many readers were looking for lighter reading-matter. On the other hand, it was also the time that saw the publication of such serious novels as Rex Warner's *The Professor*, and Jack Lindsay's *1649*. However, most of these books are rare today, suggesting perhaps that the print runs were small.[58]

Sylvia believed that her political commitments had affected the reception of her work: 'I usually had two or three amazingly good reviews, but I never had reviews from the sort of reviewers that *sell* books.'[59] It seems likely that the kind of political fable she was offering about Spain was not calculated to endear her to the literary establishment.

Was it the qualities of the fable form which alienated her readership? Certainly it is not overtly polemical and ideological – on the contrary, the novel begins as a comedy of manners; lightness of tone and acerbity of wit characterise the opening scenes set in Seville, as they take up the Don Giovanni/Don Juan story:

> The death – or rather, the disappearance – of Don Juan de Tenorio took place at Seville in the seventh decade of the eighteenth century. It happened under curious circumstances. Don Juan, a renowned libertine, was paying court to Doña Ana de San Bolso y Mexia, a young lady who was already promised in marriage elsewhere. . . . Her father, a retired Army man, had expressed his unequivocal disapproval of Don Juan, Doña Ana too averred most steadfastly that his advances were odious to her. Nevertheless, it happened that

Doña Ana was alone in the garden-court of her father's house one evening, and that Don Juan encountered her there.[60]

The smooth narrative composure of this opening and the spare recital of necessary facts belong to the traditional story-teller's art, as do the discreet pointers to the satiric intention. After relating the circumstances of the death of Ana's father fighting Don Juan, the narrative continues: 'It was expected that Don Ottavio, Doña Ana's betrothed, would avenge the Commander's death; or at any rate attempt to: Don Juan was a practised swordsman. Doña Ana, however, declared that vengeance must be the business of heaven.'[61]

Again, with a slight touch (the use of 'it was expected' and 'however') the underlying motives such as Don Ottavio's cowardice and Doña Ana's lust are pointed to. When Leporello, Don Juan's servant, tells his famous story of how the 'Commander in the likeness of his statue – or the statue animated by the Commander, have it as you will',[62] ordered Don Juan to repent and on his refusal caused him to be dragged down to hell by demons, Ana found that 'this demonstration of heavenly efficiency was too much for her'.[63] In *Don Juan* there are neither heroines nor heroes: Doña Ana and Don Juan are a match for each other in their shallow, senseless self-gratification, only for once Don Juan finds himself out-lusted. Concerned only with themselves, unable to see beyond the huge shapes of their vanity, they reveal their egoisms differently. Because she is a woman, Ana is objectively the less dangerous, if the more unpleasant; she cloaks her lusts in hypocrisy and in the respectability of the Church, whereas Juan, because he is a man, is in the position to unleash repression to promote his own interests.

Both Don Juan and Doña Ana are parasites on Spanish society and their enormous appetites for self-gratification cost their peasants and households dear. The serious side of the novel's theme, the 'message' of the political fable, concerns that cost and its outcome, which is ultimately Fascism. The novel lays bare the processes and the results of the peasantry's exploitation by the nobility, concentrating upon a small backward village in Andalucia during the visit of the Sevillean grandees to the castle.

As with *Summer Will Show*, the outsiders are brought in to point up the harsh reality of working-class lives. The poverty of rural Spain is seen through the eyes of the sophisticated city-dwellers as they make their journey to Don Saturno's castle, to inform him of his son's unfortunate death. They travel, curtained from the misery through which they are passing, in three coaches with seven mounted attendants and a baggage wagon, all draped in black and drawn by black mules: 'The hammercloths were of black velvet, crape bows obscured the scutcheons, and the servants wore black liveries.'[64] The contrast with the scene outside is stark, and related in the same flat, unemphatic story-telling manner:

> Over the wide estates of Andalucia small groups of peasants laboured, they looked no larger than hens scratching a poultry-yard. . . . Sometimes they passed the encampments which housed the labourers and their families. Only a few old women, blind or infirm, sat drowsing through the noon-day. Dogs, pigs, and infants sprawled in the road. . . . The stench was appalling, and the coachman had great difficulty in whipping the dogs, pigs, and children out of their path.[65]

The labourers are seen as insignificant as hens, the labourers' homes are only encampments, temporary, moveable, the children rate the same lack of regard as the dogs and pigs.

The subject of the novel is Spain: it is the poverty, the harsh beauty and the secret rhythms and life of the peasants that animate it. It is love of Spain that transforms the novel, little by little, from a satire of eighteenth-century aristocrats to a fable of powerful feeling and reach about the country, centering on the peasants' concern for their land. Sylvia had always been deeply sensitive to place, and her realisation of the settings of the preceeding novels forms some of the strongest inducement to the reader's sense of the solidity of these worlds. In *Don Juan* she takes this process a stage further: Spain *is* the novel: character is withdrawn and recedes before landscape to the point at which as they function within the narrative the human figures seem like tiny ants toiling, as if seen on the huge distant plains of that country. A similar distancing occurs in some of the poems of the thirties, evoking the world of labour in the fields in Dorset, in which the worker is an insignificant figure against the sweep of inhuman nature: a trait Sylvia shares with

Hardy – except that her vision is more evidently informed by political awareness.

The exploitation of one class by the other is realised through the life of Tenorio Viejo, a place so small that, as Ramon Perez, one of the leading figures amongst the peasants, says on his deathbed, when he looked for it on the map it wasn't marked: 'I have often looked for it. It is not there, though. It is too small, I suppose. We have lived in a very small place, Diego.'[66] To which his friend replies that they have lived in Spain.

It is a village in many ways probably representative of other villages in Spain, but with a difference in that in Don Saturno it has a benevolent if ineffectual landlord. In the past he has begun progressive schemes, such as opening a school to teach the peasants to read and write. When the Sevilleans hear of this, they are deeply shocked: ' "What repulsive sentiments", murmured the duena to the chaplain. "He must be mad", was the reply.'[67]

Don Saturno expounds his educational theory to his visitors that the end of all education is to impart a 'noble discontent. . . . In time the arts of reading and writing will force them [the peasants] to realise the wretchedness of their state and then to resent, and then, perhaps, to amend it',[68] much as Valentine and Sylvia had hoped their book-lending scheme in Dorset would awaken the minds of their agricultural neighbours. The nobles, who realise that educating the peasants means the beginning of the end of their social order, which is based on the rule of ignorance and fear administered through the Church, are appalled. But the school is now barely used, for the money to maintain, equip it and pay the schoolmaster has not been forthcoming, for the taxes the peasants pay are used for other purposes.

Similarly, Don Saturno has experimented with land reform, so that his peasants now hold their strips on yearly leases, but it little benefits them for the land is poor and lacks irrigation. He still taxes their land heavily, to supply not only the wants of his castle, his library, astronomy and other hobbies, but above all to support Juan. In fact, the lands are heavily mortgaged and the Don is deep in debt because of his profligate son, so the peasants are no better of for their landlord's benevolent intentions.

Don Saturno had toyed with a scheme to irrigate the lands,

and it is his revived interest in it, and the villagers' hope in its realisation, which forms the main dramatic thread in the events of the village, interwoven with the developments amongst the Sevillean visitors. Don Saturno, intellectual, amateur philosopher, sceptic, a man of reason deeply attached to his country and his people, is the most complex character in the novel. He is, at heart, a democrat, and the people are dear to him, but everything he touches fails miserably. Despite his loathing of his Sevillean guests, their prejudice and parasitism, of their hypocrisy, their lack of humour or any saving spark of intellectual curiosity, his fate remains inextricably entwined with theirs. Through the fate of the Don, Sylvia points out the way in which class interests align people despite their differences. At the end of the novel, by a twist of events, it is the Don whom the villagers see as the villain when the troops, summoned by his son, attack them. And it is Don Saturno who sits helplessly gagged and bound to his chair while Don Ottavio and Don Juan, linked in their common hatred of the people, direct the troops in slaughtering the peasants, for their unpardonable presumption in laying siege to the castle.

Early on in the novel, there is a long passage describing the old man's life-work of translating Aristophanes, which acts as illuminating commentary upon Sylvia's own methods and purposes in *Don Juan*:

> Spain could have no better teacher, no more wholesome liberator, than Aristophanes. . . . Just as Cervantes poked fun at the romancers, so did Aristophanes deride the high-minded Euripides, and on every page there was something familiar and endearing to a Spanish heart: beef boiled with broth and a slice of the tripe, pigs and chickpeas, thyme and grapes and garlic, law-suits and wool-combing, the wineskin and old women. . . . And slyly, too, the lever could be inserted, and without word of offence to church or throne the power of both might be shaken by this author whose plays included so many deities and no kings.[69]

But Don Saturno has no more luck in trying to get the insidious radicalism of Aristophanes performed than Sylvia had with her political novels – 'either something would be objected to on the grounds of the censorship or the actors would complain that there were no noble characters in the play'.[70]

But there is a limit to the Don's concern for his peasants; it is the *style* of the Spanish, of his peasants, which delights him. Appreciating them aesthetically, he enjoys their company:

> If they found pleasure in him, he no less was enjoying their company. Their sunburned faces bent over the chart, the severe comeliness of their wiry limbs, their melancholy magpie clothes, delighted him like beholding a work of art after walking through a gallery of simpering wax-works. The tang of their speech comforted his ears after so much polite conversation. . . . The Spain that he loved, pungent and austere, the Spain he studied in his library among histories, documents, charts, pedigrees, portraits and music-books: it was here in these five men talking about water; it would remain, long after his insipid and expensive puppets had gone back to their town-house.[71]

The passage contains the implicit criticism of the Don's position; for Don Saturno's appreciation of 'his' peasants is a matter of experiencing them as an art object. These same fellow human-beings which he is seeing as a work of art, he may choose not to see for months on end, while their lives are daily affected by the taxes and portions of their harvest they must give him. Their school is falling into decay and for most of the year their land is at the mercy of drought. For him it is a matter of choice whether or not he appreciates them – and it makes very little difference to the reality of their lives. Through Don Saturno, Sylvia makes a caustic indictment of the class of intellectuals and bourgeois sympathisers who do not actively align themselves with the working class by giving up their property-rights and unearned inheritance. It is the sharpest Marxist criticism in the book, directed at her own class, but it is still so lightly handled it does not disturb the even-handed satirical tone of the novel.

If Sylvia's most serious political critique was reserved for a member of the property-owning classes, her most devastating criticism of character is reserved for a woman of those classes. There is nothing whatsoever to recommend Doña Ana: she is the most unsympathetic character Sylvia ever created. Licensed by her position and fortune, Ana pursues her obsession for Juan with complete disregard of the consequences for anyone else. In the whole of *Don Juan* there is very little attention given to the women apart from the appalling Doña Ana – and her part in the narrative declines steadily from its early dominance until Don Juan reappears. As Sylvia switches her focus from the narrow world of the grandees to the broader canvas of the village community, with its miller, schoolteacher, priest, sacristan, labourers, and swineherds, its school, church, olive-yards, dusty streets and hovels, the women play an increasingly diminished role. They are seen, as in a Brueghel painting, composed and held in scenes of village life, washing the clothes in the river, combing the lice from their children's hair, gossiping in fragmentary glimpses from afar.

The only other woman character in the village to be individualised, and the only one given any sympathetic treatment, is the priest's housekeeper, a bony old woman called Doña Adriana, who has a scathing tongue and can prune the olive trees as well as a man. The village is an exclusively male-dominated society, in which women's voice is not heard; when the women speak what they say is scornfully dismissed by the men, saying, we shall go mad if we listen to these women. The women's words do not exist, have no rational status. They can only be admitted as part of the language of the irrational. Sylvia presents this society as it is, and the reader who knew Spain would draw the inference that in this respect, little had changed between the Spain of Charles III and the Spain of Negrin's republican Government.

As Sylvia does not hesitate to depict the sexism and the machismo of Spanish society, so she does not sentimentalise the portraits of the peasants. In their attempt to come to terms with the meaning of Don Juan's death, they ask Leporello to tell his story. The ensuing discussion, and the events which follow in connection with the irrigation scheme they so badly need, reveal the villagers in all their credulity, prejudice and ignorance. There are those who believe the story that Don Juan is dead; that now they will get the water to irrigate the land and at last be able to free themselves from the yoke of the estate, and there are those who, like Ramon Perez, do not place any credence in the story. Ramon realises that it will take more than the death of even their landlord's heir to right their wrongs, and give them control over their own land:

in a hundred years, though Don Juan will be dead, we shall not be rid of him. . . . We have more on our backs than the

son of Don Saturno. . . .
More than water is needed to wash away the castle.[72]

The pruning of the olive-yards offers a fable of the lives of the peasants and the way in which they are hampered in making any changes, for they lack the new, vigorous stock that would grow straight and strong and be productive. Their trees are old, with 'the prolix fertility of old age, branches bushed out everywhere, weak straggling growths obliterated the original pattern of the tree'.[73] So, in their community, new ideas are hard to grasp, for they have been isolated and turned in on themselves for so long.

The work of pruning is slow and hard and the crop uncertain because of the drought. In the groves, they work co-operatively, and the narrative highlights the way in which, in their community, each stands by each and helps the other. The hopeless siege of the castle represents the culmination of this co-operation. As the siege draws to its crisis, Ramon Perez reflects upon his life and the lives of his fellow-men; he sees the life of man having a shape as a tree does, and with as little choice as the tree has in that shape: each man is born, grows up and lives, the pattern is simple and repetitive, there is no escaping it: 'One grows up, one earns a livelihood, one marries a woman and begets children. As one grows older one gets tired and in the end one dies. That is the pattern of the life of man.'[74] He himself is a man of 'certain steadfast ideas'. They are not unusual or particularly advanced ideas, but he is uncommon for the 'steadfastness by which he lived according to his creed'.[75] (This line was inscribed by Sylvia on the flyleaf of Valentine's copy of the novel.) Life is hard, it would be better not to have been born; but since one has been born, man 'could better [his life] and amend what he could not abolish. . . . The world is not so bad as we make it. . . . There should be justice to the poor. . . . Neighbour should stand by neighbour.'[76]

Through Ramon Perez, Sylvia voiced the view of life that underlay her own political adherence, transposed into its simplest terms. She also implied that such a view of life, determinist and Marxist in origin, was the instinctive possession of an untutored rural community. At her clearest and most unequivocal in this part of the novel, she celebrates the values she admires in the peasants, which are the antithesis of the hypocrisy, cunning and self-interest of the Church and the landowners.

In *After the Death of Don Juan*, there is no talk of freedom, only of receiving one's dues, of justice to the poor man in the shape of a decent return for his hard labours. Throughout her life, Sylvia recognised justice as a key to human existence. Of those forces that stood opposed to the poor, while ostensibly on their side, and which prevented them from getting justice, time and again she attacked the Church. Although some of the villagers are sceptics and Don Saturno is an atheist, the power of the Church as an institution is still very great. No one connected with the Church emerges with any credit: the chaplain to the Sevilleans is seen to be a coward, the village priest is afraid and knows nothing of his village, barely leaving his house and near-empty church to visit it; but worst of all is the sacristan, Don Gil. Through him the novel exposes the deep connection between the Church and Fascism. It was through the Church that the sacristan acquired a hunger for power, a hunger deep, compelling and sensual; and it was through the Church that he acquired an even sweeter knowledge: power exists as a hierarchy built upon fear: 'The tyrant he knew was afraid of a great tyrant ... and behind the social order was God, the source and support of all fear.'[77]

The success or failure of *Don Juan* in engaging the reader depends to a large extent upon their reaction to a novel without heroine or hero, and their sympathy with the political viewpoint. *Don Juan* is a novel in which the dominant tone of the narrative shifts markedly from high-pitched satire at the outset through a more mixed telling in the development of the tale, while it moves between castle and village to a tragic climax. While the stooges of the castle, such as the schoolmaster and sacristan, are the butts of Sylvia's malicious wit, the villagers are treated sympathetically, not satirically, and there is nothing farcical about their final predicament as they die in hopeless symbolic resistance.

The use of the fable form provides a mechanism for the implicit communication of the political standpoint, leaving the surface of the novel largely, but not wholly, free to work upon the reader at a different level. In place of psychological realism, we are given the realism of the country, of place and atmosphere; sympathy with the peasants is balanced by the satirical treatment of the grandees; and the development throughout the novel, the shift in its tone from satire to sympathy is achieved by means of the novel's two main foci, the castle and the village, each with its appropriate mode. None the less, this is not a novel to move the reader by engaging feeling through sympathy and interest in the destiny of the individual character, as did *Summer Will Show*. It takes its sections of Spanish society and looks at them coolly, critically, from without. Only in writing of the physical reality of the Spanish countryside and people does a warmth enter into the writing, and only at the end of her novel, with the deaths of the peasants at the hands of the troops, does Sylvia become openly partisan as a storyteller. For the most part, the novel remains what she said it was: an allegory or fable of the political chemistry of Spain.

After the Death of Don Juan appeared in late 1938 and attracted little attention, except for a few brief reviews in left-wing periodicals. Meanwhile, the Spanish war had finally ended with the victory of Fascism in March 1939, and Europe was moving inexorably towards war. There was neither time nor energy to be beginning a new novel: Sylvia and Valentine sailed for the United States in May 1939.

CHAPTER 5

WARTIME AND AFTER: PARTNERSHIP UNDER PRESSURE

When war broke out, Sylvia and Valentine were in the United States. Sylvia had been taking part in the Third Congress of American Writers, held in New York, which was called in May 1939 to consider the loss of democracy in Europe. It was to be the last such conference she attended, for after the war her mood about collective action changed; there no longer seemed to be any point in it.

They left England in the company of a wealthy American friend, Elizabeth Wade White. It was to Elizabeth that Sylvia had written her long letter enthusing about the new life in Barcelona at the outbreak of the Spanish Civil War. Elizabeth had also been to stay with them at Chaldon: Sylvia wrote apologetically to Julius and Queenie postponing their planned stay because of the visit – Sylvia didn't feel their two Party friends would hit it off with Elizabeth. Sylvia and Valentine went to spend the summer after the conference in Connecticut with her, and it was during this time that Elizabeth and Valentine formed an attachment.

While she was in New York, Sylvia met her *New Yorker* editor, William Maxwell; she had been contributing stories to the paper for three years. He fell in love with her at once: 'She was dressed in black, her voice had a slightly husky intimate quality. Her conversation was so enchanting it made my head swim. I did not want to let her out of my sight. Ever.'[1]

While she was in New York, Sylvia went to visit her American publishers, Viking Press, taking with her a manuscript of Valentine's poetry for them to consider. She did not receive a reply until July of 1946, a slow response by any standards, even during wartime. When the reply at last came she was so disgusted by it that she copied it out into her

Commonplace Book, in which she wrote any incidents, brief anecdotes, sayings, comments that she wished to preserve. The publishers wrote:

> we found it somewhat difficult to arrive at a conclusion because of the nature of the pros and cons. If it had been merely a matter of merit it is obvious that we would have assented . . . but other considerations such as the unlikelihood of a sale commensurate with the cost of publication and appropriate promotion and the commitments, immediate and future, to certain other authors of books of poetry and similar hazardous enterprises, cause us to decline.[2]

Infuriating as this must have been to Sylvia, it can only have been even more disappointing to Valentine. Whether Sylvia had approached Chatto & Windus or not, there was not to be any collection of Valentine's work publicly printed until three years after her death. During her lifetime, she received no recognition for her writing. Sylvia, on the other hand, was acclaimed by the end of her life, and, ultimately, quite well-off from her writing.

In July 1939, Sylvia wrote to the composer Paul Nordoff from New York that she would be staying in Warren County, Connecticut, 'sharing a house there for the next six weeks with two other petticoats (both of them, of course, wearing trousers) . . . it is lovely country, full of wild raspberries and red-haired butterflies sitting on pink flowers, and cool mountainly airs, and a general feeling of Robert Frost.'[3] She hoped he would come and stay for a weekend. The reference to Valentine and Elizabeth may imply that the relationship between the three of them had already shifted – whether then or later, the friendship between the other two developed into a passion that was to prove increasingly troubling for all three of them, particularly for Sylvia. Throughout the next decade, and for some time on into the fifties, Valentine was plagued by this love, not knowing, as she wrote in her autobiography, whether

> I have been set aside in my judgement by those long years of drunkenness and waging useless warfare . . . or whether I am as I feel myself to be: so made that I really can, in truth, be in love with two separate and most alien people.[4]

Certainly Sylvia could not forgive the division Elizabeth wrought between them, and much later she was to say in conversation that in Connecticut she had seen one snake eating another. Some of her pain during that time in the United States is articulated in two poems in *Collected Poems*, previously unpublished. An untitled poem, 'In a foreign country', describes how other travellers buy 'something regional, a hat of grass or a fur hat', but how she bought 'a sorrow/And wore it for a half-year's stay.' She trails the sorrow through sumptuous, wild and desolate landscapes:

> embossed with mountains, darkened with forests, laced
> With summer lightening, quilted with rivers and dirt roads –
> My sorrow stately as a cope, vast as a basilica –
> My sorrow, embroidered all over with America,
> That at a word from you in mid-Atlantic I threw away.[5]

As in *The Salutation*, the sorrow has a life of its own; and whatever the germination of that strange and haunting tale, the process of distancing and control of loss and exile through the making of the poem can be seen at work here.

In another unpublished poem, 'Under the Sudden Blue',[6] Sylvia compares her exile from Valentine's affections to winter, herself to earth, and Valentine to air, a comparison to which she returns more than once in her writings:

> Poor cadet earth, so clumsy and so slow,
> how, labouring with clods, can she keep pace
> with Air, the firstborn element, tossing clouds to and fro?

Whatever the reality, Sylvia perceived herself in their partnership to be the slow, graceless, earthy one, and Valentine to be lightness, grace, quickness of spirit and feeling.[7] The poem goes on to consider the returning spring, and how slow the poet is to respond to it because of winter's hurt:

> my stammering blossoms one by one
> shoved out, and my face doubtful under the sudden blue,
>   under the embrace
> of the relenting, of the returning sun.[8]

Whatever conflicts and emotions were involved in parting from Elizabeth, there was no doubt for either Valentine or Sylvia once war had been declared on 4 September that they must return home as speedily as possible. By the 30th they were set to sail, despite the pleas of Maxwell and other friends for

5.1 Sylvia wading the Frome

5.2 Lower Frome Vauchurch and the River Frome, from across the water meadow

them to remain in safety, in the United States. Sylvia wrote to him that although she had grave doubts about the war, for she didn't feel it was being fought against the Nazis, she did feel her responsibilities lay in England. And besides, she must have come to hate the United States. By the second week of October they were back at Lower Frome Vauchurch.

THE HOUSE BY RUNNING WATER: LOWER FROME VAUCHURCH

When Valentine and Sylvia moved to the house by the Frome in August 1937 it was to be only a temporary move. They rented it from 'a bossy Anglo-Indian lady' who agreed to lower the rent by £2.10s., install electric light at her own expense, and even give them six room bells, which survive to this day. Sylvia wrote to Steven Clark: 'It is a most accommodating house, took our furniture to its bosom without any cavillings. The cat likes it, we like it.'[9]

The chief attractions were its seclusion, the garden and the river. Valentine was soon busy fishing and discovering the pleasures of dispatching trout with a priest, a small silvered kosh with which you whack the trout over the head. There was the attraction of moorhens and water-rats swimming about looking like 'half-submerged bulrush(es)', and other riparian life. The rent was £63.10s. a year: the house had three upstairs rooms, three downstairs rooms, a scullery and a sunroom. From the photographs one can see how it clings to the edge of the river bank, and in order to combat the inevitable damp it had been encased in corrugated iron. Unwisely this was removed after Sylvia died, and the subsequent troubles with recurrent damp proved unconquerable. It also boasted, in those days, a veranda.

It is a house that turns itself almost entirely to the river, and both Sylvia and Valentine's work-rooms overlooked the river. On the other side run low-level water meadows, often flooded, through which the path winds back across a bridge into the busy village of Maiden Newton. Here the life of the village coils and recoils, as people walk their dogs, take evening constitutionals or trek with shopping baskets, and young lovers go by, idling the time away. Later, when she had bought the house,

Valentine planted their bank with willows, as she wrote in a poem, every year for twenty years, to give them the privacy she so badly craved. Her fear of being invaded was such that when some bungalows were built twenty years later on the top of the rise in the fields overlooking Lower Frome Vauchurch, she was distraught, and she and Sylvia came near to selling the house.

The garden is the natural extension of the house, since the bank of the river falls steeply away from it to the south-west, and a narrow plank gangway and taffrail fence it in. From here, when I knew the house in Antonia's time, the small boys came to fish: they treated the place with a mixture of deference and rugged ownership, a mixture as much due to its long curious history in the possession of the old lady who many thought of as something of a witch, as in more recent times to Antonia's curious foreign-sounding name and title. The garden runs back towards the lane which leads over the Frome to the hamlet of Lower Frome Vauchurch, as the map shows, the name of the house being appropriated from there by the two women, for its proper name was and is Riversdale. It comprises less than quarter of an acre of fertile ground and mature trees, birch, alder, tulip tree, willows, many of which they planted.

When Sylvia lived there alone after Valentine's death, the door stood open in all weathers; and in most weathers, while Antonia lived alone there, it was the same. It is an unchanging, and indeed as Sylvia said, an accommodating house. Despite looking at several other houses throughout their lives together, in places as far distant as Ireland, Scotland, Norfolk and Cornwall, neither Sylvia nor Valentine ever moved from Lower Frome Vauchurch, except for one three-week period in 1949, when Sylvia went to live on her own, leaving the house to Valentine and Elizabeth who had decided they must live together.

LIFE IN WARTIME

When Valentine and Sylvia returned home from the United States the phoney war had begun. Already, amongst the estimated one and a half million Londoners who poured out into the country as evacuees, Sylvia's old charlady and her husband and foster-child had arrived at the house. Sylvia and Valentine were immediately plunged into the daily concerns and contrivances of civilian life in wartime.

Their lives were affected as were everyone else's in the civil population outside the big cities – by inconvenience, shortage of food, restriction of liberties and mobility, the fear of invasion, and danger from air-raids. In 1940 Lower Frome Vauchurch was hit by an incendiary bomb while they were away in Norfolk, and Sylvia's cottage at Chaldon was destroyed in 1944 by a returning German bomber dumping its ammunition. Targets for the Luftwaffe such as the docks at Southampton and Poole were not far away, and although the area was at some periods considered safe to receive evacuees, at other times it was the subject of restrictive legislation which forbade residents to move out, or visitors to enter it, as for example in the run-up to the D-Day landings in June 1944.

One of the biggest upheavals for country people was the sudden swelling of their households and villages with the arrival of the evacuees, an upheaval which formed the subject of a number of Sylvia's bleakly humorous wartime stories. (There were three families who came to Lower Frome Vauchurch, the first of whom left behind such a strong smell of mutton-fat Sylvia complained that it took four months to get rid of it.) A great deal of organisation was required to distribute everyone within the villages, and to sort out the hundred and one problems of city people pitchforked into remote rural communities, with misgivings and mismatches of expectation and behaviour on both sides. Sylvia worked for the WVS throughout the war, and recalled later the extraordinary minutiae she and other volunteer workers were required to enter into the WVS Day Books or daily records. It was work of an unremitting and relentless kind, particularly in dealing with the tender sensibilities, panics and pretensions of some of her fellow-organisers; she tried to keep her head below the parapet.

More actively, Sylvia prided herself on her prowess lobbing hand-grenades (Peg Manisty, Valentine's cousin, recalled Valentine saying she was most dangerous with them), and they were both adept with their fire-watching whistles, patrolling the nearby country lanes against incendiary bombs. (They discovered with pleasure that they could imitate the mating calls of owls.) Meanwhile, less dramatically, the problems of how to feed themselves and the evacuees increased, as food became scarcer and more unappetising, despite fish from the river and the resources of the garden: how to reinvigorate the soil with compost grew to be a problem. In a thousand small ways the war seeped into their lives and affected them as it affected everyone in the country.

Commenting to Paul Nordoff in 1940 about the quality of their lives and the reasons for remaining in England despite reiterated invitations to go to the United States, Sylvia wrote:

> It's not patriotism, and it's not obtuseness. It's realism. It is a modulation inherent in the tune, it's a variation that the ground bass demands. Sometimes I am blue with fear, but it is always the quality of fear one has before a difficult passage that has to be dealt with.[10]

She went on to describe the feeling as a 'flat-headed alleycat cautious yet passionate curiosity' which she had also felt driving over the 'bony plain' to Madrid when they were under air-attack there.

As well as the arrival of the evacuees, the blackout and the air-raid precautions transformed life in the village. But Valentine and Sylvia were not to remain at Lower Frome Vauchurch for long, for as the news from Europe grew worse and the invasion of England was expected imminently, they left for Winterton in April 1940, to look after Valentine's mother, Ruth.

Before the war, there had been a staff of five, as well as the chauffeur, at Hill House; now Mrs Ackland was alone. Valentine and Sylvia spent nearly six months with her in Norfolk, first at the house and then when the army requisitioned it in a small cottage at the lower end of the village. They stayed on throughout the summer, waiting for the invasion through the period of the worst bombing; it was a difficult time, and when they finally reached home again in November 1940 it was a great relief, despite finding the house full of feathers: an incendiary-bomb falling through the roof had destroyed a feather mattress.

They had travelled to Norfolk in strange conditions: all the trains were crammed with troops and civilians taking what they thought of as their last chance to reach safety for their families, as Hitler's armies rolled through the low countries, but the first-class carriages were empty. By June 1940, most people in Britain were prepared for invasion, and many thought it would come by air. Even while the German forces were on the Channel coast and the British Expeditionary force in France was cut off, in England, Valentine reported to the American radical magazine *New Republic*, no one thought to enter those hallowed first-class carriages: on the eve of invasion class relations and the fabric of society remained undisturbed.

Valentine wrote reports at regular intervals for *New Republic* in the early years of the war, describing what life in wartime Britain was like from a civilian point of view. She told how, in order to prevent the invaders discovering where they were when they landed, all the signposts in the countryside had been removed, but with characteristic inconsequence no one had thought to remove the parish registers from the churches, or items like postcards of the village from the village shop. (She and Sylvia had bets with each other on each of these points: they were both right.)

She described the barricades they saw built across country roads with whatever agricultural materials and implements lay to hand: they were not as well built as the ones they had seen in Spain. However, the people of her part of Norfolk were organising their defences admirably, by contrast with Dorset where the ARP defences were in the hands of a few old doddering Colonels and Admirals. The independence, hardihood, quirkiness and sheer cussed root-democratic feeling of the Norfolk people was always a source of pride to her, and of pleasure to Sylvia, compared with the conservatism and servility of the Dorset folk where deference had stamped its indelible mark for hundreds of years. The sea may be a hard master but it is an egalitarian one, in the sense that what you catch you owe to no man's favour but to your own skill and courage. Sylvia was to explore this aspect of Norfolk life fully and contrast it with the corrupting and decadent power of patriarchal bourgeois possession in her last novel, *The Flint Anchor*.[11]

By the first summer of the war most of the younger men of Winterton had already joined up on mine-sweepers, in coastal defence or the Navy. Sylvia and Valentine threw themselves first of all into the work of sorting out the village rubbish-tip; a herculean and unpleasant task, rescuing all the useable materials; Valentine worked on digging out the local bomb shelter with other villagers, to make it more safe if it were attacked. They made another exit, so that at least people could escape from it, she commented fatalistically. Sylvia became involved in local WVS work. The WVS was set up to be a women's counterpart and back-up for the fire-forces, to make use of all the talents of the housewives with young children and older married women who were not drafted into the factories or serving in the forces. Their role in organising support and aid throughout local communities, particularly in times of the worst air-raids in the latter part of 1940 and in 1944, was crucial.

Mrs Ackland, meanwhile, was organising a scheme for the distribution of vegetables throughout north-east Norfolk; she became very upset because she was not allowed unlimited supplies of petrol for her work, which she viewed as vital to the defence of the whole area. Valentine wrote to her sister Joan for help in trying to calm her down. Equally Mrs Ackland seemed unable to understand that because of the war, she needed to cut down on the household food order, while her capacity to believe that she alone was responsible for repelling Hitler, and organising everyone for that purpose, threw Valentine into despair. By July Valentine was writing to Joan saying that after the fruit-picking she thought they really must leave: there would be nothing for them to do but stay around and be another cross for 'Wroothie' to bear, as she called her mother in moments of exasperation.

It was a horrid cocktail of worries. They were anxious about Lower Frome Vauchurch, perpetually short of money having to pay rent to 'Wroothie' as well as for their own house, which had evacuees in it and was being looked after for them by a friend. Ruth's extravagant lifestyle meant they could not economise. Meanwhile, cheques from the *New Yorker* and other royalties had almost ceased. Equally, they could not take paid work while they were in Norfolk; all this Valentine poured out to her sister.

Sylvia was able to take a more philosophical and amused attitude to Mrs Ackland but she could find Ruth very trying, a sentiment that grew with the years:

Ruth is a good woman, but Riddled with Christianity, never happy unless she is suffering more than anyone else or doing more than anyone else. Preferably, of course, both. She

reminds one of that Byzantine view of Jesus called 'Jesus
reigning from the Cross'. . . . Her tactics could teach Hitler
quite a bit about overpowering resistance by surprise
envelopments and bombs fitted with megaphone devices.[12]

She later said that she thought the reason Hitler hadn't invaded
the East coast was because of Mrs Ackland, '& Ruth thinks so
too'.

However, their resistance to Mrs Ackland had to last a while
longer, for in August the army requisitioned Hill House; Ruth
had to be safely installed in a cottage in the village. They took a
tiny cottage at the 'low end of the village, where the street
peters out into sand dunes and where the village leaves its tin-
cans and bottles'.[13] The dunes were dotted with defensive
landmines, of course, so they could not walk on them; in
August, there was a week of great air-battles, from which they
escaped unscathed except for the sound of machine-gun fire
and a bomb dropped in a field. The farmers, Sylvia wrote to
Paul Nordoff, were most concerned about their harvest and
'give just the same mistrustful glances at the blue clear sky as
they gave in other years to signs of rain'.[14]

In the same letter, she described an accidental death that
occurred on the dunes when a tired soldier stepped on one of
the land mines:

an enormous stately tree of smoke and sand . . . hung on the
air, slowly dissolving; presently another soldier came running
from far away, stiffly holding at arm's length a boot with a
piece of bloodied bone sticking from it.[15]

It could be an extract from one of the stories: written in a
flat, unemotional, exact way, so much control and sharp
evocation. Indeed Sylvia's fiction which came out of the war is
exact, flat, emotionless, almost dry. It goes after no effects; the
exuberance of her early wit is tempered by a sense of levelling
fatigue, which must have been one of the most pervasive effects
of the war. Frequently the settings in these stories are bombed-
out houses, places revisited after the war, snatches of memory.
The way in which war so subtly transformed the lives of all
those who lived through it (except for a very small handful of
the rich who escaped and went on living their lives playing
bridge and canasta in the United States or Canada or country

hotels in remote parts of the Highlands) is evoked quickly and incisively in the sketches and stories of these years. It is a pervasive timbre, not only in the wartime collections, *A Garland of Straw* (1943) and *The Museum of Cheats* (1947), but also in some of the later stories in the fifties' collections.[16] The stories register the continuing impact upon ordinary people of the 'People's War' long after the declaration of peace.

Nevertheless, the letters that Sylvia wrote to her American friends, and to a certain extent those that Valentine wrote for *New Republic* in the early years of the war, are full of buoyancy, humour, a sense of the ludicrous and a love of exposing humbug. For Sylvia, they were probably a way of keeping writing and keeping in touch with people she loved, who seemed distanced by the Atlantic's treachery in wartime and by the different conditions while the United States was not yet in the war. For Valentine, the letters offered a much-needed professional outlet, she was helping to keep a progressive American readership informed of the true state of affairs in Britain. She continually stresses in these letters what is happening to ordinary people, what they are thinking and feeling; her emphasis is on describing scenes and conversations at street level. She reports on subjects such as people's reaction to the black markets, to Russia, to Churchill, and the Blitz; the behaviour of the rich; the need to protect freedom of expression and liberties; the appalling conditions of the alien camps; the desire for peace and the strength of anti-Nazi feeling.

Sylvia's letters at the time, by contrast, concentrate on relating the droller side of life. Many of them were written to American friends such as Paul Nordoff, the composer whom she had met on the New York trip, liked greatly, and with whom she would later work on an opera on the last days of Shelley. He had already set her second novel, *Mr Fortune's Maggot*, to music, and she approved his score strongly.

There were many humorous incidents to be recounted in wartime; unlike Ruth Ackland, Sylvia certainly did not like to suffer. She was adept at pointing up the ludicrous disparity between people's pretensions and the reality: 'My mother, hearing that Buckingham Palace had been bombed, instantly hoisted the Union Jack above her porch. It is a small porch, and no one visits it except the postman and a small child who brings the milk.'[17] It is the cumulative circumstantial detail that is so engaging – like her *New Yorker* editor, William Maxwell, one is immediately provoked into making lists of the incidents she recounts.

Her imagination roamed over the idiosyncrasies of the local ARP ('if there is a real raid they will dauntlessly turn up to mismanage it'), the Parish Magazine ('the earliness of Lent is causing considerable concern'), how the heat must be affecting the bowels of Sir Samuel Hoare, the ambassador in Madrid (one of the arch appeasers who wore stockings like gloves 'with a compartment for each toe') – to the feelings of the Censor:

> What will they do when they can't be censors any longer (for they can't all become village postmistresses and go into the CID)? Will they pine and languish, and feel themselves suddenly cut off from humanity? Or will they spend the evening of their days reading Mme de Sévigné and the Reverend Leman White . . . ? Or will they demonstrate their freedom by never opening another envelope?'[18]

Such descriptions could form the bones of a story. There is an inconsequentiality, a delight in the odd and unpredictable in many of these little incidents, and the intimate relaxed tone of a writer talking to close friends. Above all the letters are also continued conversation; recommending Virginia Woolf's *Life of Roger Fry* to Paul, she tells how Fry was brought up to be:

> a little Quaker with every impulse put through a sieve of conscience and scruples . . . moving on to be an industrious copycat of all the Mandarins; and ending up as free and rapscalliony and outrageously honest as any man might be, sitting on benches in dusty cheap parks talking to burglars, and laying down the law with all the bravura of the lawless. Such a nice comforting story.[19]

Bravura, a disregard of propriety, law, convention: all were dear to Sylvia's heart; and in Valentine's secretive and elegant pursuit of her own goals, her own style, Sylvia found the perfect realisation of that dash and freedom. Perhaps, too, this was one of the reasons she did not enquire too closely after the life Valentine led, for she was a very private person, and respected privacy utterly.

Sometimes the bravura is the sheer bravura of the skilled writer and humourist who cannot resist entertaining her

American friends with tales of wartime England calculated to make them laugh in disbelief at the absurdities of this hypocritical and hidebound country rumbling into the twentieth century:

> a [Red Cross] lecture . . . dealing with how to undress a wounded man. 'First of all . . . you remove the trousers.' Cries from the audience, matrons and virgins' voices mingled. 'No you don't! You take off his shoes.' 'Yes, yes. Of course. You take off his shoes. The next step is to pull down the trousers.' Renewed cries. 'You've forgotten his braces.' O tempora! O mores! How could they use an old maiden so, as the song says. To tell the truth, it's like that all over the place. The tales I hear from London would make the big tears course down your innocent nose.'[20]

As well as the humorous side, both Valentine and Sylvia's wartime letters convey a good deal of the day-to-day tedium of wartime. Valentine's are more selective, both because she is writing for a public audience and because she clearly feels she has a duty to keep the sympathies of the *New Republic* readers engaged. Their support, she assures them, is invaluable; help is needed to maintain liberties in England.

Once the blitz started, morale was high, for people's angry reaction was, what do they take us for, if they think we can be bombed into submission. Everyone agreed with rationing and was fiercely opposed to the black market. The only point in the *New Republic* letters at which she admits to problems at home and a feeling of despondency is quite early on in 1940, when she writes that if there were an invasion she thought there would be a good deal of panic-shooting, for there was a high pitch of spy-fever and people were seeing fifth columnists everywhere: 'It interests me to reflect that the same kind of thing, when it happened in Spain, was called Red Terror.'[21]

Comparisons with Spain came readily to both their minds, unsurprisingly. When Mrs Keates and her family arrived again to take shelter from the Blitz in October 1940, soon after their return from Norfolk, Sylvia wrote: 'When they arrived they looked like shadows. I felt like a hostess in hell, welcoming the dead. But I had seen them all before, in Spain.'[22]

Similarly, for Valentine, when a young soldier recounted the atrocities he had seen in Europe, the Germans burning fleeing refugees with flame-throwers, she found herself unable to say anything to comfort him: 'In Spain, oddly enough, I did know what to say.'[23] Perhaps the inability to say anything, and the repeated reference back to Spain had something to do with the shift in Valentine and Sylvia's political involvement; they had been at the centre of political struggle in that decade, but now their involvement was more peripheral. They were at several removes in Dorset from the naked agony of war.

When the Communist Party printing press moved right into Dorchester with the takeover of the *Dorset Country Chronicle* in 1942, they did not get involved again as they had before the war. Some part of militancy seems to have been burned out, an impression confirmed by William Maxwell in his introduction to the *Letters*.[24]

In November 1940 a bomb fell close enough to Lower Frome Vauchurch to wake Sylvia, who was a heavy sleeper: she remarked that if it could wake her, it could be assumed that it was too close to ignore. After the raid was over, she thought how:

> For all its violence, war is papery-thin compared to a garden with apple trees and cabbages in it. Even when it's forced down one's throat one can't swallow it. Whereas one goes out and eats great mouthfuls of cabbage and appletree and moonlight.[25]

She went on to say that she thought probably in the last analysis the horror of war was 'tantamount to the horror of boredom . . . being compelled to attend to things that don't interest one'.[26] Boredom became increasingly a daily reality as the war dragged on through four and a half more years; but Sylvia and Valentine did not lose their sense of the reality behind it. That glorifying war was loathsome, and not what the working-class cared for at all. In fact the war sharpened people's sense of humbug and the pretensions by which the ruling classes hung onto their power. In that same long letter to Paul after the air-raid on Maiden Newton, Sylvia reflected on working-class fortitude and lack of heroism: 'If more deeds of heroism could just fall flat there would be more hope for humanity.' Working-class heroes, she said, always 'disinfect' such deeds by calling any act they were involved in 'a bloody nuisance' and, most of all, 'working-class spectators pour on as much disinfectant as the performers, and say that they never saw Bert run so quick, or that Alf was unlucky from a boy . . . or that his trousers will never be the same again.'[27] It is clear where Sylvia's class sympathies still lay.

Sylvia's working week was divided: for part of the time she was involved in lecturing, at first to a class of 'young secretarial ladies' at Bridport, to which she went on foot: 'a nice walk over empty hills'.[28] (It is in fact seven miles over some quite steep hills: she must have been extremely fit.) Later on she lectured to the Army under its expanded educational programme, until sacked for her left-wing views. (She boasted they had not yet run out of topics after a year and that she still had theology up her sleeve.) For two days a week she worked in the WVS offices in Dorchester, 'pushing P.A.C. paperwork about (i.e., papers of the Public Assistance Committee which helped families in need) 'while high-bred passions' raged round her between the 'county' ladies, each hell-bent on winning the war single-handed. Sylvia reflected ruefully that there were so many people carrying out so many jobs and quarrelling as to who should do what, that their whole faculties were absorbed in vetoing as one person what they wanted to carry out as another.

Valentine's office, where she worked from late summer 1941 until nearly the end of the war as a civil defence clerk, was staffed by housewives and young women. As with all aspects of English life, class was a shaping reality in people's experience of the war: its contradictions and injustices began to be more clearly exposed under wartime conditions, and many people became impatient for a new era: they had been fobbed off after the last war and they were not prepared to be fobbed off again. The 'People's War' represented for once a positive leap forward in demands for democracy and in Popular Front ideas: the popular aspiration for wide-ranging change during the war was beyond the reach of even left-wing ideas of the previous decade. The demand for a real say, for education, better health and housing after the war all grew; perceptions of inequality had shifted radically.

The work in Valentine's office was long and tedious and she found the discipline of the hours, and the lack of holiday-time (two weeks a year), almost unbearable. Valentine later wrote to Joan that what had saved her during the war from being destroyed by the numbing discipline of full-time office-work was her political commitment: 'I was rather high-minded then. Unfortunately it all went away when I stopped being a Communist.'[29]

In a short autobiographical poem written at this time, later published in *Further Poems* (1978), she expressed her sense of alienation at being cut off from the clarity and brightness of the natural world:

> When I watch a swallow striking through the clean air
> Or see bright crests of trees over the town walls
> Or catch a thistledown erratically
> Entering my office window . . .
> I do not know how anyone can endure to live like me.[30]

It was difficult to find the time and to sustain the mood for her writing. There were many anxieties and pressures, driving her to drink. The drinking problem had become so acute by 1940 that she was forced to take a 'cure', which cost £25, a considerable amount of money to her then. The cure succeeded for six weeks.

Anxious about money, feeling the pressure of office work, which was alien and claustrophobic to her, cut off from Elizabeth, Valentine also took refuge in affairs closer to home. One was with a young relation of Sylvia's, to whom they were both very attached. Whatever else poetry was to Valentine at this time, it clearly did not provide her with the stability and fulfilment she needed in her life: she sought release in her drinking, and in relationships with other women. Sylvia, however, remained faithful to Valentine. When asked later why she did so, she replied simply that Valentine was the best lover she ever had.

In *For Sylvia: An Honest Account*, Valentine almost completely ignores her own poetry. From the story she tells there, which she wrote in 1949, one would not know that after her youth she was a writer, except for the bleak comment near the end of the book, that she had recently begun to doubt whether she was, or would ever be, a poet. However, despite everything she wrote a great deal and a number of her wartime pieces were published later in the forties. Besides the poems regularly appearing in *New Republic*, there were poems published in anthologies and West Country magazines, and in magazines such as *Life and Letters Today* which clearly belong to this time. One long poem, from which excerpts were published in *The Nature of the Moment*, covers the years 1940–4, through a number of short, linked and fiercely biting lyrics looking at different incidents.[31]

Although she did not rate her stories very highly, some of them were published. Two written in wartime deal with the emotions of women internees in camps. These stories were probably influenced by her concern about the alien camps in Britain, but may also have been written under the influence of what she and Sylvia read and heard about in Germany before the war. They had direct sources of information for the events in Germany from one of their friends, the well-known German author, Ludwig Renn, who had fled from the Nazis in the early thirties. He stayed with them at Lower Frome Vauchurch before the war, and kept in touch after he left England for Mexico. He left behind with them the draft of an anti-fascist fable written in German, about an ant who reports on the way the two-legged creatures organise their world and doesn't much like what he sees, and it was to Renn that Sylvia dedicated *The Cat's Cradle Book*, a collection of stories published in the United States in 1940.[32]

Sylvia appears to have been less than ordinarily perceptive to the difficulties Valentine was experiencing at this time. Her own life was both productive and fully occupied, even if less financially successful than before the war. Busy with her writing, with the WVS, fire-watching, lecturing, contriving meals, house-keeping for evacuees, Sylvia clearly did not give the younger woman the reassurance and support she needed – if, indeed, it were possible for Valentine to accept it. There is some evidence from her poetry that the condition of exile was a necessary one to Valentine.[33]

She was always the more anxious of the two of them; anxious about her health, about money, and later about the state of her soul. Most particularly at this time she was undergoing nerve-wracking bouts of illness, brought on, she believed, by the drinking; she was convinced she would die before Sylvia.

Despite all these anxieties, since she was a highly secretive person who placed a great deal of emphasis on formality and good manners, Valentine kept her problems to herself. Having decided early on that it was not fair to unload her drink problem on her lover, she kept to her decision to carry that burden alone.

It has been suggested that Valentine perhaps exaggerated the extent of her drinking and of her suffering in the account she later gave of those years in *For Sylvia*. A facet of Valentine's perpetual self-dramatisation, or an aspect of her vanity have both been suggested as explanations by writers primarily concerned with Sylvia.[34] Perhaps Sylvia's apparent blindness was in some measure a self-protective device too: the artist's 'necessary' selfishness. Sylvia was later to say in a letter to Valentine that the change from her drinking to her not drinking made no difference to her, beyond an opening or a not-opening of bottles.

The account Valentine gives of her misery at this time is brief but clear, and she is writing only a short time after the events she describes. Accepting that she was driven by the confessional urge to exorcise what felt to her like her heaviest sin, because it was bound up with the loss of her undivided love for Sylvia, there still seems no good reason for accepting the testimony of one part of the book and rejecting another. Either one reads the autobiography as having a basis in reality, or one reads *For Sylvia: An Honest Account* as fiction, based on the writer's life, but not to be privileged above other fictions in the insights it offers into her experience.

In later years, Valentine was to view some aspects of the life she had recounted differently: for example, she wrote to her cousin that she had maligned Joan in the autobiography by painting her so harshly, that Joan was not really so hard-hearted, although it had seemed like that to her as a young girl.

Sylvia was keenly aware that Valentine was not well throughout much of the war, and was near to breakdown. She believed that the heart of the problem was Valentine's work as a civilian clerk in a war office; what could you expect, she wrote to Nancy Cunard in May 1944, 'if you put a poet in an office doing war-work for three years on end . . . and surround it with ugly faces and loud voices and hearts like linoleum'. Her protectiveness was rewarded when she and Valentine's doctor managed to secure Valentine's transfer from the office to light duties in the doctor's dispensary (work which Sylvia had previously done), and some driving. By July, Sylvia reported, Valentine was once again looking 'all of six foot', and her skin smelling of almonds: 'It is a vast comfort to see anybody happy.'[35]

Meanwhile, two years after their return from the United States, Sylvia was absorbed in a new novel. She compared the event to having a baby:

> If things were normal I would be resigned enough, and prepared to be pleased later. But in war-time I am rather like the clerks in Valentine's office who say: 'Oh, you couldn't have one in war-time could you? – except, of course, it gets you out of being called up.' Unfortunately a novel does not get you out of being called up: or what a lot of people would now be buying bargain bundles of paper.[36]

The novel was extremely long, 180,000 words; it was also, she commented ironically, 'what one calls powerful. If dropped from a suitable height it would wipe out the state of Vermont.'[37] By April 1942 it was firmly under way; it had neither thesis nor plot, she said, and this did not in the least trouble her – her state of mind about it was 'contentedly vague'. It wasn't, she claimed, a historical novel, although most people were to read it as such, and despite its subject being a fourteenth-century abbey, she judged that, as well as having practically no love in it, there was: 'no religion, but a great deal of financial worry and ambition and loneliness and sensitivity to weather, with practically no sensibility to nature'.[38]

The Corner That Held Them remained one of her favourite novels, and was amongst her most popular despite this unpromising description. It was also clearly to her mind a Marxist novel. She wrote it, she said, whenever she could, and it demonstrated 'remarkable vitality', for despite 'an endless series of interruptions, distractions and destructions', it was as persistent as a 'damp-patch in a house wall', and living through the war at Lower Frome Vauchurch on the river's edge, she knew about what damp could do. The novel was finally finished in 1946. There were two collections of her stories published in wartime and one shortly after. *The Cats Cradle Book* (1940), composed of stories written in the thirties, *A Garland of Straw* (1943), and *The Museum of Cheats* (1947): they take a steady, un-illusioned look at human life. Frequently she uses a contemporary setting: the short story form was always the one in which Sylvia chose to explore contemporary themes, taking unremarkable scenes and characters and probing, humourously and bleakly, the idiosyncrasies of behaviour with an almost anthropological, dispassionate exactness. Unfortunately the books did not bring in a great deal of money: there was a decided paucity of royalties, and little from the *New Yorker*. (After the war she was sustained by a first-reading agreement with them, but at first it provoked more dissatisfaction for the delays caused in returning manuscripts than satisfaction through fat cheques.)

At one point Sylvia entertained the thought that her *New Yorker* cheques were being diverted straight into Spitfires. There was a nationwide popular campaign to buy the planes, with individuals, cities and factories sending in their donations and the BBC broadcasting the results. Sixpence bought a rivet, 15s. the blast tube of a machine gun, £2000 a wing and so on.[39]

Royalties from the thirties' novels never amounted to much. However, she had a philosophical cast of mind and did not worry unduly over the lack of a steady income. Valentine evidently worried enough for both of them. There was, for example, an agitated exchange of letters with Joan when Valentine tried to find a way of binding their mother to continue paying her £300 a year allowance to Sylvia in the event of her death. (Joan agreed to forego her own interest in any family money if Valentine should die.) Concern about money remained a feature of their life throughout the war years and for some time afterwards. Valentine worried relentlessly about Sylvia's impracticability and quixotic generosity, being convinced that she, Valentine, would die first, and Sylvia would be left unprovided for, and have to end her life in a state home. If she had foreseen Sylvia's income dropping so rapidly, she wrote to Joan, she would have taken out a life insurance policy.

The circumstances which caused Valentine to buy Lower Frome Vauchurch at the end of the war were bound up with these anxieties about their uncertain financial fortunes and the sudden realisation of their insecurity as tenants: the owner of Lower Frome Vauchurch, Mrs West, had announced that she wished to return and spend Christmas there. Soon afterwards she must have decided to sell, for by September Valentine and Sylvia had agreed to buy the house. Valentine borrowed £2200 from her mother, which was to be repaid at 4 per cent interest:

the deeds were entered in Valentine's sole name.

Together with the house was a field which in 1945 brought in a fair amount of money for grazing rights, in all, £88 a year. However, what concerned Valentine most was the matter of her fishing rights, how far they extended and what she should do in case of dispute: the gentleman who owned the rights adjoining on the opposite bank of the river was of a disputatious nature. Her lawyer assured her that her rights would extend to the centre of the river 'for all usual purposes', presumably including wading, but that he assumed the Frome was a non-tidal river, for if it were tidal a 'riparian owner would have no rights merely by virtue of ownership of the bank'.[40]

Soon after the war the house was redecorated: they were delighted to get rid of Mrs West's 'Irish Stew' colour scheme (Sylvia loathed Irish Stew). She reported with satisfaction that the workmen had fallen through the kitchen floor: 'As no one was hurt I look on it as providential, for now the floor will have to be mended, permit permitting or no.'[41] It was impossible of course to get any civilian repair work done in the war, even to bomb-damaged houses; and for a long time afterwards it remained a considerable problem in the rebuilding of Britain. Permission had to be obtained for all building work; meanwhile, the damp was eating away at the house.

THE COMMUNIST PARTY AND *OUR TIME*

While daily activity for the Communist Party was a thing of the past for Sylvia and Valentine, they still remained involved with the Party throughout the war and afterwards. One of the main connections was the new Party cultural paper, *Our Time*, which first appeared at what might have seemed an unpropitious moment. The *Daily Worker* had been banned the month before by the Home Secretary Herbert Morrison, as a result of the Communist Party's support for the Comintern line that the war was an imperialist affair. Initially, the Party, which had been in the forefront of the struggle against Fascism at home and in Spain in the thirties, threw itself enthusiastically into support for the war. But after the Comintern ruling the CPGB fell into line and argued that this was not really an anti-fascist war but a struggle between two imperialist powers.

Throughout the first two years of the war, until Germany invaded the Soviet Union in Summer 1941, the CP was arguing for a 'People's Peace'. During the long months of the phoney war, before the bombing began, this position was not untenable, for the Chamberlain Government retained most of the arch-appeasers of the thirties. But once the blitz began in earnest, the Communist Party argument that people's lives in the cities were being appallingly and needlessly sacrificed in the interests of an imperialist quarrel began to look increasingly threadbare. As Valentine told her American readers in *New Republic*, the mood of the British people became 'furiously and icily angry' against the Nazis. Furthermore, once Churchill replaced the ineffectual Chamberlain, 'Winnie', as he was known, and his cigar became a highly popular figure as he stomped around the streets surveying the damage after raids, talking to rescue-workers and survivors. (This may have been the stereotype of good public relations, but it was one that Valentine gave sufficient credence to retail to her readers.)

For once, the British people had a figure-head they could believe in for this time the country was largely united, although there were still many pacifists who remained outside this unity. It was widely believed that Churchill would deal with the appeasers and proto-Fascists as well as with those who were feathering their nests through the war-profiteering. The Communist Party's position in stubborn opposition to the war left it isolated and out of touch with the people. While it had previously campaigned successfully around the need to provide solidly built air-raid shelters, and to make proper provision in the undergrounds and other makeshift shelters, by the end of 1940 the Party was cut off as it had not been since the days of the doctrine of 'Social-Fascism' in the twenties, when the unions were seen as class enemies. Some Communists who lived through the period 1939–41 recall that it was a very difficult time to be in the CP: many people lost their jobs, hostility was extremely fierce in many places. Communists were frequently seen as being nearly as bad as Fascists, and the blacklists on Party members in the factories lasted for a long time. (They were also a good way of getting rid of inconvenient union activists.) However, the Party was not without influence; it was still deeply rooted in the workplace, particularly the big engineering, ship-building and armaments factories, and it also had a following amongst those who were disaffected and critical of the system. These were not a few: to many people, in retrospect 1940–1 was the time when Britain came closest to a revolutionary situation for many years.

The extent of that influence in the factories is seen by the fact that, when the CPGB swung round to wholehearted support for the war after the German invasion of the Soviet Union, armament production shot up and the CP used its considerable industrial muscle to urge workers on to Stakhanovite goals of achieving and exceeding targets. What is more, the Party had been organising through one of its 'broad front' organisations, the People's Convention, and it succeeded in getting together a convention of over 2000 delegates in January 1941, representing a wide range of workers' organisations, to demand a People's Charter. The Charter called for a People's Peace, and a People's Government. One week later, the Home Secretary, Herbert Morrison, banned the *Daily Worker*: from then on the party faced eighteen months of official persecution of any activities, including jail sentences on leafletters.

None the less, leaflets continued to be put out, and in order to produce them, the Party had bought up, ironically, the bankrupt *Dorset County Chronicle*. Sylvia and Valentine were asked over to meet the comrades who arrived to run the paper, whose printing works were in Dorchester, and to discuss ways in which they might support it. But the enthusiasm for round-the-clock activism of the thirties had waned, and it does not seem that much came of this connection. It is a revealing comment on the extent of the shift that had occurred since they returned from the United States, prefiguring Sylvia's comment to Nancy Cunard of a few years later, that her mood was 'centrifugal'. The forties saw a withdrawal from the political front-line for both Sylvia and Valentine.[42]

The Communist Party's change of line over the war came in June 1941, but the bans on the *Daily Worker* remained. Despite not wishing to be involved in the day-to-day activities of the Party press on her doorstep, Sylvia was nevertheless prepared to be openly identified with the new cultural paper of the Party: the first issue of *Our Time* appeared in February 1941. The steady flow of her contributions through the war years and after (it folded in 1948) show serious commitment to the project. Arnold Rattenbury, one of the young editors of the paper at that time, has spoken of how Sylvia's advice and encouragement was invaluable, as one of the few experienced members of the elder generation in the Party who were available during the war.

The paper was the successor to the short-lived 'Poetry and the People', edited by Jack Lindsay and Mary Watson, which in turn was the follow-up to *Left Review*. *Our Time* appeared monthly, cost 6d., and had a populist slant: it was aimed at the kind of audience that had responded so enthusiastically to Penguin Books and the Left Book Club in the late thirties. The Left Book Club's monthly subscription volumes and readers' groups had tapped a hitherto undreamt-of market for Left writing. Wartime, too, released a demand for new forms of expression, education and entertainment amongst large sections of the people, particularly in the early years of the war amongst the men and women in the forces who were based in Britain. In this atmosphere, film, broadcasting, music-hall, cabaret and theatre boomed, and many of the left-wing groups that had come into existence in the thirties, taking culture out to small towns, working-men's clubs and union halls, thrived also.

The Party hoped to tap into this new upsurge of demand, and Sylvia was involved with the new paper from its first issue. The paper was attractively presented, by war-time economy standards, with cartoons by the Grand Old Men of Thirties' Left cartooning, such as James Holland and James Boswell. It contained photographs, discussion pieces by a wide range of people, fiction, reports, poems and so on. Writers from outside the Party who were progressive in outlook contributed to it, but unlike *Left Review*, the editorial board was wholly made up of Party members. There were no women on the board.

The early pieces Sylvia wrote for *Our Time* were forthrightly political, in the vein of her 1930s journalism. Her name appears prominently on the front cover of the first issue: she contributed a notable poem called 'Here in this Narrow Room', which she wrote as the introduction to a performance of two plays by Brecht, *Rechtsfindung 1934* and *Die Gewehre der Frau Carrar* (performed by the Free German League of Culture in London). The poem, spoken at the beginning of the performance, is a powerful rallying-cry to freedom, a celebration of the great tradition of Germany's liberal poets and thinkers. It is a public poem, a rhetorical set-piece, but within those terms, a successful one:

Here in this narrow room is a wide country
Heathlands, harbours, mines, quarries, the rich bounty
Of cornfields, and the autumnal garland of vineyards . . .
                                    . . . here in this narrow
Room, as in alembic, by distillation
Of exile, by pride, sorrow, resolve, constancy
Of purpose fuelled and held in concentration
Is Germany[43]

This true Germany in exile is contrasted throughout with the false usurping Germany of 'Ueber allies': there is no direct reference to the concentration camps, but the line in the poem which refers to the smoke of books burning perhaps recalls Heine's words that those who burn books end by burning people. The poem contrasts the scattered, ill-equipped and penniless bands of thinkers, singers, creators, 'our arsenals', with the resources of the Generals who 'straddle Europe and are enriched with plunder'. The real Germans are unnumbered, and they fight

in the street and market openly with defiance
. . . in the laboratory with the verdict of science
. . . in the torture chamber with our silence.[44]

Sylvia creates a dramatic and poetic expression of resistance: the poem is not an account of the actual state of resistance in Germany in 1941. It is a rallying-cry to freedom, and a reminder of the Germany that will rise again out of the ashes of the Fascist state. It permits itself the simplicities of dramatic contrast which in a lyric poem, for example, Sylvia would not have used, but which in a poem of this public nature are appropriate. Declaimed poetry, such as Jack Lindsay wrote for many working-class groups in the war, could be a very powerful way of doing this; choral speaking of dramatic poems reached and moved audiences who would probably never have looked at verses in print.

Sylvia's other contributions to *Our Time* were all prose pieces; one written in 1941 about the ATS (Auxiliary Training Service), 'Fifty Girls Who Shouldn't', despite its humorous title, had pointed things to say about the lack of direction of the army at that stage of the war:

> women are the practical half of creation. Their training has reared them to read advertisements critically, to examine the underside of the cheap joint, to ask, as Mrs Siddons did: Will it wash? And at present the call to join the ATS will not wash. When the army gets its will, and is allowed to act like an army, women will be ready to serve with it.[45]

Sylvia's conclusion was that, for the time being, with the state the army was in, it wouldn't wash as far as women were concerned. They would rather do anything else than join what was popularly known as the 'Auxiliary Tarts Service'.

Another early *Our Time* piece was called 'The People have No Generals', which appeared in the first issue.[46] It was about the position of civilians during the blitz. The people are an army that cannot retreat; they, the people of Britain – and for that matter, the people of Germany too – hold the front line: they are an army without 'weapons, without training, without generals and therefore . . . unable to retreat'. Her comments on the civilianisation of war through the blitz were in no sense simply patriotic. Within the reasoned, calm tone there is a biting critique. In an angry satirical dash reminiscent of Swift's *Modest Proposal*, she compares the Luftwaffe to 'flocks of cornucopia-bearing angels' making a present to the country of the deaths of 'a large number of women and children', thus closing 'a large number of bouches inutiles'.

What conclusions, she asks, are the people to draw from this entirely new kind of warfare in which they make up the front line? First, they need to recognise that it takes 'more than metaphor and more than aerial bombardment to conscript them', in other words, despite the cliché that they are the front line troops, and despite the constant bombing, they are still civilians, not soldiers. From there, to realise how much war has now become civilianised – which would seem to imply civilian responsibility for it as well as their suffering – they then have to:

> ask themselves whether a civilianised (or totalitarian) war can continue without their consent and support. And then, I suppose, to consider whether they wish it to continue, and

whether they might not prefer to move forward to another front line, and a better one, giving a clearer view of the enemy.

The enemy that she has in mind here is not just the German army. It is Fascism in its entire reach, and it is the class enemy. The implications of moving forward to another front line might be considered at that time, during the Battle of Britain, to be tantamount to arguing for opposition to official policy. The call for a Second Front was a familiar Communist demand, but it was none the less a subversive demand and could have been a dangerous call to make. The article leaves no doubt that Sylvia was still, in 1941, what is called a 'hard-line' Party member.

However, with the entry of the Soviet Union into the war, and the change of political line by the CP, the political climate perceptibly shifted. Armament production soared, and people recall today their relatives sending out tanks from the factories with 'another one for Uncle Joe' chalked on the side. This pro-Soviet feeling amongst ordinary working-class communities was to last until the early fifties at least, long after official attitudes had declared the Soviet Union to be the enemy.

Valentine reported to *New Republic* that all the women in her civil-defence office were extremely pro-Russian. Sylvia wrote to Ben Huebsch in November 1942, after a showing of *The Battle Before Moscow*, of seeing the extraordinary sight of:

a perfectly respectable middle-class house leap to its feet and stand to attention through the *Internationale*. Today, to celebrate the 25th anniversary of the Soviet revolution the BBC has performed that well-known air right through, on a gramophone record. First performance by Broadcasting House.

The bans on the *Daily Worker* had finally been lifted in September: the Communist Party and the people were on course in the same direction again. Meanwhile, *Our Time* was not selling as the founding editors had hoped, although it continued to appear for another seven years.

WAR AND ITS AFTERMATH

There were times when the daily tedium of war seemed relentless, when there was no time to read or write or concentrate upon anything. Sometimes Sylvia poured out her feelings to her friend, Nancy Cunard, who during the war gradually came to be an important person in her life. Nancy was a heroic fighter in the cause of all that she considered unjustly treated. In the United States she had championed Black rights and published the massive and justly celebrated anthology of Black American writing, *Negro* (1934). In Paris her friends and lovers included jazz trumpeters and artists, black and white. Once the Spanish war broke out, Nancy threw herself into fighting for the republican cause, sending newspaper reports back to the States, raising money, enlisting the talents and energies of friends from the worlds of the aristocracy and the arts with which she mingled. During the Second World War she edited *Poems for France*, to which Valentine as well as Sylvia contributed; the poems were published in dual language versions and Sylvia later recalled how meticulously and persistently Nancy pursued the exact word for a translation.

Sylvia and Valentine had first come in contact with her when Nancy initiated *Authors Take Sides on the Spanish War* in 1937, to which they both contributed, but it was not until the winter of 1942 that they were all three to meet.

Nancy was always particularly Sylvia's confidante and friend, and perhaps her courage and gaiety made a welcome contrast to Valentine's brooding over her own health and the emotional complications in her life, and her anxieties over Sylvia's welfare and their financial situation. Sylvia respected Nancy for her work as a poet, editor and translator, and for her meticulous standards whether in scholarship, tidiness or conducting herself when drunk (which happened frequently). Nancy never compromised and she was afraid of nothing. She was amongst the rare company of Sylvia's women friends, which included her first friend Bea Howe, with whom she had an equal relationship: many of the people to whom she wrote intimate letters she did not in fact know, except through correspondence.

Nancy had come to Dorset with a friend, Morris Gilbert, and

the four of them met for lunch in Dorchester; the meeting was clearly a success, for Nancy came to dinner with Sylvia and Valentine that evening. She left her heavy African ivory bracelets with them for safe-keeping. Sylvia, in a memoir of Nancy, recalled that: 'She looked sadly at her wrists when they [the bracelets] were off. She would have felt much less denuded if she had stripped off her clothes.'[47]

Nancy came quite frequently to stay at Lower Frome Vauchurch for weekends, but usually stayed in a pub so as not to encroach on their (and particularly Valentine's) space, for she too was a great respecter of privacy. Sylvia loved her for her qualities of greatness of heart, her meticulous self-respect, courage and good manners: but she also appreciated the odder sides of her character. The bond between them about Spain was so deep, Sylvia said, that they never fell out with each other. Nancy would carry everything she needed done up in a:

> tartan haversack, supplemented perhaps by a Dick Wittington spotted handkerchief. Settled in, she began to preen: a button was made fast, a lining restitched; the bracelets were fetched and devoutly polished. . . . On a desert island, in a jail cell, she would have kept herself spruce, well-kept, clean as a cat. Her temper was notorious, her life was wilful and erratic – and she was compellingly respect-worthy.[48]

She was also a magpie collector and would go for rapid walks over the downs to collect flints, coming back with her pockets so loaded she resembled, Sylvia wrote, a cheetah fastened with panniers when seen on the skyline. Despite her violent opinions, violently expressed, she was a model guest, and Sylvia appreciated particularly the fact that she was never late for any of the many meals she cooked for her: 'Whatever she had been doing . . . she would be ready – brushed and combed and creditable; and sitting upright and slightly formalised, she would converse agreeably, as a guest should.'[49]

Sylvia herself was keen on good manners and for Valentine also, manners were very important. Both women came from a social milieu which exerted a powerful sway – however far they moved from their own class in terms of political opinion – in terms of respect for the conventions of social behaviour. Their unconventionality and iconoclasm were restricted to the spheres of politics and sexuality.

By March 1944, with plans for invading France and the big final engagement with the Germans gathering pace in preparation for D-Day on 6 June, non-residents on the south coast were forced to move away, while residents were restricted to the area. At the same time, the German buzz bombs were causing terrible casualties in the cities. Nancy, who had come early in the year to look for lodgings for her friend the writer Norman Douglas, was forced to move again, this time to Somerset. On a borderline station, between Dorset and Somerset, she and Sylvia contrived to meet. Sylvia's strong feeling for her friend shines through her concern for the difficulties Nancy was facing:

> I felt a heartless relief when this project fell through [of finding Norman Douglas lodgings where he would be 'warmed, well-fed, out of bombs' way and within reach of female attentions']: it seemed to me that if anyone needed the female attentions, etc. it was Nancy.[50]

Sylvia was not over-susceptible to the sensitive requirements of the male ego, despite her strong maternal streak.

In April 1944, Sylvia received a summons from the Labour Exchange, instructing her to attend 'with a view to taking up work of national importance'. She wrote to Nancy, fuming with anger:

> If I had taken to myself a husband, lived on him and made his life a misery (as undoubtedly I should have done, as no man has ever been able to bear me as a continuity) I should not be troubled with any of this. Being kept by a husband is of national importance enough. But to be femme sole, and self-supporting, that hands you over, no more claim to consideration than a biscuit.'[51]

It was a straightforwardly selfish response, for it was the injustice of being summoned as a single woman that enraged her. She went on: 'The great civil war, Nancy, that will come and must come before the world can begin to grow up, will be fought out on this terrain of man and woman, and we must storm and hold Cape Turk before we talk of social justice.' The comment shows how she related her feminist instincts to her socialism: unless the inequality between the sexes was sorted out first, they could whistle for all the equality between the classes for which as a Communist she was, and had been, fighting for nearly ten years. It was almost certainly a new perception, for in the thirties her attitude was that she joined the CP to fight for the working class and the causes she believed in, not because she was a woman. None the less, the first cause she ever joined was a cause of paramount concern to women, the campaign for birth control in the 1920s, for she was so appalled by the stories told her by Mrs Keates (who cleaned for her and became her friend) of unwanted pregnancies, that she became convinced contraception was the first and vital weapon that all women must have.[51]

By July 1944, after the D-Day landings, the ban on the south coast was lifted. From the fatigue and tedium of daily wartime life, Sylvia and Valentine were thrown into frenzied activity. Dorchester was suddenly jam-packed with evacuees who had fled from the bombed cities. In her letters, Sylvia mocked her own part in all the strenuous activity of trying to settle them in a quite different environment:

> I spend day after day conferring with Public Assistance, Relieving Officers, Billeting Officers, WVS ladies; and hastening from one Rest Centre to the next saying words of comfort such as soap flakes can be made out of solid soap by means of a cheese-grater, nobody need be ashamed of lice nowadays, salads will not be appreciated without vinegar, Londoners seldom like porridge . . . cows don't bite. . . . Anyway, this is now my life, and on the whole welcome to it, for I'd rather be overworked than rot on Lethe's wharf.[53]

The most heartbreaking incident of 1944 occurred in June when a German bomber unloading its bombs before returning home dropped one on Chaldon and demolished Miss Green: fortunately the tenants, Jim and May Pitman, were unhurt — the house fell round them — but they were blown outwards by the blast. Sylvia wrote angrily to Nancy of what the bombing meant to her tenants:

> Our little house at Chaldon is gone, Nancy; the little stocky grey house that sat there looking so mittened and imperturbable. . . . They have lost most of their belongings, the summer's food in the garden, and a house that they loved and looked on pretty much as their own, for they knew we

would not move them unless we absolutely had to. And the only decent cottage in that village, the only cottage kept in order, gone, while the hovels belonging to the Weld estate, God damn it, are untouched in all their filth, scarcely a bug shaken out of them.[54]

Characteristically, she was not thinking of her own financial loss, either of the 3 shillings a week rent they could ill-afford to lose or her investment. Her concern was only for the Pitmans, who were friends, and her anger was directed against the estate which owned most of the village and left its properties in such a state of disrepair and without proper sanitation.

The war was finally drawing to a close. In 1945 Sylvia went up to London to meet Louis Aragon, whom she and Valentine had known in Spain. They had lunch together and she reported to Nancy that she found him: 'triply distilled, and aromatic with pride and a queer happiness'.[55] France had been liberated in August 1944, and the French were experiencing a renewed sense of optimism and national pride, particularly those, like Aragon, who had been so closely identified with the Resistance. Aragon, by contrast, found the British little changed:

Our intellectuals . . . seemed to him to be exactly where he last saw them, planted in the year 1939. Our comfort, ease, solidity of living – like a museum piece; handsome, perhaps, and admirable, but with no relevance to the present day. Our ruins, of course, impressive, and regrettable; but only a background to people looking as usual.[56]

This viewpoint was shared by many intellectuals visiting England from Europe after the war.

Sylvia, in an article for *Our Time* in 1945, wrote of her admiration for the French Resistance and their ultimate victory. She also contributed a poem dedicated to 'The Maquis', which was published in Nancy's anthology *Poémes à la France*.[57] The poem is spoken in the mouth of a Maquisard, and celebrates in clear-cut images the hounding of the Resistance fighters to the furthest limits:

Pupil to stars and foxes
And fellow-citizen to a stone,
France hides me in a cleft of her mountains.
Tomorrow they will give me a gun.

Tomorrow they will give me a gun;
And I, that gun's man,
Henceforth shall rank among the others another,
But tonight I am France.[58]

The poem recalls the direct and effective approach of the Spanish Romanceros which she translated.

In her article 'Love of France'[59] Sylvia praised the respect for local materials which she saw to be the supreme characteristic of French culture: in this case, in the fighting against an occupying army, building of barricades and culminating in the triumphant liberation of Paris. She stressed the connection between French art and the way that the French had fought:

If France has this quality of approximating to a work of art, it is because her nationals have not failed in violence. Mother of arts, and arms, and laws, she is also the daughter of revolutions. A barricade is also *Modes*, and fighting for liberty a characteristic elegance of France.[60]

In watching the film of the Liberation of Paris in Dorchester, she compared it to watching 'sword-play ... or the flight of swallows'. The French had won back their freedom:

because they were mentally skilful, technicians of liberty ...
[it was] an exhibition of civilised behaviour in the pre-
eminently civilised act of rooting out fascism. . . . It was
another masterpiece of France, executed in local materials,
the men and women of the French Resistance.[61]

Sylvia's recognition of the place of violence in both politics and art gives the lie to those who would see her as simply a quiet English gentlewoman with a sharp Jane Austen eye for human weakness and social comedy. Too much of the reviewing of her recently published work, owing to the policies on what is being published, has presented this kind of misleading picture, neglecting the rage at the heart of her vision. Above all, Sylvia recognised, as she made Ramon Percez, in *After the Death of Don Juan* say, that there are many things wrong with society, but we do not have to suffer all of them: we can, and should, fight to change what we can.

By the time the war was over both Sylvia and Valentine were tired, and, like many others who had worked and looked for radical change, dispirited at the mood of the post-war British government. Earlier aspirations towards a society which would irreversibly challenge the crippling effects of the deeply class-divided pre-war Britain were betrayed, as many people saw it, by the bureaucratic, unvisionary post-war Attlee Government and the rapid slide, following the United States, into cold-war politics.

Valentine continued to write for *Our Time* and occasionally for the *Daily Worker* after the war. One such piece, for the 16 June 1968 issue, dealt with the history of Dorset, and, in class terms, a viciously repressive history she shows it to have been. The account goes from the days of Judge Jeffreys and his bloody assizes in 1685 (still celebrated in the name of a high street tea-room) through the public strangling and burning of a woman convicted of petty treason for murdering her husband, 'not so long ago as time is counted here', in 1705, to the assizes sentencing the ringleaders in the Labourers Revolt of 1830 to transportation. She links the background of Dorset's radical heroes, the Tolpuddle Martyrs, to present-day political consciousness and behaviour. The article points out that the descendants of those who ate with Judge Jeffreys now dismiss the story as quite sickening, and quotes from a diary of 1830 to show the alliance between the County and the judges at that date: 'The judges dined with us and we had a large party besides amounting to sixteen.' The gentry are shown to be actively complicit in putting down working-class attempts to defend themselves; her account goes on to link these incidents from history to present-day Dorset, and the behaviour of those who colonise the villages, the rural magistracy still being almost entirely drawn from the ranks of those known as the County, the descendants of the dining companions of the hanging-judge. Droves of these people have moved into the villages, expropriating the villagers, 'doing-up' the cottages and then complaining that life is uncomfortable for they cannot get anyone to work for them. (Gentrification of the countryside is not a new phenomenon.) But, ironically of course, the Powyses, Stephen Tomlin, Betty Muntz, and Sylvia and Valentine in different ways had all formed part of this pattern, even if they lived simply and did their own work. Not many years later, Valentine herself was bemoaning the lack of servants.

Despite her disillusionment, Sylvia remained strongly committed in the post-war years, and up until the end of the forties at least, was still a Party member. She wrote an acid letter to the American House Committee on Un-American Activities about their summoning of Dorothy Parker to appear before them, requesting that her congratulations be extended to Miss Parker. She wrote to the BBC castigating them for allowing a programme to be broadcast that whitewashed the Nazis. To Arnold Rattenbury as secretary of the CP Writers' Group she wrote regretting she could not attend meetings and suggesting that the group produce some kind of clear declaration to counter the increasingly overwhelming influence of *Horizon* and the right-wing cultural press.

However, she was tired. The post-war letters speak of how no one feels well or happy, there is no enthusiasm. The sound of the tedious word 'democracy' is too painful; listening to Truman is depressingly like waiting to listen to Hitler ten years earlier. 'I can't believe that the ordinary quiet coca-cola citizen . . . wants to hang over Europe like an allegory in a painted ceiling, with a bun in one hand and a bomb in the other',[62] she wrote to Paul. Valentine, Sylvia said, wrapped herself in Plotinus. She herself had yet to find 'any philosopher who will console me for the deep religious feeling which makes statesmen and politicians so ready to throw other people under the car of Juggernaut. Whoosh, they cry, their voices throbbing with piety, Under you go!'[63]

Everyone was 'more or less rheumatised', largely due to 'Mr Bevin's war of nerves on the British people, and the bleak consequence of Marshall aid.'[64] Tinned foods, cigarettes, paper, and paperclips all ran short, and everyone was fed up with austerity. When in early 1949 Nancy suggested a trip to Paris to attend the Peace Congress, organised by the World Peace Council,[65] Sylvia's response was gloomy but definite:

> I am by no means sure that I want to attend any sort of Congress or Committee or Gathering. My mood is *centrifugal*. . . . No, a quiet dust-bath is more to my mind, a dustbath and minding my own business.[66]

The next month she and Valentine went off to gather dust in Italy, where Sylvia found heavenly Baroque churches and fell passionately in love with the country. She wrote rapturously to Paul Nordoff, four months after their return:

5.3 Sylvia and Steven Clarke at Lower Frome Vauchurch, 1946

5.4 Valentine in the garden in Lower Frome Vauchurch; early morning, 1948

5.5 Sylvia in the garden at Lower Frome Vauchurch with a young relative

Oh, and the oxen, darling, so stately – one young one, unharnessed, that I saw stepping through an olive-yard like a thoughtful god; and the landscape, clasping its hands in ecstasy, its mountain hands above its valleyed breast. And everything enriched with art and poetry and history, and so deeply aristocratic, with no airs and ten thousand serious graces; and all seen hand-in-hand with Valentine. If I should ever write to you and complain of my lot, remind me that in the February of 1949 I went with Valentine to Italy.[67]

By June 1949 she had reason to complain of her lot, for Valentine had finally decided she must try to settle and choose between Sylvia and Elizabeth. Elizabeth was coming over to England, and they would try the experiment of living together. Improbably, it was agreed that they should live at Lower Frome Vauchurch. Sylvia preferred, she said, the 'sting of going' to the 'muffle of remaining'. She moved out and left the house, complete with all their shared hauntings, to the lovers, while she went to live in an unprepossessing hotel at Yeovil Junction, on the Dorchester to Westbury-on-Trym line, thirteen miles away. From there she wrote to her old friend, Bea Howe: 'I have basely deserted Valentine though it is by mutual agreement. She has an American friend staying with her, not an affliction, for she likes her; but so do not I, said the cookmaid.'[68]

Instead, she was 'wallowing in walks on Sedgemoor, I take a little train, I take a little bus, and cast myself in those willowy-green sweet-scented solitudes'.[69] The experiment only lasted three weeks; Elizabeth could not replace Sylvia, as Valentine herself seemed to have realised even before her lover arrived. Writing *For Sylvia: An Honest Account* shortly before Elizabeth was due, Valentine wondered if what she thought she wanted was perhaps only an illusion, an aberration of judgment. And yet, she thought, she might really be the kind of person who could love two people. In this she was probably not wrong, but until she put her life to the test she did not realise how Sylvia's love was for her the rock-bed she rested on. This stable part of her life made her able to love other people: without it she was lost. She wrote:

Because of that vow and because of our life together I do not think that she [Sylvia] will leave me alone, even when I am a ghost; and if she will walk with me, we will be happy. . . .

I cannot, for more than a moment at a time, realise what it will be like to be here without Sylvia – or anywhere without Sylvia. . . .

But I know beyond any doubt that my whole being is rooted in Sylvia – that out of my being, however base and bad it seems to be, this matchless love and faith has grown.[70]

More prosaically, it seems that Elizabeth lacked Sylvia's sense of humour, and any trial relationship undergone in that house – 'muffled' with all the hauntings of the twelve years Sylvia and Valentine had lived there together – could have stood little chance against such in-stored power. Unsurprisingly, for many years, there was to be no neat and final healing of the wound.

CHAPTER 6

MATURE ART: SYLVIA – THE WRITINGS OF THE 1940s

A NOTE ON THE POETRY OF THE THIRTIES AND FORTIES

Poetry remained for Sylvia an important medium. It was as a writer of fiction that she was known, however, and that was the genre in which her mature art was displayed. It was not until towards the end of her life that she became known as a poet once more. She once said that she proposed to be a posthumous poet; when she came to look through her manuscripts to choose pieces for the Aldeburgh Festival celebration of her work in 1977 – her poems were set to music by John Ireland and Alan Bush, and Peter Pears performed some of her work – she found so many that she wrote 'One would think I had never done anything else but write poems.'[1]

Without the opportunity to study the unpublished material it is only possible to guess at the significance of poetry to Sylvia at this time, a point on which Claire Harman's biography will certainly be enlightening.

She had written a number of poems for publication in left-wing periodicals in the thirties, and some also appeared in places like the *London Mercury, Life and Letters Today, Time and Tide*, the *New Statesman* and *Nation, New Republic* and *The Countryman*. Poems continued to appear in periodical publications in the forties. Some which were published in pamphlet form much later at the end of her life date from this time, and a number of unpublished poems of both the thirties and forties appeared in *Collected Poems* (1982).[2] Poems such as 'An Acrostical Almanac 1940', which used the letters of Valentine's name, and of her own nickname, Tib; 'The Story of a Garden';[1] 'Death of Miss Green's Cottage'; 'Monsieur de

Grignan' and many others belong to this period. Sylvia's editor in the *Collected Poems* describes these 'out of earshot of an audience' poems as 'extraordinary', and suggests that they read as 'a sort of journal . . . a record of small events breaking on the surface of daily life'.[3] But there is a wide range to these uncollected poems of both the thirties and the forties, from personal and passionate poems such as 'Under the Sudden Blue' and 'Drawing you, heavy with sleep', the close-brooding stare of some of the Dorset poems ('Mangolds' and 'Man in a landscape'), the intense realisation of Spain in poems like 'Port Bou'; 'Journey to Barcelona'; 'Waiting at Cerbere' and 'Benicasim', to the concentrated bite and anger of 'Some make this answer'; 'Recognition'; 'We Accuse'; 'Exile'; and 'Trial of Marshal Pétain'.

THE SHORT STORIES

The first collection of stories was *The Cats Cradle Book*, which was published in 1940 by the Viking Press in the United States. Here all the stories are supposed to be traditional ones told by cats to their kittens, collected and transcribed by a Mr William Farthing of Spain Hall, Norfolk. The stories were written in the thirties, some at Frankfort Manor, two of them originally for the *New Yorker*. On the surface a witty, light-hearted collection illustrating human weaknesses from the cats' point of view, some of the stories have a darker undertone: 'The Magpie Charity', for example, is a biting attack on institutional charity, which was published in *Our Time*. A darker note also sounds at the close of the long introductory story which is a half-realistic, half-fanciful account of how 'the editor', a young woman who stumbles upon the house by accident while motoring in Norfolk, comes to have the stories in her possession. This 'Introduction' was written either at the time Sylvia and Valentine were living at Frankfort Manor, or soon afterwards, and is imbued with the heightened, romantic atmosphere of those days, and of the house and garden that their letters convey so intensely. The Introduction is bathed in an almost Pre-Raphaelite glow, mellow, ripe and still, an air at once unreal, slightly out of focus and at the same time hyper-real, in which the talking cats and their handsome young master appear like figures in some stately old-fashioned dance:

the general tint of the house was that of a ripening pear with streaks of vague rose and pale madder flushing its sallow skin.

With trees all around it, with a deep mossy lawn in front of it, the house lay like a pear fallen from a tree – a pear beginning to grow sleepy, I thought.[4]

The handsome young man is a veritable fairy-tale prince, but a fairy-tale prince out of Grimm or Perrault, not of the Victorian imagination. He appears out of nowhere, untouchable, beautiful and autocratic:

I had not seen him approach. He might have come down a tree, he might have come out from under a lilac or a syringa: no hunting cat could have arrived more stealthily, more disconcertingly. Like a hunting cat, he was on his guard, and concealing it under an appearance of being there more or less by accident and on his way to somewhere else. But there was ownership in every inch of him – ownership of house, and trees, and cats, and privacy, and solitude. He was holding a rake, and a lock of hair fell over one eye.[5]

One of the most notable features of Valentine's appearance when she was young was the lock of hair that fell over one eye: compare this with Sylvia's (undated) letter to Llewellyn Powys, 'Her face is pale with sleep, and a lappet of hair dangles forlornly over her left eye.'[6]

The young man relates his life-story; how he came to talk cat through his love for a beautiful Siamese cat, and his life with her in Bangkok. The story has mock-heroic and satirical elements, but also this fairy-tale, surreal quality in which anything may and does happen. Over a fine supper of cold pigeon pie, asparagus, Vin d'Anjou, sugar biscuits, coffee and brandy, they discuss the stories and how to publish them. Then he leads her out onto the lawn:

deftly he knocked me over, and with a sigh began to make love to me. The mossy grass was deep and cool, and in an interval of love I praised it. 'It has never been cut', said he, 'except with a scythe. While I am here it never will be.'

A cuckoo woke me. I was lying on the lawn alone, and it was green now, and the sun flashed on the dew.[7]

That morning, the young woman returns to London; at intervals he sends her copies of new stories the cats have told him. Then she receives a telegram, summoning her to Norfolk: there is a murrain among the cats. They are all dying.

This had happened to Valentine and Sylvia in March 1934: over twenty cats and four dogs in Sloley died of a mysterious plague, including four of their cats. But the story communicates a darker foreboding than simply the death of the animals, for in it the cats' civilisation represents the best of culture: their narratives are the most pure, their manners the most exquisite. And that civilisation, which is appreciated by and matched in the young man, is doomed. The concluding sequence has a nightmare quality, moving swiftly to a grim close. The unspoken sub-text is the murrain at work in Europe.

Far from being simply a collection of children's stories, then, as it seems to have been regarded when it was published twenty years later in England, *The Cat's Cradle Book* points in some of its contents to the darkness a great many writers were preoccupied with at the end of the thirties. The book was dedicated, appropriately, to their friend Ludwig Renn, the anti-Fascist author and fighter.

By the time Sylvia came to write the stories that make up her next two collections which were published by Chatto, the imaginary had become real; *A Garland of Straw* and *The Museum of Cheats* are less visionary; they are also firmly rooted in the contemporary, in particular in the experiences of wartime. In *A Garland of Straw*, for example, there are stories dealing with evacuation, the village school in wartime, an air-raid during a funeral, and older themes from the thirties: unemployment, the feelings of a young Fascist soldier sent to Spain. There is little exuberance or gaiety in the collection, and certainly none of what Valentine called, in one of her *New Republic* letters, the 'jingoism of war or the jingoism of peace', but quite a lot of black humour. Some of the stories lack ease and spirit, perhaps because Sylvia 'knocked them off' to try and bring the raven to her door again.

Although not all of the stories in these two collections are about wartime, the sour flat tang of war and its aftermath hangs over most of them. Sylvia's writing about contemporary times and contemporary characters in a story like 'The Trumpet Shall Sound' illustrates this atmosphere. At a family funeral, a bomb falls onto the graveside. The mourners are already split by family feuds and the explosion throws them all scrambling pell-mell regardless into the freshly-dug grave for shelter. The grieving and aggrieved Lotte Mullen is thrown up against Dodger Blackbones, whom she cannot forgive for making off with the big family mahogany sideboard, after Aunt Mabel died, along with the dumb waiter 'and the eight chairs so solid you could hardly lift them'. 'Dodger had got them and Mrs Dodger had dusted them.' When the mourners pick themselves up out of the grave afterwards, Lotte gives vent to her wrath to her sister:

> All those Blackbones tumbling in without so much as a by-your-leave, and Mr Kedge and that poor old parson left to perish on the brink. Trust Dodger! Trust him to find a safe place to start blaspheming in! Dodger by name, and Dodger by nature.[8]

There is a quality of distance, an implicitly patronising low-life humour in this dialogue which elsewhere Sylvia was at pains to denounce. In her Royal Society of Arts lecture on 'Women as Writers', for example, she discusses what she calls the kind of 'workaday democracy' that characterises women's writing, which has:

> an ease and appreciativeness in low company. It is extremely rare to find the conventional comic servant or comic countryman in books by women. A convention is a *pis-aller*, a stopgap where experience is lacking. A woman has to be most exceptionally secluded if she never goes to her own back door, or is not on visiting terms with people poorer than herself.[9]

And she makes a similar point in her article on Mrs Gaskell in *Our Time*. The critic and biographer Hilary Spurling described Sylvia as a distinguished novelist and biographer, poet and musical scholar, but said that she would be chiefly remembered for her 'incomparable stories'.[10] Contrasting the intense and classical expression of the Elfin stories with those which Sylvia wrote in the post-war period, she concluded the latter were a 'little flavourless' by contrast, and that the characters were a 'contemporary standard post-war cast of genteel villagers, elderly queers [sic], drunks and dropouts, and the fifty-seven varieties of cultural snob'.[11]

With some of this judgment one must agree: contemporary times did not engage Sylvia's art at its deepest level. The paradox was that Sylvia, whose life and work were so involved with the social and political events of her time, produced no fiction that spoke memorably of it, while a writer like Elizabeth Bowen, for whom those events were peripheral, created in *The Heat of the Day* (1949) the novel which many people felt epitomised for them the feeling of wartime. Arthur Calder-Marshall wrote of Elizabeth Bowen in *Our Time* that she 'wrote superbly about those who didn't know effects have causes or didn't care'.[12] He went on to say how it was possible for anyone living in Regents Park to ignore events such as the Wall Street crash, the Manchurian incident, the burning of the Reichstag, the invasion of Abyssinia, the civil war in Spain, the Anschlusss, because 'Some chickens take a very long time to come home to roost'. Finally, however, the chickens did come home to roost: 'Not only Limehouse and Whitehall were bombed, but Regents Park also. The class structure was levelled by conscription, direction, misdirection, rationing and blitzing.'[13]

Sylvia, on the other hand, had been deeply aware of and involved in making an active political response to all those events of the thirties. She was the direct opposite of Bowen: in France one would have called her 'une écrivaine engagée': a 'committed' writer. She was, for all her later disclaimers, a writer for whom the act of writing was predicated upon her engagement with the society she lived in, however much she disguised it with fantasy and remote historical setting. That engagement took many different forms, and shaped her writing for the most part implicitly. She was most at home in some reversal or removal from the immediate scene, and one in which she was able to expand into the period and the place through leisurely disgression and idiosyncratic but telling example. Dialogue and the intimate exchange between characters she did not excel in, and while the epigrammatic quality of some of her later stories is indeed beguiling, she herself recognised towards the end of her life that in a sense, wit had been her enemy: unless harnessed it could too easily merely entertain.

In her stories of contemporary life there is a loss, a withdrawal from immediacy. The themes of loneliness, failure, betrayal, are often summarily treated: the corner of the coverlet is twitched back to reveal a glimpse of humiliation and pain, but the reader is kept at a distance. It is a controlled, cameo art, and one misses that sense of the writer at ease in her work, disporting herself with delight, in the way that she writes of Jane Austen as doing. She conveys that sense of delight in her own writing during the early gestation of *The Flint Anchor*, for example:

> about ten days ago I got started on a new book . . . my hair is uncut, my letters are unwritten, the house is a shambles, and I sit here as happy as Mrs Jellaby, though I am in 1836, not Africa.[14]

At its best, Sylvia's fiction has something of the flavour of the old cookery books, travellers' tales and memoirs which she loved. The reader loses herself in the physically powerfully present world of the fiction, and, as Sylvia demanded she should do, the author vanishes off the page. Sylvia's art is richly worked and rifted, the product of a sensibility and a consciousness imbued with a sense of history and of materialist dialectics. In these two collections, however, the social comedy of the lower classes and of her 'genteel' characters has a more dated air. There are exceptions, for example the moving sketch in *A Garland of Straw* of two young people, homeless and caught up in the law, called 'An Unimportant Case', in which the reader's sympathies are drawn to the sense of helplessness of the young couple, trapped by poverty and inexperience.

A more substantial exception is the title story of *The Museum of Cheats*. The curator of the Museum of Cheats, in the small town of Tipton Bacchus, has returned from the war and, when summoned to re-open the museum, decides to make of it something rather different from the intentions of its benefactor and the upright citizens of Tipton Bacchus. Much of the story is a humorous account of how the museum came to be founded, the vested interests and warring parties which had arisen through the course of its history over such vital matters as which of the museum's many and curious exhibits should actually be displayed, whom to admit and when, and so on. It is familar ground for a Warner short story; a collection of characters as eccentric as the elephant casts and other objects of the museum itself, the warring passions raging over matters of small import to anyone but the inhabitants of Tipton Bacchus, while greater events outside go by unnoticed. The curious, caricatured intensity of village life, where the minutest happenings get blown up like a nose in a Cruickshank etching, is something Sylvia was only too familiar with from life in Maiden Newton and Dorchester.

While the *Museum of Cheats* is an entertaining story, it is at the same time highly informative about English social change in the immediate post-war period. Sylvia deftly sketches in the background of the conservative baronet with parliamentary ambitions looking nervously at his neighbour's slender majority in the recent election, and beginning to mouth some of the catchwords of the Labour triumph – 'democracy', 'progress' – in case he needs to stand as a Labour candidate. The various social strata, and the museum's colonial inheritance are all done surely and swiftly, 'con brio', but the story has serious issues at stake, to which it leads up through twenty-six pages: Mr Colet the curator has spent two of the war years with the Maquis in France and has come back to Tipton Bacchus with new ideas.

He reopens the first floor of the museum, gets permission to install a wireless, and soon there is a constant stream of visitors to the museum's first floor and sounds of merriment and convivial discussion going on late into the evening. Downstairs, the bland exhibitions, lemonade and talks on the creator are not so well patronised – the creator who, 'as usual was badly in need of a little assistance, and could not be expected to do everything single-handed'.[15] Sylvia could rarely resist an ecclesiastical side-swipe: during the war she had observed how many clergymen there were in the villages, 'They are not even rationed yet, there is one to every village.'[16]

When Sir Alexander, the Tory baronet, smells a rat at the unusual popularity of the museum's first floor and makes enquiries, the local builder, Mr Hawke, tells him that it's due to 'education. People were more educated than they were in the old days.'[17] Hawke triumphantly repeats the exchange to the curator, pleased at having put the baronet off the scent. Mr Colet remarks that he wonders Hawke didn't mention culture. ' "Durn it I went and forgot he." Colet said that he daresayed education would do.'[18]

Culture would have been the safer reply, for education was then perceived to be a powerful weapon. Once people are educated they may start to demand things. Culture is merely soothing, anodyne.

The curator reflects philosophically on what he learned from a comrade in the Maquis: how easily political advantages can be lost, 'because an immature rank and file that has not learned caution when first seeing it displayed suspects it to be cowardice'.[19]

Colet does not smile at the disproportion between the scale of his concern in Tipton Bacchus with events in France and Spain for he reflects that 'he was handling a much smaller gun; but the target was equally the same'.[20] In the denouement of the story, all his hopes are overturned as the upright citizens finally discover what kind of satirical revolutionary socialist horrors have been being perpetrated on the first floor of their august museum. The building is found to be unsafe and the museum is closed.

The combination of political seriousness, rapid and sure-fire wit, caricature, and a deep, directed hatred of the hypocrisy and inertia of the ruling class and its allies – even in its smallest most pusillanimous form – characterise the best of Sylvia's political fiction. Where she loses touch with her anger she becomes what the polite reviewers see: simply a superb entertainer and stylist.

WRITING ABOUT WOMEN:
WRITING WITH COMMITMENT

Throughout the forties Sylvia's writing had a markedly partisan tone. It was of course apparent when she wrote for *Our Time*, but it also surfaced in less likely places. One of the inadequacies of her society that she was most impatient of, and which brought out a particular mordancy in her style, was the position of women.

Like many other women novelists, Sylvia was frequently invited to pronounce upon the subject of women writers. As she pointed out at the opening of her Royal Society of Arts lecture on 'Women as Writers' in 1959, it was questionable, to say the least, whether, if she had been a 'gentleman novelist', she would have been asked to lecture on 'Men as Writers'. She thought it improbable.[21]

For *Our Time* Sylvia wrote a long piece on Elizabeth Gaskell, with whose work she felt great sympathy. Her greatest praise of Mrs Gaskell was that she was someone who felt clearly – an unusual distinction: 'though she was not a deep thinker, she was a clear feeler. She knew her own heart. People who know their own hearts (women, perhaps, especially) are quite as subversive as people who know their own minds.'[22]

It was to women, she points out (especially middle-class women) that the opportunity came to observe the actual daily life of the poor in Victorian England: for it was the women whose social duty it was to go visiting the poor. Characteristically, this point is made with a good deal of wit at the expense of the nineteenth-century capitalist patriarchy (shades of Lolly Willowes' brother, Henry):

> To the stern businessman of the early nineteenth century the fashion for visiting the poor must have seemed a godsend. Visiting the poor was woman's work, it kept wives and daughters quiet, and as they visited with broth and blankets as well as with tracts it kept the poor quiet too.[23]

However, the consequences were not at all what those same stern businessmen had envisaged: in fact, they were the cause of as much consternation in middle-class households of the nineteenth century as the admission that 'Chloe liked Olivia' was to become in twentieth-century households.[24] For, 'Wives and daughters, instead of concentrating on the family mutton chops, began to air their views on the absence of mutton-chops in other families.'[25] This comment brings the whole relationship between men, women and their domestic economy into sharp focus, at once deflating and making the patriarchs' authority look ridiculous.

What Sylvia particularly valued in Mrs Gaskell's art was her ability to observe and to render what she saw in her society with a mixture of 'coolness and intimacy' a 'Vermeer-like quality of pure and scrupulous verisimilitude'. But she also valued Mrs Gaskell because her art did not, any more than Vermeer's did, 'harangue or argue'. Mrs Gaskell was 'armoured in the artist's essential limitations'; she 'attacked no abuses, she preached no remedies, she supplied no answers, she barely questioned. She presented her characters and told their story.'[26]

This celebration of the story-teller's art is particularly relevant in considering the art of Sylvia Townsend Warner herself: she was the last person to preach in her novels, and a great part of her success as a novelist and short-story writer derived from the combination of wit, serious feeling and impersonal narration. It is quite possible for the casual reader to catch only the humour and the richly evoked sense of place and time from Sylvia's work, while missing the essential warp and woof in her mature novels: the critical examination of society itself. If the hasty reader might miss the critique for the sake of the entertainment, it was nevertheless there, embedded within fiction's 'essential limitations'.[27]

Sylvia conveyed a spirited loathing of the hypocrisy of capitalist society when she analysed the difficulties Mrs Gaskell faced over the subject of illegitimacy:

> Victorian rancour against the lost maidenhead, a mixture of
> religious feeling and property sense with which society
> regarded the fallen women, as householders might regard a
> plate-chest which had deliberately thrown itself into the
> embraces of a burglar.[28]

These kind of comparisons have an almost metaphysical life of their own: they stand out from the text like three-dimensional baroque ornamentation. But the essential point is made: that it is a property-relation that is at stake in the Victorian attitude to the 'fallen woman', not just an outraged religious sensibility.

Sylvia wrote the British Council pamphlet on Jane Austen for their 'Writers and Their Work' series, which was first published in 1951, and reprinted over many years. This gave her the opportunity to make some telling points about women and writing. The pamphlet is written in faultless Austenian prose and shows quite as steady a hand and straight an eye as Austen herself was reputed to have in her family. Sylvia draws out a wealth of social meaning implicit in a sentence such as 'Miss Tilney always wears white', in *Northanger Abbey*:

> Behind Miss Tilney she sketches in, not the park or the
> stables, but the laundry-court of Northanger Abbey, the
> family wash-tubs and the laundry-maids. Her five words do
> more than that. They illuminate Miss Tilney also. Not only is

Miss Tilney so fortunately circumstanced that she can afford always to wear white, she does so from an inherent elegance of mind.[29]

And, some might think, from an inherent disregard of the laundry-maids. Again, it is a woman's viewpoint which recognises the social and economic cost implied in the choice of a colour: and, by extension, the social and economic cost of *choice*, of expressing one's 'inherent elegance of mind'. With such details, Sylvia points up the fundamentally social and realistic concerns of Jane Austen's art, how her 'outward gaze on the world was alert, but cool'; she contrasts Austen's use of the white gown with Hardy's in *Tess of the D'Urbervilles*, and Richardson's in *Clarissa*:

> It is of the world, worldly. Jane Austen is a completely worldly artist: as worldly as Fra Angelico was heavenly, and working with similar conviction and serenity in the field of her choice. . . . Though in her case the saints and angels are ladies and gentlemen, and the patriarchs are playing whist, and the act of martyrdom has been replaced by the act of marriage – to a worldly talent a theme of prime importance, since the world is peopled by it'.[30]

The emphasis on marriage which was Jane Austen's theme was not, of course, Sylvia's. Only rarely could men–women relationships be said to be significant in her work. Her 1929 novel, *The True Heart*, while dealing with a man–woman relationship, was an exercise in narrative form: the most powerful relationships between men and women in her longer fictions are those between the patriarch John Barnard and his daughter Mary in *The Flint Anchor*; the elderly Englishman and the equally elderly Spanish widow in *The Salutation*; and in the stories, the tale of the incestuous relationship between a brother and sister, 'The Love Match', published in *A Stranger with a Bag* in 1966. This story won the Katherine Mansfield short-story prize that year: much of its poignancy derives from the intimacy between the brother and sister which is rendered with such conviction and dignity. The empathy critics applauded in it came, it seems fair to suggest, from Sylvia's own experiences of living in what society judges a deviant relationship, however tolerantly it judges. (And it does not always judge tolerantly.) The sense of unease and the petty persecution, so quickly magnified into something unendurable, which can undermine the most trusting relationship is acutely, yet undramatically, realised.

But if Sylvia's themes were very different from Jane Austen's, in that they were wide-ranging in time and place and little concerned with individual human relationships, she was also very much a writer of the world, worldly. In her critique of Austen, Sylvia pulls aside the then accepted view of Jane Austen as a harmless writer whose work charms, soothes, refreshes, to replace it with a far more complex portrait. Jane Austen's unfinished novel, *Lady Susan*, for example, 'where Miss Austen's eyes are those of a hunting cat' – a reference to G. H. Lewes' comment about Jane Austen's 'mild eyes' – is an indication of the power Austen's work contained:

> In harshness of plot and nakedness of satire it looks back to the *Juvenilia*; in controlled grimness it looks forward to a masterpiece never written – a masterpiece that even without her untimely death the intervention of nineteenth century timidity might well have made impossible.[31]

Sylvia's awareness of the social and economic forces which bound and controlled women, like Virginia Woolf's, was an essential part of her perspective, only in Sylvia's case it was a perspective which embraced all classes of women in society, and not only the inevitably middle-class women writer. And, as we are beginning to understand to our cost today, the 'nineteenth century timidity' which repressed the range of what women could, and did, treat of in the novel after Jane Austen's time, has still a reach into the late twentieth century.

In her Royal Society of Arts lecture on 'Women as Writers', Sylvia took as her theme the way in which women got into literature in the first place:

> It would appear that when a woman writes a book, the action sets up an extraneous vibration. Something happens that must be accounted for. It is the action that does it, not the product . . . this extraneous vibration may be differently received and differently resounded. . . . It is also subject to the influence of climate, the climate of popular opinion. In a fine dry climate the dissonance caused by a woman writing a

book has much less intensity than in a damp foggy one . . .
volume increases with the mass – as summarized in
Macheath's Law:

> One wife is too much for most husbands to hear
> But two at a time sure no mortal can bear.

Finally, it would appear that the vibration is not set up until
a woman seizes a pen. She may invent, but she may not write
down.[32]

Thus, in 1959, Sylvia disposed of the patriarchal culture's
exclusion of women.

The early women writers caused so little alarm because 'they
only went off one at a time'. But, after the retreat from the
Renaissance, the vibration became truly jarring. By then many
women had learned to read and write, which was well enough
if they could be employed to keep account books, to 'transcribe
recipes for puddings and horse pills'. But thus far, no further;
they must be 'kept within bounds'; they must subserve. If they
broke the rules, then there was that most effective whiplash,
ridicule, to drive them back into their corrals, and in recent
years feminist literary historians have shown how effectively
this was done. Sylvia comments:

> It is more damning to be shown as absurd than to be
> denounced as scandalous.
>   It is more damning still to be thought old-fashioned.
> Margaret Countess of Newcastle was derided not only as a
> figure of fun but as a figure out of the lumber-room. . . . (I
> doubt if Pope would have laid so much stress on Lady Mary
> Wortley Montague being dirty if she had not been inky.)[33]

Again, the tone is light, but the matter is sharp and serious. To
write was to lose caste if you were a woman: but women were
determined, and they were cunning. They grasped every
opportunity they could, masking what they did behind blotters,
slipping their manuscripts aside, and ultimately, to avoid the
Angel-in-the-House, assuming men's names to get their work
published. Sylvia's points may be standard feminist literary
criticism today, but they weren't generally being said when I
went to Newnham in 1959.

Sylvia's conclusion is, that for women to have done all this
and got away with it, having started writing at the kitchen table

and ended up inside the palace writing on the same footing as men (which she concludes they do), they must have been and must still be, 'obstinate and sly'. And that is the distinguishing assertion that she can make about 'Women as Writers':

> I deliberately make this assertion in the present tense. . . . Obstinacy and slyness still have their uses, although they are not literary qualities. . . .
> But I have sometimes wondered if women are literary at all. . . . They write. They dive into writing like ducks into water. One would almost think it came naturally to them – at any rate as naturally as plain sewing.[34]

This is an argument more usually associated with male critics and writers (for example, John Crowe Ransom on Emily Dickinson as a 'little home-keeping person'), which Sylvia subverts here by implying throughout her lecture women's 'natural' affinity for writing, both because of what they do, and because of what they have been denied. Women still need obstinacy and slyness to enter the public world of literature because the demands upon them have in fact changed very little: once, women were encased and dragged down by their supposed moral superiority; now it is their physical superiority which interferes with their creativity. For 'it is well-known that a woman can be in two places at once'. Sylvia sees the dual labour of women, the woman writer's enduring complaint, as the reality most women still have to deal with. She imagines the woman writer:

> pinning down some slippery adverb while saying aloud, 'No, not Hobbs, Nokes. And the address is 17, Dalmeny Crescent.' Her mind is so extensive that it can simultaneously follow an intricate train of thought, remember what it was she had to tell the electrician, answer the telephone, keep an eye on the time, and not forget about the potatoes.[35]

The poor woman writer of the twentieth century turns out to have a worse deal than her sisters of previous centuries, worse too than that arch-exponent of the art of reflecting men, Mrs Ramsay in Virginia Woolf's *To the Lighthouse*.

It may come as something of a disappointment to the present-day feminist reader to find Sylvia saying that, after all, women's disadvantages turn out to be their real advantages: 'it is easier for a woman to make herself air and vanish off her pages than it is for a man, with his heavier equipment of learning and self-consciousness'.[36]

But, in short, she argues, precisely because they were debarred from education, and had to steal into literature through the pantry window, women have a quality or tend to have (with notable exceptions, such as George Eliot) of immediacy in their writing, whether as writers of memoirs, books, visions, medical records or indeed fiction. Furthermore, their very disadvantage puts women on the same footing as those other great writers who have entered through the pantry window, and 'left the most illustrious footprints on the window-sill'. Notably, of course, Shakespeare. Now they are in the palace, sitting writing:

> with great clearness what they have in mind to say – for that is all they know about it, no one has groomed them for a literary career – writing on the kitchen table, like Emily Brontë, or on the washstand, like Christina Rossetti, writing in the attic, like George Sand, or in the family parlour, protected by a squeaking door from being discovered at it, like Jane Austen, writing away for all they are worth, and seldom blotting a line.[37]

In this lecture, Sylvia made a clear statement about the quality in writing which she rated most highly; it is the classical quality of the writer disappearing off the page so that one no longer feels the author's 'chaperoning presence'. One is not aware of a writer at all. Her definition of this, or recipe for it, is that it occurs 'When the unequivocal statement matches itself to the predetermined thought and the creative impulse sets fire to them, the quality called immediacy results.'[38]

By this token, there are many occasions in Sylvia's own work when we are conscious of the writer's presence: of her humour, her delight in bravura and digression, of her sly and subtle, mocking tone of voice. When that tone becomes paramount, as it frequently does in the stories, we are entertained but not challenged. The Sylvia Townsend Warner whose work we should re-evaluate, is the novelist and the poet of the later works, of *Azrael, King Duffus* and *Twelve Poems*. One of her earliest, most perfect achievements in distilled impersonal immediacy is the 1932 novella *The Salutation*. Amongst the novels, *Summer Will Show* and *After the Death of Don Juan* are both uneven as whole works, whereas in *The Corner That Held Them*, Sylvia evolved for herself the perfect loose-limbed medium in which to express the materiality of the created world. It was to be her major fictional achievement, and one still firmly rooted in her Marxist outlook, even if less obviously and dramatically so than in the thirties' novels.

FABLES AND ANGER: *OUR TIME*

These examples of Sylvia's critical writings do not exhaust her treatment of the position of women in the forties and fifties; but the position of women in society was not the only shortcoming in society that she used her pen to expose. Arnold Rattenbury wrote of Sylvia in *Our Time* that she was one whose hatred of the society they lived in was so tempered by subtlety of technique that it made satire her prerogative. Hatred is perhaps too strong a word, but certainly right from the early *Lolly Willowes* she showed that her bent was satirical, and many of the pieces she wrote in the forties for *Our Time* display her fine use of that weapon. But she was above all a writer who enjoyed her art, and in the forties she extended her range both of technique and subject. In many ways this was creatively a very successful decade for her.

During the war, *Our Time* had gone through a succession of editorial changes but had maintained a consistent political outlook; after the war, under Edgell Rickword's editorship, it continued to hold to a policy of unswerving support for the Soviet Union despite the growth of cold-war attitudes in Britain. Sylvia contributed to the paper up to the end of its existence and she was still a card-carrying Party member in the late forties, if a somewhat inactive one, maintaining her interest in the activities of the writers' group.

Our Time abruptly ceased publication in July 1949, having been going, to all appearances, from strength to strength. (In the early part of that year it had halved its price from 1s. to 6d., and increased both its circulation and content.) It represented no small achievement for the Communist Party: apart from some lean years in the middle of the war, when it was hard to get contributions, it was a consistently stimulating, wide-ranging and varied review of the arts, which lost nothing in freshness by the steadiness of its left-wing commitment. In the earlier years, its policies and platforms had not sounded so far distant from other cultural magazines with a populist slant, particularly in its campaign for a genuinely popular State arts policy. But in later years, after the war, it was to find itself increasingly arguing alone, as other groups fell back into the cultivation of their 'mandarin' sensibilities, and lamented the passing of youth, and the inroads of standardisation under a Labour Government.

One of the forms in which Sylvia contributed to *Our Time* was the political fable. 'The Magpie Charity', published in the United States in *The Cats Cradle Book* (1940) and in England first in *Our Time* in May 1948, was one of her fiercest. The story is an attack on that peculiar capitalist institution, charitable relief. A dying magpie provides in his will for the relief of indigent cats, because he loathes all cats and amongst cats he loathes starving cats most of all, for 'a starving cat is a menace to society'. He appoints a rook and a crow to be his executors: they invest the money and with the interest stock a refrigerator with mice, as the will instructs, for 'a genuinely indigent cat will not mind if a mouse is not perfectly fresh'.[39]

At first no cats come to apply to the charity; and when they do, after a long spell of snow and floods, the few that arrive look ashamed. But none of them measure up to the strict criteria to be wholly indigent; either they are too young and strong, or good-looking, or they have savings, or family. At last one comes who seems to fit all the criteria. He is blind, lame, old, stone-deaf and without family. The rook and the mouse retire to consider his application and are about to grant him one mouse, when the rook realises that he is not eligible after all, for cat skins 'fetch a very high price in the market. This old imposter is walking about with a good sixpennyworth on his back.'[40] After all they need not disturb the neat packing of their refrigerator, or mar the pristine cream-laid page of the ledger.

Comment seems superfluous, but those who have had dealings with our DHSS may feel the force of the fable. Sylvia articulated her disgust at society's hypocritical treatment of the poor and socially destitute through the fable form. During the Spanish Civil War she had published a fable portraying the Spanish people as sheep set upon first by a band of wolves and then, under the even-handed justice of the bailiff, who above all 'loved to hunt', by those who were supposed to be their guardian dogs.[41] Another 1940s fable called 'The Jungle Blossom' appeared in *Our Time* three months later.[42] Sylvia homes in upon her target with a merciless and unerring Swiftian relish: in many of the fables she wrote the style is terse and epigrammatic, but 'The Jungle Blossom', while employing a concise narrative style, is more picaresque. It traces the fortunes of a young Indian poet who lives in the age of post-atomic disaster. Rajendra comes across a few lines of Shakespeare in his exam paper for the Madras Riparian and Forestry board (leftovers from a former era) and he is hooked. His uncle tells him they are by the English poet 'Shakspere', but knows no more of him and Rajendra sets off to rediscover what he can of the poet.

This device of the poet's journeyings allows Sylvia to present her distopia of a world in the aftermath of atomic destruction, and a highly topsy turvy one it is. The hero accepts everything at face value, and gobbles up every scrap of information he can find; but sadly most of the relics are misleading, plastic replicas of downright lies. All the countries he travels through, except one, are controlled by the Atomic Board, which, in gaining control, has wiped out most of their individual cultures. In England, though it is a 'favoured nation', ony carbon copies remain of Anne Hathaway's cottage, 'Shakspira's girl-wife'. In the United States, where the Vatican has been re-sited in Utah while Europe was being 'democratised', Shakespeare has been put on the index in the Library, for presenting a favourable view of a Jew, in 'Big Business in Venice', and perpetrating the heresy that Jews are biologically different from Christians. For Sylvia by this time it was the Americans who were the Fascists.

In the capital of the United States, Tombstone, Rajendra is told there are three copies of Shakespeare first folios, belonging to a Mr Dwiddle, a Mr Popplefest and Mrs Melchior Sponger, which are all held in 'Sealed wrappings . . . in safes . . . in vaults . . . specially hollowed out during the period when we in this country were defying the menace of unauthorised atomic reprisals.'[43]

The United States is clearly responsible for starting the Atomic war in this scenario. It was during the late 1940s that Communist Party members in Britain as well as in the United

States were campaigning hard to get a 'no first use' of the atomic bomb guarantee, and being branded Commie-lovers and Reds for their pains. Hundreds of thousands of signatures were gathered against the Bomb, and the petition was taken, fruitlessly, to the United Nations.

Sylvia's language in this fable shows all her contempt for the authoritarian bureaucratese that must have so dispirited her during the war, and perhaps helped to contribute to her lack of enthusiasm and withdrawal to the sidelines of political activity. This story was being written at the height of the cold war in the United States, and amidst growing anti-Red feeling in Britain. The House of Representatives Committee on Un-American Activities, the notorious McCarthy committee, was at its peak of witch-hunting; Brecht's collaborator the composer Hanns Eisler was being deported, and in England Sylvia was yet again affirming her colours by appearing in a pamphlet edited by Edgell Rickword and published by the Writers Group of the Society for Cultural Relations with the Soviet Union, *Soviet Writers Reply*. (This pamphlet was advertised in *Our Time* as an 'up-to-date and informative book on Russian cultural problems in which questions are asked by Sylvia Townsend Warner, Montague Slater, Phyllis Bentley, Jack Lindsay and others and answered by eminent Soviet writers'.[44] J. B. Priestley wrote the foreword, and it was published in June 1948.)

At the conclusion of the fable, after Rajendra has been through many adventures, he arrives at the limits of the Precautionary Zone, which is the outer limits of the known world for those who live under the control of the Atomic Board. By the time he gets there he is already an old man, and crossing the Precautionary Zone (the territory that lies adjacent to that of the Soviets) is the most depressing experience yet of all his wanderings. 'Every feature of its geography had been obliterated; forests had been felled, rivers and lakes filled up, mountains and valleys levelled to an unvarying flatness; finally all this had been covered by a thick layer of concrete.'[45]

Below all this, the natives worked and the administrative authorities controlled them; and beyond, on the Eastern boundary, rose the wall which defended the territory of the Soviets and marked the furthest limits of their quest: 'A wall of polished red granite . . . over a hundred feet high . . . and above it to a height not known, rose the magnetic defences which forbade the passage of any kind of machine or projectile.'[46]

It is here that Rajendra finally hears news of his beloved Shakespeare being performed. His travelling companions, officials of the Atomic Control in the Precautionary Zone, are complaining of outrageous activities they have heard of going on behind the red granite wall: dramas which, one of the officials reports, 'take place almost every night, and people throng to them. But instead of being film, or radio or television, everything is done by a handful of propagandists who actually appear in the flesh.'[47]

His companion agrees that this is outrageous – 'totally undemocratic' – and the subjects of the scenes are equally scandalous: 'a friar is shown poisoning a young girl. That's to work up anti-clericalism of course . . . abandoned love-scenes between two young men . . . a white girl of social standing is made to dote on a negro.'[48]

Rajendra has reached his goal as nearly as he may; his search is a failure, for his permit has expired and he must return to devastated Europe where he has left behind his wife and family, to concentrate on his 'Critical Remains' of the great poet. Safe behind its polished red granite wall, the Soviet Union continues to enjoy Shakespeare.

The humour of the story is matched by the bleakness of its vision of a totalitarian, physically and culturally annihilated world after an Atomic war, except, contrary to the usual viewpoint, that world lies on this side of the 'Iron Curtain', not the other. It is not possible to read 'The Jungle Blossom' and think that Sylvia did not take sides.

Clearly, there was not much sympathy for this kind of partisanship by 1948, at least not amongst the intelligentsia; popular attitudes may have taken longer to shift from the belief that the Soviet Union was our ally, without whom, and without whose heroic resistance and loss of twenty million of its people, England would not have emerged from the war. However, for the majority of those who had 'fellow-travelled' before the war, the stories of the purges in the Soviet Union, the 1936 show trials and the reports from refugees of the treatment of Jews, all combined with the post-war division of Europe, the agreement at Yalta, and the 'democracies of a new type' surrounding the Soviet Union to create an atmosphere of something considerably more sinister. Even before Stalin's death in 1951 and the

revelations of the Twentieth Party Congress in 1956, information about 'Stalinism', as well as disinformation, was
beginning to emerge. At home, the Communist Party bore the
brunt of these developments, and for the first time, Communist
speakers and leafletters were physically attacked at public
meetings.

One example of the West's new fears was the formation of
Nato in 1949 as a defensive alliance, originally for twenty
years, to confront the perceived threat of the Soviet Union and
the satellite states (the Warsaw Pact followed some seven years
later). However, the anxiety about the new face of Europe was
not confined to the military and right-wing opinion. *Left News*,
still a Left monthly paper if a rather different animal from its
pre-war issues, devoted a good deal of space to critical
discussion of the 'new democracies' and their failings. The only
genuine popular nationalist leader, the paper thought, was
Georgi Dimitrov, the great anti-Fascist hero in Bulgaria.
Politically Europe had changed drastically within four years,
and the changes did not favour those who felt like Sylvia. The
only solution was retreat, as she was to say later, with reference
to *The Corner That Held Them*, an adroit and calculated
retreat.

'Minding her own business', throughout the 1940s, produced
a number of stories, mainly for *The New Yorker*: reviews;
some biting fables; a guide to Somerset; an edition of Gilbert
White; and above all, the novel written throughout the war and
finally published in 1948. It would be six years before she
began another, and it would be her last: a study of that most
oppressive of bourgeois institutions, the family, set in the East
Anglian sea-faring landscape which she and Valentine loved so
much. With *The Flint Anchor*, Sylvia returned to her study of
character and society, and created a world of nineteenth-
century patriarchy, posessiveness, oppression, guilt and hypocrisy almost unrelieved by any suggestion of escape. Only the
free, hardy, and homosexual society of the fishermen in that
novel – enclosed, literally peripheral, at the land's edge, and
dependant on the sea's unjudging expanses for its livelihood –
offers any glimpse of another kind of life.

Meanwhile, in *The Corner That Held Them*, if the theme
was retreat, or rather dissolution and break-up, the technique
was for Sylvia another step forward, a further experiment.

THE CORNER THAT HELD THEM

> I think that is my most personal book probably . . . I had to
> include religion . . . I began that book on the purest Marxian
> principles . . . if you were going to give an accurate picture
> of the monastic life, you'd have to put in all their finances,
> how they made their money, how they dodged about from
> one thing to another and how very precarious it all was, how
> only the rich orders had any sort of financial security. The
> smaller houses just dodged about on the edge of the abyss:
> they were nearly always bankrupt, except just three or four
> and they were so rich that everyone wanted their money. But
> it's a strictly capitalist story.[49]

It might seem strange that this long, loose chronicle of an
obscure fourteenth-century Benedictine nunnery, with no main
characters (except perhaps an anti-hero in the person of the
fraudulent priest Sir Ralph and a succession of prioresses),
should be the novel which Sylvia considered her 'most
personal'. Her readers and critics concurred in thinking it one
of her best books. It also represents a significant assay in the
form of the historical novel, although she in fact denied that it
was a historical novel.

In *The Corner That Held Them*, Sylvia succeeded in distilling
her love of the fourteenth century; of the progressive forces in
art, music and literature which were gradually sweeping away
the influence of the French, and asserting a new English
confidence and vigour. For example, with the national
Perpendicular style in architecture, 'at once more lucid and
more ambitious' than the old Decorated Gothic; and with
literature: the greater expressiveness of Piers Plowman.

Oby, in the fen country – her microcosm of the medieval
world – is touched by these changes. The new music, the Ars
Nova, enchants Bishop Walter's secretary when he encounters
it on a visit to a leper chapel with its 'ease of movement and
euphony', 'concords so sweet that they seemed to melt the flesh
off his bones'.[50] At the nunnery itself the dream of prioress
Dame Alicia of building a spire cripples and imperils the
community. The convent's priest, Sir Ralph, encounters a blind
poet's widow who hands on to him her husband's poem, the
Lay of Mamilion, an English epic written in the barbarous
demotic tongue which he comes to recognise as a masterpiece.

The nuns too demonstrate the new-found untrammelled creativity, embroidering an altar-hanging with all the skill and subtlety of the renowned Opus Anglicanum, which was sought all over Europe for its intricacy and richness.

The changes signalled in the arts are set in the closely observed texture of a society undergoing change. For the first time, as Sir Ralph observes, 'labourers move about and live on the country, just as kings do. For if your house has no roof you can leave it without regret. And if you have no land, you do not have to stay on it.'[51] Events lead up to the stirrings of revolt signalled by the Peasants' Revolt of 1381, which touches Oby in a serio-comic way and by which time the nunnery is, through a series of misadventures and a lack of 'capital' (or good dowries) practically bankrupt. English readers were expected to understand the historical events that lay behind the novel, but for the American reader an instructive gloss was provided. Noted in the American edition were: the decimation of the labour force by the Black Death and the peasants' greater mobility and increased bargaining power as a result; the landlords' response in changing farming practices from arable to pasture and enclosing land; the rise in wages and correspondent rise in prices; the subsequent fixing of wages and prices by parliament to control the mobility of the peasants; and the culmination of all the peasants' grievances against the Church, ignited by its evidently expanding wealth, which exploded in the Revolt.

One of the themes running through the novel is the way in which the peasants perceive the nuns to be idle and living in luxury while their lives are hard; consequently their service is given grudgingly to the manor of Oby and the nuns are often cheated. The workmen run away in the middle of a job and skimp their duties if the bailiff lets them, while conversely the nuns treat the peasants with contempt and refuse to do anything practical to help which might improve matters. When a nun suggests teaching the peasants' children, others object because of the fleas and the smell and the uselessness of the occupation: religion, in short, is a matter of obligations and ties, a worldly affair, affording at its highest the ascetic pleasure of music and silence. On Christian charity the community is short.

However, there are no dramatic reversals of fortune in this

novel, and no sudden comeuppance for the arrogant ladies who sit sewing and singing while others work their fingers to the bone for them: this nunnery, like others of the time, has servants, contrary to the original Benedictine rule. Just as this is a novel without conventional protagonists (unless Oby itself can be seen as the central subject) so it is a novel without conventional plot development, crisis and dénouement. In this novel Sylvia succeeds in breaking all the rules: even *After the Death of Don Juan* had a dramatic crisis and resolution in the siege of Don Saturno's castle.

Hilary Spurling praised *The Corner That Held Them* for its 'slow, orderly, painstaking, gradually entrancing accumulation of medieval detail';[52] She goes on to criticise it as merely a string of separate episodes and to affirm that Sylvia was defeated by the sheer bulk of her historical novels. Perhaps John Updike was nearer the mark when he wrote that Sylvia was one of the last 'bardic intimates of rural England and a witty, erudite explicator of those myths and sensations in which the agricultural underlay of civilisation makes itself felt'.[53]

There is a quality of total absorption and sensual abandon in the sheer physicality of material experience, of plainsong, cooking carp, recipes for madness, harsh winter landscapes, gaunt, dark interiors of cathedral churches, and the intense intermittent experience of journeys, meetings, feasts, mourning and politicking which made up social life for people whose lives were pre-eminently isolated. All of this closely woven texture does have the kind of freshness and immediacy which old records and memoirs have, and gives the reader an entry into that fourteenth-century culture. But that is not all that the novel achieves.

The Corner That Held Them is also about a fourteenth-century community in a period of transition and rapid social change: just such a period of change as England was going through during the middle part of the twentieth century. The insecure and unimportant religious institution Sylvia had chosen to write about (for all the important institutions, and indeed the whole of public life, was religious in foundation then, although a few lay people were beginning to be employed also), signalled the crisis of the times more acutely than the great religious institutions, whose greater wealth cushioned them against the break-up. When Sylvia said that she was inclined to call the novel 'People Growing Old', her fancy was partly serious: the novel had a relevance beyond its own day – it was in this sense that she denied it was a historical novel.

She was not setting out to write a fictional version of H. S. Bennett's classic text about medieval life *Life on the Manor*. Nor did she set out to write about a community of nuns for any feminist reason, but she centred the novel upon women because she could write in greatest detail about their everyday lives and so come at the feeling of the period.

Her method was always to work from material details, from fish-kettles or gold thread, from rushes or beeswax, from poultices or pillows, outwards, netting the complex pattern of expectation, frustration, conflict and gratification in the tapestry. There is no sentimentality about her community of women and very little sisterhood. The nunnery is as full of spite, lechery, boredom, and fantasy as a girls' boarding-school: there are some unselfish, loving and patient nuns, but they are more pitied and taken for granted than revered and have little effect in their community. The nuns who make the most impact are the efficient ones, who fulfil their offices of treasuress, prioress, cellaress with skill and foresight; but the democracy-in-action of electing the new prioress frequently results in a bad choice and several miserable years to follow for the nunnery. Prioresses, like prime ministers, could change their spots with alacrity on assuming office.

The absence of traditionally constructed plot and of the realist novel's convention of character development from the inside frees Sylvia to pursue the anatomy of a society. No longer attempting to mediate conflict and change through character, she wields her cast giving each their moment: when it is past they disappear and others take their place, through whom the action flows like a stream through different topography. If character is not in this novel 'process and unfolding', history itself is precisely that: each nun, bailiff, peasant, bishop, priest, and knight plays his or her part in it, while throughout the small community the reverberations of wider social change are felt. And in that context, individuality as such is unimportant, except in so far as the characters, who are treated almost like the traditional 'humours', affect the life of Oby. The ambitions, anguishes, sufferings and desires are sharply painted, but like the butterfly their life is transient.

The effect of this technique was to free Sylvia from treating of a traditional foreground and background, and to allow her to give equal attention to every part of her narrative. It also made her feel, she said, 'as providential as Providence', so much 'creating and killing off'. Only Sir Ralph, the nunnery's imposter-priest, who arrived with the Black Death at the beginning of the novel, was allowed to live on to the end and die of old age, 'serene and bright ... without a pang of conscience'.[54]

Where there is no longer background or foreground the reader's traditional processes of moral judgment and analysis are dislocated and for a time have to be suspended; one is forced to pay far greater attention to every corner of the canvas. A mouse may be as important as a christening feast, a singing friar as significant as a murder. Some incidents, such as the Peasants' Revolt, seem to pass far away in distant focus, while some are held in close-up. Some years are quickly catalogued: at some the action slows down and a scene expands and develops. The technique is in one way like that of Brueghel, in a painting such as the *Fall of Icarus*, or John Clare in *The Shepherd's Calendar* and *The Rural Muse*. But, more closely, this technique of giving equal emphasis to all the details presented, and convincing the reader with a sense of the inclusiveness of that vision, recalls the Russian cinema. In Sylvia's own time the work of a director like Eisenstein, or in our times of the Armenian director Paradjanov, who has equally employed his sense of history to explore the forces at work in his society, in his case most particularly the power of Armenian nationalism.

Detail as dominant motif

In writing *The Corner That Held Them*, Sylvia avoided using the novelists' key techniques of dramatic contrast and developing narrative crescendo, providing no central exploration of character. She was not the only novelist on the Left to have abandoned traditional techniques, but she was perhaps unique in maintaining and developing this strategy during the forties. Inevitably, because of its publication date, *The Corner That Held Them* is classified as a post-war novel. In fact, as we have seen, the bulk of the writing was done during the war, and only the last touches were made to it after the war's ending.

The story opens many years before the founding of the abbey

whose history forms its subject, in lust, summer heat and murder: 'Alianor de Retteville lay on her bed and looked at Giles who was her lover.'[55] It ends with the covert departure on a pilgrimage to the Holy Land of a nun whose spiritual ambition is thwarted in the convent of Oby, founded two centuries before by Brian de Retteville in his wife's name. The pilgrims sweep past the cathedral, where a thief is about to be punished by having his hand cut off: they 'swept on unimpeded. Their singing swelled out like a banner on the wind as they fell into step and marched southward'.[56]

It begins in contraries with passion satisfied, the rhythm of post-coital sleep, light and birdsong from the forest interspersing; it ends with the pilgrims' march, the swelling song of faith and hope, posed against the mutilation of a thief.

The nunnery was founded in the twelfth century, and from the first the isolation from the world proves to be problematic: the prioress reflects that while men 'with their inexhaustible interest in themselves may do well enough in a wilderness', 'the shallower egoism of women demands some nourishment from the outside world'.[57] This even-handed, clear-eyed tone is the dominant note of the novel. The outside world is extremely important to Oby. Oby's fortunes to that outside world may be of small concern – for it is a poor, struggling religious community, set in a remote and infertile countryside of marsh and moorland – but Oby is inextricably bound up with the larger world. In the matter-of-fact, scrupulous way of the chronicler, Sylvia details the material possessions of the nunnery:

> [Lady Alicia de Richenda] brought several servants, a great deal of household furniture, three dogs, one of the Magdalen's tears in a bottle, and twelve chests stuffed with law-papers and inventories. She also brought a great deal of method and efficiency.[58]

The fortunes of a nunnery depended on what the inmates brought to it by way of dowry, but equally they depended on fire and flood and natural hazard; the Plague; church edicts; the passing of one bishop and the succession of another; the condition of the peasants; the taxes imposed by the king.

Although Sylvia had denied that the novel was historical, the pre-publication notice in *Our Time* in 1948 stated that she was 'seeing through the press her new historical novel . . . [which]

deals with an East Anglian nunnery between 1348 and 1381 studying the approaching social break-up'. In the two thirties' novels (*Summer Will Show* and *After the Death of Don Juan*) she had dealt with social and historical forces: in the first with the interaction of the individual and revolutionary social forces, and in the second with the changes wrought on a small peasant community when it was finally confronted with the brute reality of the power oppressing it. In *The Corner That Held Them* she attempted to focus on one large area of social unrest and change in the years preceding the Peasants' Revolt by dealing with an insignificant religious institution at a time when the large ones held the great power and were amongst the most hated institutions in the land. The nunnery is a social cosmos for, like a social class, it contains within it the seeds of change; people rise and fall, new interests are represented, the relationship with its surrounding community shifts. At one point the nuns reflect that:

> nowadays a manor was not what it used to be, and little more than a tiresome way of supplying oneself with milk and poultry, bread and firing. More tiresomely, a manor these days was a camp of malcontents, and one must be on good terms with one's people and not press them too much, lest they should take part in the rebellions which were jumping up, here, there, and everywhere.[59]

But the peasants' rebellion, and the uprisings which preceded it, do not form the central motif of the book. They are seen, as the nuns would see them, through a slit window, or as the peasants might hear of them, in snatches repeated from mouth to mouth and transformed in the telling by the pedlars and pilgrims passing along the Hog Trail, one of the old medieval bridleways linking that part of Fenland to the rest of the country. The major events are far-off and distant; the ones which change everything are the Black Death, which comes into their villages and homes and brings the Nunnery its priest (the illegitimate imposter Sir Ralph Kello), and the enthroning of a new bishop who descends to inspect the nunnery and finds it to be 'a house builded upon sand ... full of pride, sloth, greed, falsehoods ... pet animals and private property ... spiced meats, soft cushions, perfumed and flowing mantles, better befitting harlots than brides of Christ'.[60]

Main characters are absent, drama is infrequent, the closest the reader gets to a sense of inwardness with a character is with the wretched priest's craven fears of being found out for his imposture, of the judgment that he will suffer for pretending to be a priest and for his venal sins of gluttony and sloth. Interspersed in the dark medieval realism are shafts of light, music, the soaring spire chequered in light and shade like the days that pass under the wide revealing fen sky. All is open to inspection; everything is as it is, not as metaphor and symbol. Nothing stands for something else; each thing has its own exact weight and value.

To try and placate their bishop the nuns set about making a costly and beautiful altar hanging; the work is evoked in detail, the stitching, the cloth, its sumptuous and richly sensual texture worked in gold thread, pearls and satin. The embroidery is presented in sharp contrast to the austerity and uncertainty of medieval lives, above all of the poverty of the Oby Manor peasants. One of the poor women who comes to the nunnery to be fed pours out the hatred of the poor for the wastefulness of the religious at this work:

> [sitting] all day by a fire embroidering gold thread upon
> satin . . . you will stir your fingers for God's altar, but when
> did you ever prick your finger for God's poor? We go in rags.
> And you waste on one yard of your fancywork as much gold
> as would clothe and feed ten of us for a year's length.[61]

The novel makes no indictment of the nuns for the way they live, nor does it stress any connection between the way they and their superiors live and the unfortunate lot of the labourers. The community:

> now spoke of the labourers as though they were some
> unknown kind of beings, people from under the earth or over
> the sea. No one remembered what a few weeks before
> everyone had known and feared: that the revolt had sprung
> up from the soil as naturally as nettles, and that from every
> manor men had gone out in hope and desperation who were
> now coming back in despair.[62]

By the end of the novel Oby has lost its altar-hanging, all its wealth in plate, and been attacked by some peasants in a bungled raid which has left its bailiff dead. But none of this is highlighted: it is almost as haphazard and fortuitous as the sunshine, plague, floods, the murrain among the cattle. The decline and fall of the convent of Oby looks set to continue, but that matters little. It is, we feel, inevitable; institutions rise out of family pride, jealousy, ambition, the desire to make restitution for sins committed, to honour a family name; they play their part, shape and are shaped by the dynamics of the time, they decline and wither away. Similarly the lives of individuals: no one individual is more important than another. Some make their mark and things shift slightly for what they do, but their reign is short, whether as prioress, custos, bishop or vilein. The determinism of Marx and the fatalism of the medieval mind, its resignation, cruelty and indifference to human suffering as well as its capacity for enjoyment, shape the movement of the chronicle. Event follows event in indifferent, yet significant, sequence.

The book leaves us with the sense of a journey travelled, of history in the making, of the abundance and confusion of detail heaped up in human lives, and underneath, the immense tug of slowly shifting, muddily moving social change. Pure as a bell above it all rises the spire of Oby which cost its nuns and prioress so dearly over so many years; the manuscript of the lay of Mamilion, that came at last through chance into the possession of one who appreciated its beauty; the Ars Nova, the new music, which soars in counterpoint between monk, priest and leper in an obscure leper chapel. Unremarked, accidentally saved and passed on, long in the contriving and making, human art remains lastly, confusingly, our one clear legacy of those ages. Ages which, as Sylvia showed her readers, were far from clear or pure, untroubled or unproblematic in their spirituality. Ages which, like the post-war period, reflected the possibility of profound social change.

Sylvia's mature writings show her to have still been a committed left-wing writer in her fifties. In *The Corner That Held Them*, the vision of injustice in the previous two novels is broadened out to peel back the structures of a whole community, exposing with a level and humorous glance the priorities, preoccupations and oppressions of a community of women, and rendering their place in the hierarchy of medieval exploitation. Sylvia's re-evaluation as a novelist, and the recognition of her stature amongst British left-wing writers, is long overdue; it cannot be long before this compassionate and engaging novel assumes its rightful place amongst the finest novels of the post-war period in Britain.

CHAPTER 7

VALENTINE ACKLAND, POET

UNSPOKEN PRESENCES, CONTINUING TRACES

Throughout the 1940s Valentine continued to write a steady output of poems, the greater number of which were never published. From the first, she sought to resolve conflict through her poetry, and dealt with the tensions between self and feeling, truth and the moment. Her perceptions were both subtle and complex, as well as being searchingly exact, although she chose most frequently to explore them in traditional poetic forms.

Early poems of Valentine's showed a lyrical gift with delicate precision of phrasing, if little particular pressure of feeling. In the later poems there is sometimes less certainty of technique but greater emotional intensity. 'Early Poem', a poem of 1931 which was not published until after 1969, reveals the intense and secretive working of the self and the freshness of observation that were to characterise much of her later work:

> Ash boughs grey and smooth, and withy wands
> Silk-berried still, and the lamb's tails falling . . .
>
> No one is near. The sunlight on branches,
> On black ash-buds, on my glittering hair –
> The sunlight and the trees conspire,
> Banish time, outwit time –
> There is no one to come here.[1]

The vision of the poem in its celebration of wood, sunlight and the poet's own youth and beauty shows a sense of oneness with nature. The sunlight glittering through her hair, the birds 'threading through the hedge', 'the lambs' tails falling', all are in motion and she is part of it, 'solitary and glad', telling the jewels of her hidden kingdom. This 'I' is the secretive, haunting person whom Bea Howe so sensitively sketches in the introduction to *For Sylvia: An Honest Account*; 'she' is unreachable, as immune from human spoiling and mortal ravage in that moment as the branches and black ash-buds. Pleasure in her own beauty was a marked feature in the young Valentine, and there were many photographs and drawings in the house at Frome Vauchurch that testify to that beauty.[2] (Later she would have none taken: she never resigned herself to the loss of her looks and figure.)

Some eighteen years after this poem was written, Sylvia recorded in her Commonplace Book a dream she had had about Valentine, in which Valentine was the legendary priestess of an old faith. In this dream, Valentine was leading the bride and groom to the marriage ceremony with a look of most unvirginal shyness on her face. She was dressed in a long white robe, a helmet and a corselet of golden lizard skins, and carrying a spear.[3] The dream captures something of the quality Valentine's beauty had for her lover.

In the mid-thirties Valentine had been faced with a particular problem as a poet. Believing that her art should be at the service of her politics, she found herself frequently baulked by the problem of *how* to achieve a poetry appropriate for her purpose. In 1935 she wrote to Julius Lipton:

> I am still uncertain how to write poetry as it has to be written. Whether to carry on . . . for the present, trusting that (as has happened before) the difficulty of reading a 'new' style will wear off. . . . Or whether to make a partial return to the old, simpler forms – renouncing the pleasures of inverting words and phrases; of using three-syllabled words; of using semi-scientific words; of assonance and rhyme . . . But we need something really *hard*. Not noisy and bombastic . . . but definite and deliberately reasonable, . . . well-devised and musical.[4]

At the same time that Valentine was struggling with poems on themes such as the burning of the Reichstag (that one did not work and she said that she felt sick about it) other poems had appeared which were personal and intimate in tone and where her lyrical gift and the characteristically clear feeling of her mature poetry are married. Some of these poems appeared in the *London Mercury*, to which she contributed for many years: 'New House' appeared in 1935, and evokes the feeling of estrangement a new place can create between lovers:

> We pass about the house
> Fearing our isolation, calling each to each.[5]

Another poem from the *London Mercury* was a love-sonnet which speaks of the poet's inability to say 'I love you' and to remain present in what she has said:

> I cannot find
> Any speech in any country of the mind
> Which might inform you whither I have fled.

Paradoxically, by saying 'I love you' she is exiled to a place where her lover may not find her, 'a star /Till now deserted'; she can only wait there to be found;

> Islanded here, I wait for you to come –
> Waiting the day that exiles you to home.[6]

One of the sharpest twists to this characteristically unsentimental love-poem is that 'exiles' in the last line; for their love to be reunited the beloved too must go into exile to reach her. 'I' can act no further.

It is this kind of wrestling with the paradox of feeling which marks Valentine's poetry at its best. Writing continually from a place of exile, her quest for 'home' – for the resolution of conflict – sharpens her acute awareness of the 'thisness' (Manley Hopkins' 'haeccitas') of creation. Never reaching that 'home', finding, in the course of her quest, every place and every relationship, every authority, religious or political, offering only a transitional refuge ensures that her best work is informed with an urgency not easily forgotten.

A more mature technique had begun to fuse with intensity of feeling in some of Valentine's political poems in the thirties too, though there were some ambitious failures. Perhaps the best example is 'England 1936'.[7] Another such poem, 'Badajoz to Dorset, August 1936', written at the outset of the Spanish Civil War, appeared in Bryher's innovative international magazine, *Life and Letters Today*, which, under the editorship of Robert Herring, published a range of fine writing in the avant-garde and contemporary world. The poem is a simple, unforced reflection on the sense of isolation and helplessness, of being so helplessly far distant from the place where the action is beginning:

> Telephone wires cry in the wind
> And make song there . . .
> Hear voices from a far distance . . .
> Hear sounds, from Spain.
> The mist muffles all but these; blankets perhaps the reply –
> But the wind plays the wires still, and the wires cry.[8]

Sometimes the poems are satirical, or bitterly ironic, as in 'England 1936', or 'Time for a Quick One'. (The latter also appeared in *Life and Letters Today*.[9], In it, Valentine contrasts the British Medical Association's pronouncements on what poor families could eat on Public Assistance level incomes (they 'starve with a flourish') with the diet of the middle classes. It is not the most polished of her lyrics but it has a fierce, rough energy, and is an honourable example of satirical verse. It also marks a movement away from subjectivity, a determination to engage with themes that are politically difficult, and an attempt to do in poetry what she had been doing in *Country Conditions*: letting the material speak for itself, allowing the voices of the protagonists to emerge. Other left-wing writers in the thirties were attempting this through satire, ballad and choral speech, so it was not an unusual thing to be doing. In their different ways, both Valentine and Sylvia were affected by these developments.

In wartime, Valentine continued to write biting lampoons upon the ruling classes. There is a long poem called 'War in Progress: A running commentary, Spring 1941–1943'[10] which is made up of a series of short satirical pieces, lyrics capturing the reality of civilian war, such as the blackout or an air-raid. The writing is uneven: some parts of the satirical verses rise little above doggerel, but some have a compressed rage in the tradition of political invective going back to Dryden, Rochester and Pope, such as this dated 1 March 1940:

> How hard the task of men who try
> To find out when a man should die
> And whether he, being justified
> In dying, is happy to have died.

In another section, (dated 6 August 1940), Valentine looks back at the twenty years between the two wars and in a sweeping glance of controlled and bleak hopelessness, confronts the reality of men's unthinking and muddled aggression:

> No peace now. In conformity with custom
> Men will fight on till idiots only left
> Creep to a thieves' den and condone the theft,
> Blink at the murderers and agree to trust 'em
>   And wait again. Ten years to mourn the blunder
>   Which beggared them. Ten more to muse on plunder.
>
>   And half of ten to mass sufficient armies
>   T'avenge defeat. Oh tell me where the harm lies?

It is the poetry of a person who is not hoodwinked, it is wide-awake and angry poetry. That anger reaches its most concentrated and savage moment in the 7 October section, after the devastation of the first wave of Blitzkrieg. In this Valentine contrasts sentimental and hypocritical attitudes about birth ('fecundity par excellence is here/Lying in labour even on the bier') with the reality: 'Fear not, there's one deep shelter/Open alike in Free and Fascist State,/Vast, private, silent and inviolate.' She continues:

> Maternity's the holiest thing on earth
> (No man who's prudent as well as wise
> Concerns himself with what is in the skies);
> Drain-deep below the slums another birth
>   Sets angels singing – the other noise you hear
>   May be the Warning, may be the All Clear.
>
>   Comfort ye My people! These reflections
>   Should help them die politely who must die

Turning to another section of the same poem, 'Black-Out' shows the greater assurance with which Valentine handled her lyrical, descriptive poems in this sequence. In the first stanza, the rhythms and delicacy of phrasing suggest the tentativeness of the gradual transition from dusk to dark:

>   the surprising
>   Last minute turn aside into a modulation,

The lines catch their breath in exactly the 'artistry of hesitation' she perceives in nightfall; and in the second stanza, the flat, mechanical certainty of the black-out is realised through the staccato phrasing:

> a sentence everyone's learned to utter,
> Undoubted and certain,
> Too stupid to interest anyone at all.

In March 1941 Valentine wrote a letter to Elizabeth, an extract from which Sylvia copied into her Commonplace Book. It gives an insight into the author of these poems, into the almost Herbertian simplicity and plainness with which she could express herself. George Herbert was one of her poetic as well as later her religious mentors, for she admired above all clarity, lack of fuss and adornment, and purity of line. The things that her spirit delighted in, which sustained her in the worst moments and still made her heart 'swirl' (as she wrote in a late letter to her sister Joan,) were quite simple things:

> small animals moving, eating grass, tomtits flying, making love; trees in winter, spring, summer, autumn; rivers and little small puddles and streams, clouds and stars and the moon on rooftops and lights in Dorset at night and the sound of people walking and the sight of trees over walls in a city and the grunting sound of trains on rails on a wet night, and the rattle of a bedroom window in a storm, and myself in bed with my love. . . . If there is one thing certain for me, it is that I am certain of me, and lunatic or maimed, unpleasant or perfectly the same, if I come out of this war able to crawl or be pushed, I shall know exactly what delights my eyes if I have them, or what would delight them if I have them not.[11]

Valentine does not have the power to convey in her prose, as Sylvia does, the latent magic in such commonplaces; she cannot transport us as Sylvia's letter to Paul Nordoff does, about the papery-thinness of war and gulping down great mouthfuls of apple tree and moonlight,[12] but her response is a kindred one, and in its quite different, bare and honest way, it is a moving testimony.

Another interesting poem, the product of wartime experiences, 'I am thinking of France', was published in 1944 in Nancy Cunard's anthology, *Poemes à la France*.[13] It shows how Valentine had learned within ten years of the publication of *Whether a Dove or a Seagull* to interweave her personal and political feelings with such a degree of tautness that they are inseparable, but to do this within a traditional framework. The poem begins stiffly, formally:

> With all the world at woe
> And time keeping
> Evenly its flow

The alliterative sounds and awkward prepositional phrase 'at woe' (frustrating the expected cliché 'at war') pin down the remoteness of the generalisation 'all the world'. But the whole feeling of the first stanza is remote and archaic, a feeling completed by the pathetic fallacy in which the river is 'weeping . . . as if it cost such tears to go'. In the second stanza the poet addresses the absent beloved, who usurps her attention from the world's woes, 'And so compel my seeing/That unlit other truths go by.' The implicit shame for the poet is that she knows it is a species of trickery:

> You, by the sleight of eye,
> In bright being
> Appear continually

The harshness of that realisation is echoed in the harsh consonantal sounds and sense of closure in the last line 'unlit other truths go by'. It is a richly patterned, imprisoning texture. In the final stanza, the two realities of love and death are brought together in inescapable paradox:

> But all the worst is true;
> The world dying
> That was alive in you
> (O love with War complying!)
> This loss makes all destruction overdue.

There are a number of other wartime poems, some of which were published in an anthology published by Chatto & Windus in 1947 called *The Pleasure Ground*,[14] some of which appear later in the privately printed or small press booklets. There are undoubtedly a great many more poems of Valentine's scattered about, and in the Dorset Museum.[15] What is clear is that by the mid-forties Valentine was an accomplished poet, with a distinctive voice, an accomplished, traditional lyric technique, and a range of subjects that could encompass and harness the political as well as the personal.

She could convey the sharp physical reality of an air-attack, as in 'November Night':

> in the silent-moving frost
> Stars crinkle and shiver, flashing in the sky
> Unabashed by the trespassing sharp light
> Of shell-bursts.[16]

The adjectival 'trespassing' fixes the intrusiveness of the shells, but the culminating image of outrage is that of the moon, which is compared to an angry host 'whose guests outrage him': 'one vast angry eye/Blank with that meticulous stare of the host . . ./So the moon glares tonight.' Or she could, with equal aplomb, create a dazzling Dantesque vision of the moment of the atomic bomb being dropped on Hiroshima (quoted here in full):

> When out of the clear sky, the bright
> Sky over Japan, they tumbled the death of light,
> For a moment, it's said, there was brilliance sword-sharp,
>
> A dazzle of white, and then dark.
> Into that cavernous blackness, as home to hell,
> Agonies crowded; and high above in the swell
> Of the gentle tide of the sky, lucid and fair,
> Man floated serenely as angels disporting there.[17]

This unsentimental and compelling vision of man's complacent self-delusion was called simply 'August 6th 1946'. The Valentine who was painfully groping her way out of despair, self-reproach and alcoholic dependancy towards a spiritual renewal did not do so in any spirit of retreat or refusal to face the truth as she saw it. Nor was she using her religious quest as a crutch, or refuge.

'Poem in September 1945' (later published as 'Autumn River' in *Twenty-Eight Poems*, 1957), captures something of the uncertainty Valentine felt at this time. While life in the aftermath of war superficially resembled a sharply indrawn breath, a period of tranced suspension of business, underneath change was fermenting rapidly. Emotionally and intuitively

Valentine was more attuned to the complex post-war zeitgeist than Sylvia, who after the fourteenth century was then immersed in the eighteenth century with her edition of the life of Timothy Tortoise, extracted from *The Journals and Letters of Gilbert White of Selborne*. This was published in 1946. She also produced a wonderfully idiosyncratic guide to Somerset in the Paul Elek series *Vision of England* which was published in 1949, edited by her old friends Clough and Amabel Williams Ellis, in which her fondness for digressions took her at a stately pace around the timeless world of stone carvings and middle dwelling houses in Somerset, taking in blackberries, willows, apple-blossom, and mosses on the way.[18]

Valentine's sensibility in her poetry was at once personal and in a wider sense political, deriving in part from the intuition of impending change in her own life. As usual, the images she employs are traditional, pastoral ones, and the landscape of river, meadows, sky, varies little throughout her work. In 'Autumn River', the different levels of water in the river offer the metaphor for the processes of change:

> underneath the rapid water travels,
> Unmanageable, to the sea.[19]

In the next stanza, with its echoes of Shakespeare and Gray, 'All things wear silence during such a night', evening is lightly pencilled in in the quick flickering movements of the swallows that 'Shuttle their airy threads across the sky' and the bats that 'flick past, inheriting the meadows /As dark spreads from the West unhurriedly'. The last stanza returns to, and sums up, the sense of foreboding, the conflicting movement between the hope of a certain formal, resigned quietude, and the inevitable and irresistible force of change:

> All things . . .
>   have put on formality and serious
> Airs of compassion, resignation, state;
> And swift and dark the tide goes racing down.

The changes are focused in the poem through the contrast between the tide with its rapid, cumulative movement, and the stately, rather beautiful image of life putting on 'formality and serious/Airs of compassion'.

In her own personal life, these years were filled with change and conflict: perhaps the purchase and renovation of Frome Vauchurch in 1945 was a stay against some of the uncertainty. One of her most complex poems of this time 'New Paulus Silentarius', published in *Poetry Quarterly*,[20] deals with themes of change, the transformations occcurring with ageing, the chicanery of desire; the central image is of the lover who complains that he is dying of cold, the fire no longer burns within him:

> the altar flames, having devoured the sacrifice,
> Would slacken, grow grey and die for lack of fuel,
> Leaving the altar cold:

The image, in the original work, 'is no more than a lover's device/Reproving a mistress transiently cruel', against which the poet states her own condition: 'But I am dying of cold'. Her words are to be heard as a different kind of signifier, not as poetic convention but as literal statement, and they are inserted into a context in which another 'truth' has been asserted, a general 'truth':

> In these days we know other flames beside desire
> But the most fearful still, of private distress,
> Is life growing cold.

In the second section, the poet takes the subject of her pain, the beloved 'you', and shows her to the sun, the shadows, the night and the river in turn in an attempt to free herself, but each attempt fails: 'as if you were a burning-glass' the sun 'throws the weight of his light against you/ And you direct it to consume me.' The river 'Dark and stilly-flowing receives you, wears /You bright as the moon set silver on its deathly water.' There is no escape.

At one level one might read this as a love-poem, a cry of anguish to be released from the torment of a fading love. But the poem has a more poignant intensity when read at the level of dialogue between self and heart, as the last line suggests: 'What fool, my desperate heart, would call that stream Lethe?' The struggle between the recalcitrant heart which consumes her and the self, or soul, haunted her. She could not, she felt, arrive at a wholeness, a balance: she could not jettison that old stinking cur, as Yeats called it, the foul rag-and-bone shop of the heart. She would willingly consign it 'to the Shades', but instead is forced to confront it in the image on the glittering water.

A less successful poem called 'Autobiographical'[21] charts the divisions in herself more openly. As she felt she could love two people, so Valentine was always aware of different possibilities within herself: in some way she was unfinished, uncertain, and this led her later on in life, writing to Joan, to consider how self-conscious she had always been as a younger woman, and what a burden she had found her own self.[22] 'Autobiographical', which has the air of being an early poem in its transparency and self-advertisement, uses melodramatic contrast to give the pitch of her self-division – lying down on a battlefield, making love to the tune of 'Greensleeves':

> The day is not only the dove in a morning waking
> But noon at white stare of light, and evening when bats replacing
> The twilight swallows in flight, precede themselves the owls
> Who cry 'Woe, woe,' and shriek 'Tis he! Tis he!'

There are a considerable number of poems of this time which are lyrical, descriptive poems, dealing with the landscape and seasons amongst which she and Sylvia lived and which plainly formed an important part of their shared experience. Indeed, it is impossible to live by that constantly changing river, enclosed by the willows and alder, with the wild cyclamen and snowdrops, the grape hyacinths, primroses, tulips, roses in their season, and the continual call of birdsong, without feeling enmeshed in nature. Valentine's 'nature' poems, some of which were published in places like the *Wessex Review* and the *West Country Magazine*, sprang out of this setting as genially and luxuriantly as the long grass. Some are 'occasional' poems, some go after the wrestle with the exact apprehension of changing truth which is characteristic of her best work, and some express a concentrated physical apprehension of the 'nature of the moment': a cat, a drop of water, a cloud passing.

The Valentine who wrote the hauntingly lovely and passionate lyrics of *Whether a Dove or a Seagull* never ceased to be a poet. When she died in 1969, she left behind literally hundreds of drafts of poems, many of them worked to a fine degree. Writing the book-jacket 'blurb' for *The Nature of the Moment*, Sylvia spoke of how the poems were chosen from: 'a life-time of taking poetry seriously, they show the interaction of a remarkable talent and an implacable regard for truth'.[23] She went on to say that they are without 'dogma, solemnity or witticism', and that they do not 'sprawl' from the point at issue. 'This integrity makes them – a rare commendation – "interesting" as well as moving . . . the subjection of technique to truth results in a style of Purcellian flexibility, spareness and unexpectedness.'

Sylvia makes no mention here of one of the most characteristic of Valentine's qualities, her absorbed and rapt celebration of experience and of the moment, but arguably it is a dominant note. Valentine lived very much in the present, and if she could be utterly heartbroken with melancholy one moment, she could equally quickly the next moment have her heart lifted by the sight of a feather, a light glancing on the river, the swans' stately drifting. After Valentine died, Sylvia kept coming across such small fragments as feathers and leaves which Valentine had picked up as she walked, and they are to be found in letters and notebooks, carefully taped to the page. Her heart would 'swirl' at the slightest chance, and as readily she would turn to poetry.

The best of the later poems show the conflict intensified but disciplined; in the search for spiritual accuracy some of the mawkishness of the earlier poems is refined. The poetry, though, is always varied in quality, sometimes as clear and hard as a bell, sometimes swathed in sentiment. Throughout, Valentine never ceased to search for her own identity, which makes reading many of the last poems an exciting and humbling experience, for she was prepared to cast off everything she knew in pursuit of it, to write, as Sylvia said, 'the kind of poetry which would convey truth and the moment with plain-dealing integrity'.[24]

Most of the prose of this period, by contrast, is less intimate and less challenging, although there are one or two exceptions. Valentine contributed quite a number of articles and stories to periodicals, as a cursory examination of, for example, *Housewife; The Countryman; Lilliput; Life and Letters Today; Our Time* and the *West Country Magazine* reveals. But she had a clear sense of where her real power as a writer lay – she never valued her prose writing as she did the poems, and at the end of her life she wrote that she did not know what to do about the mass of papers she would leave: 'there are one or two stories which may be good. . . . But probably nothing of much use.' The poems, on the other hand, she thought might, after a time, come to life; a tentative enough appraisal, but at least an admission of her belief in them.

The most pedestrian of her prose-pieces were probably the reviews, such as the ones for *Our Time*, which one senses were done only for the guinea or so they brought in, for there is little sense of pleasure in the writing. The post-war ones are more assured than those she contributed to *Left Review* in the thirties, and give a modest and clear account of the books' qualities and themes. She does not attempt any theoretical statements, confining herself to her own careful reading of the works in question. As reviews they are informative but not compelling, and unless one had an interest in subject or author one would probably not give them a second glance.

In the articles about village life her unpretentious way of writing can be seen to advantage. Her familiarity with, and feeling for, the village people gives that quality of immediacy to her writing that Syvlia claimed as one of the hallmarks of the woman writer.[25] Valentine turned her experience of Dorset life to good account. When writing of the old village woman whom some called witch, Granny Moxon, she succeeds in bringing the old woman sharply before the reader, without either patronising her or turning her into a folk-heroine:

> Most evenings, winter and summer, she crossed her garden and climbed over the fence to the village inn, where she settled down to talk and tell stories and sometimes to play her accordion. She had a variety of songs, some of them very mysterious. . . .
>
> Her speech was as supple as her movements . . . and she spoke a pure Dorset dialect of which she was very proud. But at times her words became stately and had great grandeur, and that was when she conversed about death and the fate of man. We do not live after death, she said; there is a hole made in the ground and there we are laid in the earth, and that is the end of all. 'Never you go looking to live', she said, 'for you ha'ant never seen no-one come back from the dead.'[26]

The character sketch is affectionate, shrewd and clear-eyed:

Valentine describes the old woman as bawdy, strong, fearless and independent, a rare person who never judged her fellow human beings but would treat their follies with laughing affection, as she treated her caged goldfinches. Late in her life Granny Moxon became very ill with cancer, and Valentine recalled going to see her before she died. Holding her hand, Valentine asked Granny what she expected of death; the old woman repeated her words:

> 'Never you go looking to live'. Holding her hand brown
> hand I looked down at her and she gazed back at me. I
> remembered the image used by Bede in our seventh century
> and by a Chinese sage two thousand years before Christ: 'As
> he entered death he did not hang back. Like a bird he flew
> away, just as like a bird he came.'

Valentine made use of her personal experiences of Dorset village life in a number of semi-documentary pieces, which de-mythologised and de-sentimentalised rural life. She also sometimes used this material as settings for short stories, but usually with less success. The stories are sometimes marred by a rather unpleasant kind of whimsy, a sort of sub-Powys fey or supernatural element, as for example, in 'The Last and The First'[27] and 'A Multitude of The Heavenly Host'.[28]

Another kind of story features wartime experience. In *Life and Letters Today* there were two published, 'Sunlight on the Camp', and 'When I was in Basle',[29] both of which are fragmentary, terse pieces dealing with women living together in alien and hostile surroundings. The stories are concerned with the emotional tensions and conflicts that build up between the women; too slight to be more than jumping-off points, they remain as sketches for stories.

There is one story that has a greater interest and more feeling to it, also from *Life and Letters Today*, called 'Two Occasions':[30] this deals with a triangular situation between a man and his ex-wife or lover, and her new companion. Although the characters are involved in a heterosexual triangle, the situation paralleled the triangular situation that Valentine, Sylvia and Elizabeth found themselves in, and the story bears a greater pressure of feeling than most of her other prose pieces. The central character of 'Two Occasions' is a man living peacefully on his own in his country cottage, tending his garden, absorbed and self-sufficient in a quiet humdrum routine, into which, unnerving him and upsetting his calm, reappears the woman he used to live with and her new man. The hypocritical and antagonistic exchanges which take place between the two of them, flavoured with an all-too-conscious sense of what existed between them once and a faint, trace of their old attraction, like sharp but fleeting patchouli, are finely done. The sense of place in the unchanging cottage and garden contrasts with the febrile stirrings between the petty human protagonists, giving substance to the sensation of physical release that the ex-husband experiences when his unwelcome guests depart.

Valentine returned to this theme of the triangular situation in a longer and more ambitious piece, 'Urn Burial', which was published in the American periodical *Modern Writing* in 1953.[31] Founded by two ex-editors of *Partisan Review*, *Modern Writing* drew contributions from a range of prestigious writers, mainly American. In it, Valentine was advertised as a 'new talent'. (She was by then forty-seven.) The triangular situation in 'Urn Burial' concerns three women, with one onlooker, male, accompanying one of the women. Valentine had at last chosen to speak out directly about jealousy and possession between women.

Dulcie, an Englishwoman on a business trip in the United States, arrives to stay with her ex-lover Janey and friend Sara; she is accompanied by her young associate Peter, through whose eyes much of the outward misunderstanding and ghastliness of the American social experience is relayed. But it is the tensions and emotions between the three women that Valentine is concerned with, and it's not always clear what the author's perspective on the melodrama is. The characters are presented in a very unsympathetic light, especially the American couple. One can only agree with the departing visitors when, on the train going home, they muse on the black comedy of the evening before, saying that one might be very unhappy in New England. Or happy. It really doesn't seem to matter.

The Americans are seen as wealthy, complacent, cloyingly possessive and absurdly thin-skinned. The English are seen by the Americans as arrogant, faithless, sneering: 'Secure with their poets and their poverty, their "European" standards and their faithlessness, they came to gibe, to mock, to tread underfoot'.[32] The English have gone through the war and are harder, freer of illusions; for Dulcie, the experience of the love affair with Janey seventeen years ago, to which Janey clings so desperately, is distant and finished: it ended because Janey never really knew her. But Janey has clung to this illusion, even through ten years with Sara, while Dulcie thinks:

> how thin it all became, a thin little trickle of unidentifiable juice, squeezed through the wire mesh of Janey's words; while the lovely summer-ripened fruit it had been was nothing now but pulp, and someone must clear it up and throw it away.[33]

At the high-farce climax of the evening, after an unbearably silent and long-drawn out dinner in which every conversational gambit sinks dismally into the ground, Janey makes a last desperate bid for some time alone with Dulcie. Sara, however, has been watching hawk-eyed and adroitly steps in to nip that little manoeuvre in the bud. The story is assured but heartless, which is perhaps Valentine's point. Certainly the ease and luxury of the American standard of living is stressed: at the end of the story Peter and Dulcie wonder if they have tipped the servants enough.

From the savagery of some of the writing it would appear that Valentine was attempting to lay ghosts to rest in 'Urn Burial'. Elizabeth was wealthy, at least by Valentine and Sylvia's standards, and Valentine was quite conscious of that. (One year, when unable to make the obligatory yearly meeting with Elizabeth, she wrote to Joan to say that their mother Ruth was having lunch with her instead, which she would enjoy greatly for Elizabeth would treat her to a slap-up meal.)

If 'Urn Burial' represented one of Valentine's most ambitious, and at one level, most successful stories, there were other prose pieces that were rather more interesting. One was a piece called 'In the Emporium', one of a series of Christmas offerings written either by Valentine or Sylvia or both of them, neatly typed on onion paper, with a stapled card cover and greetings, and sent out to friends. This one was written for Christmas 1951. It is a macabre interior monologue by a fat woman in the bridal department of a department store, where the dummies dressed as brides remind her of her own wedding-day, and the contrast between then and her life now. As the sight of the white, satin-draped figure calls to mind her wedding-day, her recollections pour out in a jingling, mocking tumult of a folk ballad: 'hadn't he nudged her elbow then, called her Dear to her inclined ear; through the modest well-permed hair didn't he declare with grin and shake of head and crunching cake it seemed almost a Sin.' The voices in the woman's head rise and swell to a crescendo, jeering at her:

Lonely and cold the bed and everything silent except the
fools in your head beginning to sing:
    Am I still your heart's desire
    Am I light as you require?

    NO. Sorry, mother; but definitely NO.
Then the mother (she's no mother!)
Then the matron (she's no wife!)
Sees him turn unto another,
Sees him go – and takes her life!
How the words swell and ring like a bell. Stupid!
You stupid thing! It's morbid.

The story evokes a vision of desperate loneliness, of that feeling of being quite unloved and unlovable – the feeling which Valentine had, according to the autobiography, when Sylvia came into her life in 1930. In 1951, in the throes of wrestling with herself and her feelings for Elizabeth in the aftermath of the break-up in 1949 – when the experiment at Frome Vauchurch had failed and Elizabeth had returned to America – Valentine was plunged into deep despair. The half-mad aslant vision of the fat woman of 'In the Emporium' gives a powerful poetic expression to the grim sense of pointlessness which characterised these days:

Now is the further side of winter again and they say as the
days lengthen so the cold strengthens and Oh how the left-
over butterflies labour to live! Cold and without the sun's
favour or the savour of nectar from flowers, they drag weary
days and spend their hours stuck up with cobwebs in
corners, cobwebs heavy as ten tons of muck –
    Why do they last out the summer?
    Why do they last out the summer?

'In the Emporium' was possibly Valentine's most radical

experiment in story writing; under the emotion, the prose was already dissolving into verse. Had she continued the experiment, there might have been interesting results.

A NOTE ON THE LATER POEMS

When you look at me, after I have died,
And note the tidy hair, the sleeping head,
Closed eyes and quiet hands – Do not decide
Too readily that I was so. Instead,
Look at your own heart while you may, and see
How wild and strange a live man is, and so remember me.[34]

There were two privately printed collections of the poems, the first one, *Twenty-Eight Poems* – selected by Valentine – came out in 1957. The first poem of this collection, a short untitled lyric 'O Flame Do Not Die', celebrates the intensity and passion of her life, the quality of wild strangeness. It is the same quality that characterises the haunting 'When you look at me', which Sylvia chose as the epigraph to *Later Poems*, which appeared as a memorial tribute after Valentine's death.

'O flame do not die' recalls, in its lyrical simplicity and passionate charge, the Blake of *Songs of Innocence and Experience*. If the flame, the creative heart, dies, everything is extinguished: the 'leaping tongue, the kindling eye', hearth fire, the heart all wasted 'If in this night you die'.

The predominant mood of *Twenty-Eight Poems* is one of melancholy, the harvest of the bitter years of wrestling with herself, and the most memorable lines are frequently the bleakest. The poem 'In Dreams, In Visions Of The Night'[35] (a vision of a magical under-ocean world where everything is 'turned to the same/ Compatriot colour of skeleton bone') concludes with the blind bones in the darkness saying: 'nothing is lovely without the light'. The tough 'Poem With No Title',[36] which was written in the 1940s, exacts a look at the worst, 'Whatever of life or time passed by outside,/ Within it was midnight, fallen at heart of day.' The poem follows a journey of spiritual agony, in which images of 'the crazed beggar / Locked in a churchyard dank at winter dusk' jostle each other, and the landscape wears a half-familiar look as death comes near, 'Half-known, half-strange'. This poem does have some hope in its resolution: the poet returns,

I . . . sightless heard:
Spirit breathes light as man breathes air, and spirit
Has not permission to die. I heard light tossing
The tall-plumaged forest; I heard the darkness breaking
And saw clear sky, and returned.[37]

The sense of loss of freedom is captured in compact images like this from 'Turn The Captivity Of Thy People':[38] 'They had wired all earth and heaven /While I was in prison.' There is a perpetual contrast made in these poems between the airy freedom of spirit and the leaden-weighted movement of man, the 'hybrid monster'.[39] The most extreme expression of this despair is in a poem called 'Accept The Cold Content'[40] (which was one of the few of Valentine's poems to be broadcast) where the final solace of the grave offers the release that there can be no further change:

The sure and certain stronghold of that North
Withstands all foes that beat upon its wall;
No joy, no season's change, no spring to come
Can storm or charm you now; no love at all.

The last few poems signal the transition in Valentine's life towards finding some kind of spiritual resolution, and three of them are in a new mood of joyful praise. The last short lyric in the collection reasserts the hungering, all too human, poet as watcher:

But lord! to follow the swallows with one's eye
As they fly, as they fly
Over the darkening meadows, and hours flow by
Smooth as the river flows, as the summer goes;
To watch them for ever and never and never to die![41]

After Valentine's death, Sylvia put together another small card-bound, stapled collection of forty poems called *Later Poems*, which, like *Twenty-Eight Poems*, was printed by Clare & Sons. It opens with the poem quoted at the beginning of this section and concludes with 'Early Poem' (above, p. 206), whose concluding lines stress the solitariness of Valentine's nature: 'I with the world gone, with earth my own, /Sit solitary and glad, watching my kingdom thrive.'[42] Similarly in 'The Heron', the poem emphasises the solitariness of the bird and the stillness of the spectator. The ache and intrusion of the human in these poems ricochets through the stillness of the natural world, jars against its perfect, self-absorbed creation: the poet's eye watches and in turn, watches itself watching as in A Young Cat:

> I watch you spring through the grass . . .
> You play imperturbably – now pensively handle
> The small dead mouse the morning gave you to keep,
> Very much as the sea thoughtfully fingers the spars,
> The coconut shells, the bottles, the litter and wrack[43]

Many of the poems deal with grief and heartache: the heartache of growing older, of uncertainty and loss of feeling, of the search for the other in the shifting disguises which love wears. Two poems dealing directly with this are 'Love Poem' ('When we are for the dark, my Love')[44] and 'A Not-Poem About Love, Written During A Sleepless Night',[45] written during the 1940s. Neither show Valentine's writing at her best; they lack the concentration and the complexity of feeling of some of her love-poems and the spare truthfulness of a poem such as 'Where the hills'.[46] This latter poem has the transparency of some of the lyrics in *Whether a Dove or a Seagull*, an exact and undramatised rendering of the thing seen. The seeming ordinariness, the use of ordinary language and refusal of poetic stances or disguises, again recall John Clare, an objectivism entirely English:

> by the hut the shepherds come together
> a thin smoke rises from their fire
> on the no colour of the hillside
> their washed clothes hang along the fold
> the scattered pattern of the flock waiting
> night draws into full circle.

This is exemplary in its refusal to exploit the scene the poet is presenting for effect, allowing the reader, in the two stanzas, to move freely through hills, evening sun, sheep, valley, shepherds, fire, and the washed clothes, creating a complex interweave between the anonymity and emptiness of landscape and its human shaping. It is a simple poem with rich effects.

More obviously a lyric such as 'Snow',[47] which is only four lines in length, attains this impact, in this case through the more conventional use of metaphor:

> From the white swan flying invisibly,
> Whose wing-beats matched the heart-beats of the night,
> Fell this light scatter of feathers, transient and bright,
> Now spread like a cloak over the naked morning.

'Love Poem', relies for its impact upon a lyrically cadenced and musically-pleasing use of cliché: 'darkness dazzles and light blindness brings'. Some of the lines have almost the unworked fervour of exclamation: 'How close the scentless earth comes when we stand in the scent of the rose!' And the final rhetorical question, the completion of the opening phrase 'When we are for the dark', is arrived at after a crescendo of cloying self-pity:

> Oh, muted then
> Is all this summer sound of wings and lost the scent of
>   the rose;
> Vanished this delicious, delicate warmth
> And the sweet safety of our garden close.
> When we are for the dark and all is gone –
> Your hand, my hand, and all we touched and held –
> What then?

If wit was Sylvia's enemy, one might say that lyricism was Valentine's.

More interesting are the two bleak poems written at the time of Great Eye Folly: the short 'Poem in Norfolk',[48] which concludes 'Speechless, I hold your silence in my hand', and the even more bleak 'Salthouse: New Year 1951':

> How dare we stand alone on this empty shore . . .
> We who believe in Time, in passing and coming?
> We do not dare; we stand because we must.[49]

This poem, none the less, like several in the collection, ends with a note of hope. As they stand, watching the sea, the:

> round earth heels over,
> Bearing the living sea, leaving the moon;
> Heavy with night and winter, the earth turns over . . .

The poem remains within the terms of the movements of sea, moon, and earth, and within the moment of the New Year, except in the last line where Valentine's liking for traditional metaphor signals the return to some sense of security and expected order, of the eventual rebirth of the year and of life, in contrast to the dead and stony images of the opening.

Later Poems also contains the fine 'August 6th 1946', (see p. 213) and two complex and interesting poems, 'Exile', and 'P.D. Obit September 1964 A.D. Obit June 1965', the latter reprinted in *The Nature of the Moment*.

The two most recent collections of Valentine's work, *The Nature of the Moment* and *Further Poems of Valentine Ackland* represent a combination of poems which had appeared in magazine publication, some from *Twenty-Eight Poems* and *Later Poems*, and some unpublished work. *The Nature of the Moment* (1973) which Sylvia selected and for which she wrote an explanatory note, is a somewhat confusing collection because most of the poems appear untitled, even where previously they had titles, and many short pieces are doubled upon a page. There is no certain chronology, despite the note that the poems are roughly in chronological order. None the less, it was Valentine's first major book, some thirty years after Sylvia had first tried to persuade Viking Press to publish her. Only after Valentine's death did Chatto & Windus, Sylvia's English publisher, respond. The book was published on both sides of the Atlantic, by Chatto in England and by New Directions in America.

Further Poems, the last collection which appeared in 1978, from Welmont Publishing (a small press run by her friend Julius Lipton) contains a wide selection of poems including many from the first two pamphlets. This again is confusing because there is no chronology; some early poems appear towards the end of the book; poems are retitled; and different drafts followed. But it is a useful collection in that it is in print and makes available earlier work no longer accessible.

Finally, there is the great body of unpublished work. This late love poem to Sylvia was amongst a number of poems Valentine enclosed in her letters to her cousin Peg Manisty in the 1960s. They were sent for Peg's enjoyment, and because they were intended to be read. This poem was still in the process of being worked on; the last two lines have near-illegible and crossed out alternatives.

> I have tried very hard to write
> Some poem abut love which might
> Explain to those who sift our dust

> When we have gone what rite they must
> Perform, what ceremonial dance
> Follow in its intricacy
> If they would make their love as we
> Made ours: out of a moment's chance
> A timeless immortality.[50]

Classical, distilled, lyrical: Valentine's work at its best was of a timeless quality, apparently out of reach of the turmoil and experiment of the twentieth century and twentieth century poetics. It is attached only to that long tradition of meditative, English lyric poetry stretching back through the centuries through which she increasingly came to speak in her last years. But her concern as a woman for life shines through: in 'For all that takes place under this dome of the sky',[51] it is her concern for:

> The desperate last cry of the hare;
> For the small cubs flung for hounds to tear;

The poem ends:

> And we turn on each other, father on son and brother on
>   brother;
> And the flood rises and the blood flows –
> And carelessly, every summer, blooms and burns and falls
>   the rose.

She felt each act of destruction; she was one of those to whom the agonies are agony and will not let them rest. Restlessly she haunted life, in her own words, 'for a moment's moment . . . . Like thistledown on the wind, between life and life', 'Only so truth is seen'.[52]

By the end of her life, poetry came to be an extraordinary outpouring of her spirit. Not the least surprising thing about this surprising woman was that by the end of her life she was a poet reaching the height of her powers, all unknown.

EPILOGUE (1951–1978)

Six months after the trauma of Elizabeth's departure in the early Autumn of 1949, Sylvia had written to Alyse Gregory of the agonising time she and Valentine were living through. She felt they had never needed each other as much as they did then: 'We hold on to each other like convalescents.'[1] But in a letter she wrote to Valentine two years later, the agony of that winter was more starkly revealed. Sylvia asks how, having seen Valentine's love for her at once to be her greatest torment and her greatest happiness, how she, Sylvia, can possibly draw the thorn from Valentine's heart. And she draws a vivid picture to illustrate that torment, a picture out of some half-forgotten children's book (for only children's books are permitted to deal in such cruelties) of a man caught and trapped by some octopus-like monster which is dragging him backwards down a hole, pinning his arms and gagging his mouth until all that can be seen are his imploring eyes.

This grotesque vision has a quality similar to the vision in Valentine's story of the butterflies, labouring to live, stuck up with cobwebs, 'cobwebs heavy as ten tons of muck'[2] which she wrote at Salthouse on the North Norfolk coast. It was to make an escape from such chimeras that she and Sylvia rented Great Eye Folly, Salthouse, in the winter of 1950–51.

They had spent a holiday in Ireland, looking at a house in County Clare which they nearly bought: they were always looking at houses with a view to buying them. On their return, they found the folly at Salthouse, built by a mad nineteenth-century speculative builder, Onesiphorus Randall, to entertain his women. It had been modernised and extended as a holiday home in the twentieth century, and the owners wished to let it for the winter. Onesiphorus (the name means Bringing Profit)

8.1 Great Eye Folly, Salthouse, in Norfolk, where Sylvia and Valentine
stayed, 1950–51

had an eye for a view, for he built his 'spectacular castle-like structure'[3] right on the beach. In 1953, two years after Sylvia and Valentine's tenancy, most of that part of the beach and part of the house was swept away in the great floods and the rest of the house had to be demolished. (The guidebook relates how after the flood the owner, walking along the beach looking for her possessions, is reputed to have said to a driver working for the river board whom she met also searching, 'Oh my good man, if you should find any silver forks and spoons, they will be mine.' To which the driver is said to have replied, 'Yes Ma'am, and if you find a bloody bulldozer, that will be mine!'[4])

Before going to live at Great Eye Folly, Sylvia and Valentine went to the Auvergne where, Sylvia wrote to Paul Nordoff, she hoped to find 'a nice extinct volcano . . . preferably with a lake in its crater . . . and sit on its slopes for days and days and days, quietly emptying myself of an infinity of crumpled yawns and deferred groans.'[5] She, too, was paying a price for the events of 1949.

Great Eye Folly proved to be a success; they let Frome Vauchurch and spent from November to March 1951 in Salthouse, where Sylvia joked that she was much more of a social success: 'I don't look forward to being just that peculiar Miss Warner again, after being loved and laurelled all the way down Holt High Street, and knowing the Christian names of everyone's cat.'[6] Valentine too was in her element – Sylvia wrote that all her beauty had come back to her: 'she walks about like a solitary sea-nymph . . . a sea-nymph who can split logs with an axe and manage a most capricious petrol pump, and cut up large frozen fish with a cleaver'.[7]

The dismay of returning to Frome 'in this gentle air and beside this sly subtle river'[8] as Sylvia put it, brought back many of the ghosts that had been laid to rest in the rough air of Norfolk, with the bracing noise of the waves continually crashing on the pebble beach all round them, and that curious sensation one has along the North Norfolk marshes of being suspended between sea and land. Within six months Sylvia became immersed in her new novel, *The Flint Anchor*, which was set in a Norfolk fishing town and was published in 1954. In conversation with Arnold Rattenbury, Sylvia called it 'my work on Hypocrisy', and said that she believed it was neglected

8.2 Lower Frome Vauchurch after the war

8.3 Valentine with one of the treasured
cats at Lower Frome Vauchurch

because 'by 1954 the worm of McCarthyism had got into English critical fashion as well and corrupted it'.[9] Meanwhile, once more, Valentine was facing the lonely battle with herself, her feelings for Elizabeth, and her search for the real and enduring in her life. It was these conflicts that fuelled and shaped the development of her later poetry, and most particularly, her religious poetry.

For Sylvia and Valentine, after the return from Salthouse in March 1951, there were nearly two decades of their partnership left to live. Writing in 1969, Sylvia commented sadly that it was not until Valentine knew she had cancer, in 1968, that she was able to trust in their love. There were still difficult years ahead.

The niggling ghosts may have been laid to rest while they were at Salthouse but on their return to Dorset the attachment between Valentine and Elizabeth, the continued correspondence and occasional visits, still caused reverberations of anxiety and tension between Sylvia and Valentine. It was to be many years before that attachment was no longer disruptive to their lives. During these years, Valentine's letters and poems show her working towards an understanding and acceptance of herself, and convey the imperilling searches she had to undertake throughout her life in pursuit of love and truth. For her these two ideals were inseparable. Her searches were the quest of a poet, made with a characteristic abandon and quick susceptibility to the fullness of the moment, and a rigorous dedication to capturing the exact impression and feeling in the poems. It was hardly surprising she suffered melancholy, depression, self-doubt and a sense of perpetual division, as well as a strong dose of Puritan guilt, the inheritance of her childhood.

During the years 1951 to 1958, Valentine was trying to find her way to a faith; she was finally received back into the Catholic Church on the anniversary of her first reception in 1925, 17 July 1961. In the last two years of her life she left the Church again, a prey to many doubts, and unable to bear the Anglicisation of the Mass. She became a Quaker, in which faith she died.

Although the 1950s and 1960s were not easy times, both Sylvia and Valentine retained their capacity for enjoying life, and even in her last two years when she was already ill, Valentine's letters are full of humour and zest for life. They reveal a wealth of concern and kindness towards her friends, and give detailed accounts of her reading, together with much searching commentary upon spiritual life. There are wonderful descriptions, such as of the palaver of a fashionable wedding of their friends' children, anecdotes about the cats, local life and the journeys she and Sylvia made.

Valentine had begun her antiques business in 1952, establishing a shop at the side of Lower Frome Vauchurch in the room known as the 'Long Room', which brought her into contact with a great many more people. She would take infinite pains to obtain a particular request for a customer, and soon built up a reputation for this. She also built up a successful mail-order business, a great deal of it with the United States. Some customers who came to the shop proved painful to deal with, so Valentine and Sylvia evolved a ploy to escape them, as with the unwelcome visitors at Chaldon. Valentine would discreetly ring a bell which alerted Sylvia, who promptly appeared to summon her away to attend to urgent business.

Despite the antique shop, finance still proved a worry. Valentine wrote to Joan in 1957 that she and Sylvia lived: 'on such a very sharp knife-edge financially: sometimes it widens a bit and is easier, but other times it is uncomfortable'.[10] At one point Sylvia had made over some capital to her, and £500 on deposit at the bank, the income from which they used mainly in joint living expenses: without this money, in earlier years, Valentine declared she would have been totally dependent on Sylvia's earnings and income, which were 'hazardous'. Presumably this act on Sylvia's part was an attempt to reassure Valentine, for it is difficult to see why the income from the capital would have been any more 'hazardous' if it were still in Sylvia's name. However, Sylvia was well-known for giving away her money to anyone she felt needed it, so perhaps this act was intended as some security for Valentine against her quixotic generosity.

Another difference between them in later years was the extent to which their political views had changed: with her reconversion to Catholicism, Valentine became increasingly right-wing, seeing a Communist plot everywhere in Europe, and in the sixties railing against Harold Wilson's Government. (She was angered because her dividends were dropping.) She thought Wilson too much of a fool or a knave to perceive what the Soviet Union was up to and to resist their scheming. In the 1966 election she voted Liberal which, she reported to Joan, caused considerable coldness at home.

The issue of religion caused a great deal of unhappiness, bringing them nearer to a split than Elizabeth had ever done. Sylvia wrote to Paul Nordoff in October 1956 of this period when Valentine was becoming a Catholic, being:

> full of unexpected jabs and pitfalls, and a completely unresolved perplexity as to what on earth a mind and a heart like hers can require from that extraordinary mingle-mangle of pettifogging little ordinances and assumptions of such incredible ambition. . . when I think of them I feel swamped and overshadowed by some nightmare variety of tree, a perambulating tree with no roots, such as I used to dream of when I was a child.[11]

There is in this passage a sense of deep gut loathing, and the nightmare amorphous quality that all Sylvia's worst fears and horrors took: a kind of enveloping chimera, such as she had described in the octopus–monster vision of Valentine's unhappiness in the letter referred to above. or her own vision of death being as if one were pulled along to the end of a pier with a shapeless ragbag attached to one's back, and one fell into the sea and drowned, dragged down under the water by its clinging weight.[12] All Sylvia's fears were of shapelessness, of something amorphous, smothering, clinging: the opposite to the rationality, order, wit, and solid material reality she loved and celebrated. It was what she feared about senility and madness in old age. Her art was a stay against shapelessness, against the chaos of insanity. Because she was a very private person, little of that territory of madness she so feared (there was a history of madness in her family and her mother was senile in her last years) was permitted to seep through into her published art.[13]

Sylvia's reaction to Valentine's conversion back to the Catholic faith shows how she had come to realise what a distance had opened up between them: 'I realise more and more sadly that this could not have happened to her without a long spell of previous unhappiness and dissatisfaction, which perhaps I was instrumental in, and in any case was incapable of mending.'[14]

The extent to which Sylvia buried herself in her work and

8.4 Sylvia on the front step at Lower Frome Vauchurch, 1964

8.5 Valentine's snapshot of Sylvia on one of their holidays (Berkshire, 1963)

8.6 Sylvia and Fougere in the upstairs sitting-room, at Lower
Frome Vauchurch

was capable of ignoring what went on around her seems to be indicated by her comment that the Proust translation she had been working on in the early fifties (*Contre Sainte Beuve*, published in 1956), was a 'secure private life', without which she felt extremely 'desolate and oddly unprotected'.[15]

The pattern of life which built up in the last two decades was one in which Sylvia was extremely productive. She was steadily producing stories for *The New Yorker*, working on the translation of Proust's *Contre Sainte-Beuve*, and later, in the sixties, on the very difficult and time-consuming task of writing the biography of T.H. White (published in 1967). She also took care of the cooking and a great many things about the house besides keeping up correspondence with friends. Sylvia rarely went out of the house and they did not entertain a great deal: they had a few good friends locally but were not in sympathy with Dorset county society. Valentine was still the indefatigable one, who busied herself doing 'good works', as her mother had done, when she was not working in the antiques business. Her good works consisted in helping to care for many of her friends who were in need, such as her lover and friend of many years ago, Bo Foster, who had first introduced her to the Catholic faith and who had come to live nearby. Valentine wrote long letters daily, both to her sister Joan, who had suffered a mental breakdown, and to a friend who was undertaking a drinking cure; the letters are detailed, sympathetic and wise. But she also wrote many hundreds of poems, the typescripts of which are now in the Dorset County Museum. In every direction she drove herself constantly to live a life more in tune with her exacting ideals. Valentine was never satisfied. Once found, her Catholic faith drove her with the intransigence of the convert to live in every moment the truth which she believed. To that end she gave herself no mercy; every sin was scrutinised and noted down, including frequently those of arrogance and spiritual pride in the course of her arguments with Sylvia.[16]

Looking back on their lives, both Valentine and Sylvia separately stressed the great span of happiness they had enjoyed together, and Sylvia came as near as she ever did to a religious use of language when she exclaimed after Valentine's death, how nearly she might have lived unblessed.

Illness dogged Valentine throughout the last twenty years of her life. She first had pains in her breast in the 1950s and

8.7 Sylvia reading, Lower Frome Vauchurch

8.8 Sylvia and one of the cats in the garden at Lower
Frome Vauchurch, 1968

cancer was diagnosed, which proved to be a false alarm at this stage. Later she suffered from a thyroid condition and in 1960 she fell ill with temporal arteritis. This lasted for some months and could have affected her eyesight. Valentine was sure she would go blind and went so far as to order Braille books: an operation was recommended, which would have been a risky procedure at that time. Fortunately she recovered without surgery.

The years 1958 to 1964 were almost continually marred by illness: it was, she wrote later to Joan, an 'almost daily experience'. Another of her illnesses, a back condition, she decided was largely to do with physical frustration. Humorously, but revealingly, she remarked that with all six foot of her, she could not show physical violence. But for all that she remained a source of support and comfort to many people, not least her own sister and mother, with whom Sylvia had little patience. (Sylvia described 'V's mamma' as the 'iron hand in a moth-eaten rabbit-fur glove; she appears to be warm-hearted, full of understanding, a brave old poor thing with an Anglo-Catholic smile.'[17])

Sylvia thought that Valentine's relations were vampires. She was often extremely angry at the thought of the demands the family were making on Valentine, and was 'frantically, unavailingly angry' not only at the 'vampire-relations', but also at 'her vampire Church'. Sylvia consoled herself that she was by now more often 'saddened than infuriated'. However, she was her mother's daughter, and Nora had been, as she said, 'quite a considerable tigress'. Sylvia herself could not help but contain 'a considerable charge of dynamite'.[18] It was impossible to accept calmly anything that drained and taxed her beloved Valentine.

In June 1961 Valentine's mother died, and they were faced with the appalling task of clearing out Hill House which had stood empty for two and a half years since Ruth left it to live with relations in Sussex. However, conscience and duty were sloughed off when they escaped on one of their recurrent 'jaunts' – for which money was always found. At the beginning of the T.H. White project, Sylvia went to Alderney: on her return she started work in earnest. There were about five hundredweight of papers, she reported, and she was hard at work in total solitude, from six o'clock in the morning onwards. (Unusual for Sylvia, who was rarely an early-morning riser; when she was woken with her breakfast in bed, however, she would immediately begin a brisk and intelligent conversation, picking up from where she stopped the night before.[19]) In 1966, after Valentine had recovered from a car-crash, they went to Scotland, and went again in 1967. It was to be the last of their long jaunts in search of 'quantities of sea air and salt water',[20] for early in 1968 Valentine was diagnosed as having cancer. The pain in her breast had at last been revealed as a malign symptom.

She underwent a masectomy and by September she was sufficiently recovered for them both to make another expedition, this time to Portmeirion 'summoned to see Clough and Amabel' (Williams-Ellis; Amabel had been one of the founding editors of *Left Review*). Valentine underwent radiation treatment after the operation and because of this, what had come to be the 'painful annual meeting' with Elizabeth was avoided. Soon after they returned from North Wales, the doctors found that the cancer had spread: a second operation was necessary.

Valentine was principally concerned about what would happen to Sylvia if she died: she wrote to her cousin Peg imploring her to help keep Sylvia 'out of the hands of the Welfare State'.[21]

By February 1969 she was sufficiently recovered to be tearing round the country in her car: 'Her brio is unchanged', Sylvia wrote to William Maxwell; 'but she has not the same reserves as she had and tires easily . . . when I can sit on her head and make her rest she does pretty well'.[22] By August the disease had spread to her lungs, and two months later Sylvia wrote to their American friends Marchette and Joy Chute:

> Ten days ago we were still going on in a narrowing pattern of our daily life. She could still drive, though only for short journeys; she could walk in the garden with me and pick figs, her eyes sharper than mine to see them; and though she could not be up for more than half a day we could talk and discuss and laugh together at the antics of the cats. And in the morning she still brought me my breakfast, the habit of over forty years, and we read our letters together.
>
> But suddenly she has begun to fail. Only love and her invincible fortitude is left. *And the fact that we are together.*[23]

8.9 **Drawing** of Valentine on her death-bed done by Joy Finzi at
Sylvia's request

Valentine died two weeks later, on 9 November, in the morning. On the 4 November they had heard an anti-Vietnam war speech on the radio which roused her; three days later the doctor increased her morphine. She was barely conscious, but roused a little to talk with Sylvia the next day.

On the 9th 'The wind raged round the house, her body raged round her, and she knew nothing of either.'[24] Sylvia wrote to William Maxwell that death had brought back all the beauty of her young days: 'It was like something in music, the re-establishment of the original key, the return of the theme.'[25]

It was not a hearse that came to take her coffin away, but a bright, forget-me-not blue van: Valentine's spirit was laughing beside her at this, Sylvia thought. Later she said it was one of the worst things: you turn to share and laugh, and there is no one there. And it is so.

At that time she did not feel alone: she felt rather that she was in a 'new country', and that Valentine was the compass she travelled by. She was to live on in that new country for another eight and a half years.

SYLVIA ALONE

In the aftermath of Valentine's death, Sylvia could not bear to leave Frome Vauchurch. She remained in Valentine's ambience. Friendships were resumed, with David Garnett for example, whom Valentine had not liked, and new ones forged, such as that with Peter Pears, who was also living a solitary life as a 'one-winged partridge' (the emblem of fidelity, she told Joy Chute). Sylvia's greatest consolation was putting in order the letters she and Valentine had written to each other once or even twice a day when they were apart. She found it hard to accept the suffering of the last decade, the 'slow grinding accumulation of ill-health, calamity and self-exile'.[26] Only after Valentine knew she had cancer was she able to trust in their love.

Sylvia finally made a trip away two years later, to stay with Paul Nordoff in Denmark. Soon after her return, she was introduced to a young woman, the widow of an Austrian count who lived at a farm six miles away in Litton Cheney. A friendship sprang up between them that was to grow and to last for the next six years of Sylvia's life. Gradually the void left by Valentine's death was filled.

With Antonia von und zu Trauttmansdorff, Sylvia recovered her youthfulness and her carefree spirit: Bea Howe remarked that she reverted to being the person she had known in the 1920s. In the last years of her life Sylvia was both happy and at last well-off from her writing. She was also beginning to receive something like her proper recognition, particularly with the collection of stories called *Kingdoms of Elfin* (1977), was published the year before she died to wide acclaim.

Between them Sylvia and Antonia shared a lot of good food, wide reading, witty conversation, and above all a ridiculing turn of humour which they indulged by composing a great many spoofs and parodies, either jointly written or written by one for the other. These were fantastically illustrated by Antonia, who was a very talented illustrator. They liked to talk of childhood, to travel, gossip, and cook; they did not like to engage in earnest or portentous conversation and avoided any company in which they might be exposed to it. They had both lost loved partners through cancer and had the harrowing experience of nursing them to the moment of their deaths; when you have seen the other thing, said Antonia, you live at the level of flying pigs. But what they had each been through was a deep bond between them. They also enjoyed the sharpness of each other's own acerbic characters and their common refusal to be taken in by appearances. After one particular occasion when Antonia felt Sylvia had been living up to her sweet-old-lady-writer image and patronising her, Antonia sent her a caricature of herself as a knowing, malicious old owl: Sylvia replied that it was an unexpected pleasure to find herself so well understood in her old age. 'I was beginning to feel sweetness growing over me like mildew.' She signed herself 'Strix'.[27]

Probably the last adventure of importance in Sylvia's life was her journey to Aldeburgh in 1977, when a programme of her work was put on in her honour at the Aldeburgh Festival. There were excerpts from her opera libretto on the last days of Shelley, which had been a joint project with Paul Nordoff, and her poems were sung in settings by Nordoff, John Ireland and Alan Bush. Peter Pears read a short story and her fine last poetry collection, *Twelve Poems*.[28] She was chauffeured and companioned by Antonia, and on the way home they made a 'circumbendibus' to see Ely, which Antonia had never visited.

8.10   Sylvia in the 1970s (photo by Nigel Luckhurst)

'All things are possible if you have an Antonia', Sylvia said, for as she grew more frail physically she became increasingly dependent on Antonia.

As late as 1974, Sylvia had travelled to North Wales on her own to see her friends Sim and Arnold Rattenbury, two of the few people she could still discuss politics with who had not reneged on their earlier socialist commitment. But by the winter of 1977 her health was failing. The winter was extremely severe, and Antonia walked over the fields and tops of hedges from Baglake Farm where she lived to look after Sylvia, inbetween rescuing and feeding the cattle and keeping everyone at her home fed and sheltered. When the thaw finally came, Sylvia said she felt ten years older: and she could no longer always guarantee her legs. Throughout March and April it was clear that she was failing: her last letters were written at the end of March. She was looked after at home by Antonia and Mrs Cleall, staying in the big bed in the room looking out over the garden and the river.

She died of chest complications brought on by old age on 1 May 1978. It was an appropriate day for this Fellow of the Royal Society of Literature and member of the American Academy of Arts, who was also a lifelong opponent of Fascism, sometime member of the British Communist Party, and friend to the Soviet Union, to die. Eleven years earlier, William Maxwell had written to tell her that she was now regarded in the United States as one of those who were 'prematurely anti-Fascist'. His letter arrived on May Day and she greeted it as a present:

> It soars above all other mortal distinctions. Oh, the inexhaustible solemn fatuity of the official mind. . . .
> Pre-maturely anti-Fascist. Not in step with us, but we will overlook that. Thank God you told me. I might have died in the night and never known.[29]

East Chaldon Church Dorset

8.11 Drawing of East Chaldon church – Valentine and Sylvia are buried there together. The stone reads 'Non omnis moriar'.

ABBREVIATIONS

By Sylvia Townsend Warner:

CCB	*The Cat's Cradle Book*
CTHT	*The Corner That Held Them*
CP	*Collected Poems*, ed. by Claire Harman
GS	*A Garland of Straw*
Letters	*Letters*, ed. by William Maxwell
MC	*The Museum of Cheats*
SOC	*Scenes of Childhood*
SWS	*Summer Will Show*
WDS	*Whether a Dove or a Seagull*

By Valentine Ackland:

FSHA	*For Sylvia: an Honest Account*
TNM	*The Nature of the Moment*
WDS	*Whether a Dove or a Seagull*

Other titles & periodicals:

LR	*Left Review*
LLT	*Life and Letters Today*
NR	*New Republic*
OT	*Our Time*
PNR	*Poetry Nation Review*
SCWV	*Spanish Civil War Verse (The Penguin Book of)*, ed. by Valentine Cunningham
SFWCW	*Spanish Front: Writers on the Civil War*, ed. by Valentine Cunningham
T&T	*Time & Tide*

Names:

AR	Arnold Rattenbury
AT	Antonia Trauttmansdorff

ER	Edgell Rickword
JL	Julius Lipton
JW	Joan Woollcombe
NC	Nancy Cunard
PN	Paul Nordoff
SC	Steven Clark
STW	Sylvia Townsend Warner
VA	Valentine Ackland
WmM	William Maxwell
WM	Wendy Mulford
PSUC	Partita Socialista Unificat de Catalonia (Catalan Communist Party)

NOTES

INTRODUCTION

1 Peter Pears, *Twelve Poems* (London, Chatto & Windus, 1980) Preface, p. 7.
2 *Lolly Willowes* (1926); *Mr Fortune's Maggot* (1927); *The True Heart* (1929).
3 AR, 'Plain Heart Light Tether', in *PNR* 23 (1981), Vol. 8, No. 3, pp. 46–8.
4 STW, *Jane Austen* (1964), p. 5.
5 Letter, VA to JW, Manisty Papers (no date).
6 Letter, STW to AR, 1968.
7 STW to WmM, *Letters*, 2 May 1967.
8 Letter, Claire Harman to WM.
9 The letters were put together with a linking narrative by STW after VA died. They will be published when certain restrictions placed on them in STW's will are met.
10 Letter from STW after VA's death, recipient untraced, quoted in unpublished memoir by AT.

CHAPTER 1: TOWARDS MEETING

1 STW, 'The Way By Which I Have Come', in *The Countryman* (July 1939), p. 472.
2 Letter, VA to PM Manisty Papers, (1960s).
3 Ibid.
4 Ibid.
5 Information courtesy of William Goffin, Winterton-on-Sea.
6 VA, *FSHA*, p. 16.
7 Ibid., p. 6.
8 Ibid., p. 69.
9 Letter, VA to PM Manisty Papers, (1960s).
10 STW, *SOC*, p. 132.
11 Ibid., p. 138.
12 VA, *FSHA*, p. 8.

13 Quoted in *Letters*, p. xiii.
14 'On Being a Lily', in STW, *SOC*, p. 142.
15 Ibid.
16 Bryher, *The Heart to Artemis*, (1963), p. 207.
17 'Behind The Firing Line: Some Experiences in a Munition Factory. By a Lady Worker', in *Blackwoods Magazine*, February 1916, pp. 191–207.
18 VA, *FSHA*, p. 75.
19 Ibid., p. 82.
20 Ibid., p. 75.
21 Ibid.
22 Ibid., p. 88.
23 Ibid., p. 84.
24 Ibid., p. 86.
25 Ibid., p. 89.
26 Ibid., p. 93.
27 Ibid.
28 Ibid., p. 97.
29 Ibid., p. 98.
30 Ibid., p. 117.
31 See Nina Hamnett's autobiography of these years, *Laughing Torso* (1932).
32 VA, *FSHA*, pp. 115, 119.
33 Ibid.
34 Ibid., p. 113.
35 Ibid., p. 115.
36 *Letters*, p. xiv.
37 VA, *FSHA*, p. 108.
38 Ibid.
39 Letter, T.F. Powys to STW, quoted in *The Powys Review*, No. 5, Vol. 2 (i), p. 17.
40 Ibid.
41 Information from unpublished memoir of STW by AT.
42 Ibid.
43 Quoted ibid.
44 Dorset was not unusual in these conditions. An informant in Bedfordshire reported that water was delivered by hand-cart to their village in the 1930s.
45 Jean Starr Untermeyer, *Private Collection* (1965), p. 145.
46 Ibid.
47 Information from unpublished memoir, AT.
48 Ibid.
49 Quoted ibid.
50 Ibid.
51 VA, *FSHA*, p. 123.

52 Ibid., p. 123.
53 VA, *FSHA*, p. 123.

CHAPTER 2: PARTNERSHIP – THE EARLY YEARS

1 STW to Harold Raymond, 17 June 1933, in *Letters*.
2 VA, *FSHA*, p. 127.
3 Discussed in Chapter 6.
4 STW to WmM, *Letters*, 21 February 1965.
5 STW to Llewellyn Powys, ibid., 16 August 1933.
6 VA, *FSHA*, pp. 129–30.
7 Quoted in Kenneth Hopkins, *The Powys Brothers* (1967), p. 205.
8 VA, *FSHA*, p. 131.
9 Review in the *London Mercury*, 1934, p. 656. The reviewer also said that though he thought he could recognise Sylvia's work 'by its somewhat esoteric character there are many instances in which I found myself wrong', showing that one reader at least did consult the key to the poems' authorship.
10 *CP*, Preface, p. xx.
11 Letter, VA to JL, Lipton letters, April 1935.
12 STW & VA, *WDS*, p. 52.
13 Ibid., p. 43.
14 Ibid., p. 33.
15 Ibid., p. 39.
16 The book was dedicated to Robert Frost, also a poet of transparent and delicate attention in his craft.
17 STW & VA, *WDS*, p. 94.
18 Dorset County Museum archive, Dorchester.
19 STW & VA, *WDS*, p. 131. The last part of the collection comprises some equally remarkable, passionate and tender love-lyrics from STW to VA.
20 Ibid., p. 24.
21 Ibid., p. 49.
22 Ibid., p. 29.
23 Discussed in Chapter 4.
24 Storm Jameson, *Journey from the North* (1969), Vol. 1, p. 322.
25 STW, 'The Way By Which I Have Come', *The Countryman* (July 1939), p. 475.
26 AR, letters.
27 John Strachey, *The Theory and Practice of Socialism* (1936), p. 10.
28 G. Dimitrov, *Letters from Prison* (1935).
29 'STW in Conversation', in *PNR* 23 (1981), Vol. 8, No. 3, p. 35.
30 Lower Frome Vauchurch library.
31 Leonard Woolf, *Downhill All the Way* (1967).
32 STW, 'The Way By Which I Have Come', p. 485.

33 The title of Stephen Spender's influential book, published by Victor Gollancz and the Left Book Club in 1936.
34 Margot Heinemann in conversation with WM.
35 STW, 'The Way By Which I Have Come', p. 485.
36 Ibid., p. 475.
37 Vera Brittain, *Testament of Experience* (1957).
38 AR, letters.
39 The 1935 Jubilee of King George V. STW & VA were amongst many distinguished writers who signed a protest against it in *Left Review*, and later demonstrated against the obscenity of celebrating such an event, when so many had died in the First World War, and so many were unemployed and near starvation.
40 Tom Wintringham, poet and author of many books on military and international affairs, founder member of the Communist Party of Great Britain and of *LR*. He fought in the Spanish Civil War as a Commandant with the International Brigade.
41 Letter, VA to JL, Lipton letters, Summer 1935.
42 Letter, STW to JL, ibid., 24 December 1935.
43 *Letters*, p. 33.
44 Roger Miller in conversation with WM.
45 VA to JL, Lipton letters, 3 April 1936.
46 STW to JL, ibid., 24 February 1937.
47 'Plain Heart, Light Tether', in *PNR*, 23, 1981.
48 Editor of *Britain, Fascism and the Popular Front* (1985) and author of *The Signal Was Spain* (1986).
49 STW to JL, Lipton letters, 12 May 1936.
50 VA to JL, ibid., 6 May 1936.
51 Sir Stafford Cripps, later Labour Chancellor of the Exchequer in the post-war Labour Government, was at that time a leading speaker on Unity platforms.
52 The Dorset Peace Council, of which STW was elected Secretary in 1936, at which she and VA worked extremely hard.
53 STW to JL, Lipton letters, 24 February 1937.
54 STW to JL, ibid., 19 January 1938.

CHAPTER 3: WRITERS IN ARMS

1 Editorial in *LR*, Vol. 3, May 1938. *LR* was originally published for the British Section of the Writers' International.
2 J.B. Priestley, in *LR*, Vol. 1, October 1934.
3 Naomi Mitchison, 'The Reluctant Feminists', ibid., December 1934. Philippa Polson's piece, 'Feminists and the Woman Question', later in the year, was another exception to the general disregard of women's position by *LR*, pointing out that the family as an economic unit remained 'unassailed and the double

exploitation of working women continued unchallenged. . . . Every day sees the tightening of the bonds of women.'

4 STW, 'Red Front', in *LR*, Vol. 1, January 1935.

5 VA, 'Communist Poem 1935', in *LR*, Vol. 1, April 1935.

6 Jack Lindsay in converstion with WM.

7 VA to JL, Lipton letters, May 1935.

8 STW, review of 'Concert of Soviet Music', in *LR*, Vol. 1, June 1935.

9 STW, 'Competition in Criticism', in *LR*, Vol. 2, January 1936.

10 Ibid.

11 Ibid.

12 STW, 'Underlying Morality: review of *New Writing*, in *LR*, Vol. 3, July 1937.

13 Ibid.

14 STW, 'Recommendations to Starvation', in *The Countryman*, January 1936.

15 STW, 'The Way By Which I Have Come', July 1939.

16 VA, 'Country Dealings 1', in *LR*, Vol. 1, March 1935. There were three articles published in that year, from which the book grew.

17 'Country Dealings 2', in *LR*, May 1935.

18 'Country Dealings 3', in *LR*, June 1935.

19 Ibid.

20 Sylvia also wrote about this to Julius Lipton. See *Letters* p. 36.

21 VA to JL, Lipton letters, 21 March 1935.

22 *Daily Worker*, 18 November 1936.

23 *LR*, Vol. 2, 1936.

24 VA, *Country Conditions*.

25 'Country Dealings 3', in *LR*, June 1935, p. 507.

26 *Dorset Daily Echo*, 3 August 1936.

27 In his report for *LR* of the first months of the Writers' and Readers' Group, Julius Lipton ascribed the germination of the idea of the group to a remark by STW on the May Day demonstration in 1936, that here for the first time 'writers and readers were combining and . . . had found a unity of expression'. *LR*, Vol. 3, November 1937.

28 STW, review of H. Newitt, *Women Must Choose*, and J. Peterson, *Our Street* in *Left Book News*, April 1937, and January 1938.

29 STW to QL, Lipton letters, 29 May 1936.

30 VA to JL, ibid., 31 May 1935.

31 Ibid.

32 Ibid.

33 Ibid., 13 May 1935. VA also wrote that it was 'a thousand times more difficult for a woman poet to get a hearing' – a viewpoint which STW may well not have shared.

34 Ibid.

35 Julian Symons, *The Thirties: A Dream Revolved* (1966), p. 31.
36 STW to ER, 13 June 1938, AR, papers.
37 Cecil Day Lewis, reported in *LR*, Vol. 1.
38 Erwin Piscator, reported in *LR*, Vol. 1.
39 Christina Stead, report of the First Congress of the International Association of Writers for the Defence of Culture, *LR*, Vol. 1, August 1935.
40 Ibid.
41 Ibid.
42 Programme of Association of Writers for Intellectual Liberty meeting, 'In Defence of Freedom – Writers Declare Against Fascism', p. 2.
43 STW to ER, 13 June 1938. Frederick Prokosch was then known as the author of two volumes of poems, *The Assassins* (London, 1936), and *The Carnival*.
44 See, for example, J. Fyrth, *The Signal Was Spain: The Aid Spain Movement in Britain 1936–39* (1986).
45 NC article in the *Daily Worker*, 12 September 1936, Marx Memorial Archive.
46 VA, letter to *The News Chronicle*, 14 September 1936, ibid.
47 VA to JL, Lipton letters, September 1936.
48 STW to Elizabeth Wade White, 14 November 1936, in *Letters*.
49 Ibid.
50 Ibid.
51 Sue Bruley has pointed out that party members, and women in particular, devoted more time and energy to relief work than to political work. See S. Bruley, 'Socialism and Feminism in the Communist Party of Great Britain 1920–39' (1980).
52 Reported by Margot Heinemann.
53 See, for example, M. Heinemann, 'Remembering 1936: Women and the War in Spain', in *Women's Review*, October 1986, and Jim Fyrth's forthcoming book on women in the Spanish Civil War.
54 STW to Naomi Mitchison, *Letters*, 17 July 1937.
55 STW to JL, Lipton letters, 24 February 1937.
56 Ibid.
57 Ibid.
58 Nan Green, unpublished memoir, 'A Chronicle of Small Beer', quoted in *SFWCW*, p. 240.
59 STW to ER, Rattenbury papers, 10 November 1937.
60 Sir Peter Chalmers Mitchell, at one time Secretary of the London Zoological Society, who frequently spoke at anti-Fascist meetings. He was thrown out of Malaga by the Fascists in 1937.
61 STW to ER, 4 February 1938.
62 Asunción Lou Fleta to STW and VA, letter in John Johnson Collection, The Bodleian Library, Oxford. Translation courtesy of

Tony Morgan.

63 Ibid.

64 Reprinted in *SCWV*, p. 372.

65 VA, *Daily Worker*, October 1936.

66 As yet there is no bibliography of STW's works.

67 STW, 'Harvest in 1937' in *New Statesman*, July 1937. Reprinted in *SCWV*, pp. 233–5.

68 STW, 'Barcelona' in *LR*, Vol. 2, December 1936. Reprinted in *SCWV*.

69 Reprinted in *SCWV*, pp. 135, 150. Also reprinted in *CP*.

70 Cockburn wrote for the *Daily Worker* under the name of Pitcairn; his book, *Reporter in Spain* (London, Lawrence & Wishart, 1936), was one of the first eye-witness accounts of the war to be published and was enthusiastically reviewed by VA in *LR*, Vol. 2, December 1936.

71 VA to ER, AR papers, 22 July 1937.

72 There is a battered photograph of STW and VA standing smiling on either side of a Spanish woman, likely to be Asunción, with their arms about her.

73 'O'Donnel' is presumably the 'O'Donnel' who had no authority to attach STW and VA to the Medical Aid Unit. On p. 57 of *The Signal Was Spain* (see note 44), Fyrth reports that he was not a success in the Barcelona office and left shortly after to work at the headquarters of PSUC, the United Socialist Party of Catalonia, affiliated to the Communist International.

74 The Spanish nickname of an English woman in Barcelona who, apparently, 'could not love the Spaniards'. Footnote in *Letters*, p. 49.

75 Ibid.

76 Stephen Spender, *World Within World* (1951).

77 Ibid., p. 244.

78 Ibid.

79 *SFWCW*.

80 A woman's brigade was involved in the defence of Madrid in 1936, but that was the last frontline action in which women were permitted to take part.

81 VA, report on the Second Congress of the IAWDC, Madrid, 1937, in the *Daily Worker*. 21 July 1937.

82 STW, 'What the Soldier Said', in *T&T*, August 1937. Reprinted in *SFWCW*, pp. 92–4.

83 Ibid., p. 93.

84 Ibid.

85 Ibid., pp. 93–4.

86 Ibid., p. x.

87 Ibid., p. 93.

88 It is a rare collectors' item and fetches a high price.
89 *SFWCW*, p. 51.
90 Ibid., p. 230.
91 STW, *The Countryman*, April 1939.

CHAPTER 4: SYLVIA: THE NOVELS OF THE 1930s

1 STW, review of S. Spender and J. Lehmann (eds.) (1939), in LLT 1939, pp. 101–2.
2 STW to JL, Lipton letters, 13 September 1936.
3 Ibid.
4 STW, *Lolly Willowes, or The Loving Huntsman* (1926). Quoted here from The Women's Press reprint, London, 1978, p. 247.
5 Ibid., p. 101.
6 Ibid., p. 102.
7 Ibid., p. 234.
8 Ibid., pp. 234–6.
9 Ibid., pp. 238–9.
10 Review by Louis Kronenburger, reference untraced.
11 The American reviews were unanimous in their lively appreciation of STW's subtlety and originality of style: her early novels were highly successful with the American reading public.
12 Katherine Anne Porter, *New York Herald Tribune*, February 1930.
13 In F.R. Leavis, *New Bearings in English Poetry* (London, Chatto & Windus 1932).
14 STW, review of F. Le Gros and Ida Clarke, *The Adventures of the Little Pig and Other Stories*, in *Left News*, September 1937.
15 *Letters*, p. 39. Since completing this book, *SWS* has been reprinted by Virago, with an introduction by Claire Harman.
16 Ibid.
17 Ibid.
18 Ibid., p. 40.
19 STW, *SWS*, p. 96.
20 Ibid., pp. 96–7.
21 Ibid., p. 135.
22 Eleanor Perenyi, 'The Good Witch of the West', review of works by STW and VA, in *New York Review of Books*, July 18, 1985.
23 STW, *SWS*, p. 143.
24 Ibid., p. 138.
25 Ibid., p. 145.
26 Ibid., pp. 150, 151.
27 Ibid., p. 156.
28 Ibid., pp. 156–7.
29 Ibid., p. 160.

30 Ibid., p. 162.
31 *Letters*, p. 40.
32 STW, *SWS*, p. 217.
33 Ibid., p. 274.
34 Ibid.
35 Ibid., pp. 287, 288.
36 Ibid., p. 214.
37 Ibid., p. 382.
38 Ibid., p. 390.
39 Ibid., p. 405.
40 Ibid., p. 406.
41 Marvell, 'The Definition of Love'.
42 STW, *SWS*, pp. 290–1.
43 Ibid.
44 Ibid., p. 184.
45 In conversation with AT towards the end of the life, STW stressed the modesty of her art.
46 STW, *SWS*, p. 214.
47 Peter Quenell, *New Statesman*, September 1936.
48 Reviewer in *T&T*, September 1936, p. 1286.
49 Ralph Wright, the *Daily Worker*, 23 September 1936.
50 A contemporary example of this selective reading of the novel by a left-wing writer occurs in AR's otherwise excellent article 'Plain Heart Light Tether', in which Sophia and Minna are only named as the 'wife' and the 'mistress'.
51 Eleanor Clark, *New Republic*, 12 August 1936.
52 STW to NC, *Letters*, 28 August 1945.
53 'STW in Conversation', *PNR* 23, Vol. 8 No. 3, 1981, p. 36.
54 Ibid., p. 35.
55 Ibid.
56 STW, 'The Bear', *PNR*, 1981, pp. 48–50.
57 *PNR* 1981, p. 35.
58 Information courtesy of Ian Patterson Books.
59 *PNR* 1981, p. 36.
60 STW, *After the Death of Don Juan* (1938), p. 1.
61 Ibid.
62 Ibid., p. 2.
63 Ibid., p. 3.
64 Ibid., p. 14.
65 Ibid., p. 15.
66 Ibid., p. 301.
67 Ibid., p. 54.
68 Ibid.
69 Ibid., p. 73.
70 Ibid.

71 Ibid., pp. 173–4.
72 Ibid., p. 148.
73 Ibid., p. 145.
74 Ibid., p. 248.
75 Ibid.
76 Ibid., pp. 248–9.
77 Ibid., p. 155.

CHAPTER 5: WARTIME AND AFTER: PARTNERSHIP UNDER PRESSURE.

1 *Letters*, p. xv.
2 The Viking Press, New York, N.Y., 5 July 1946.
3 STW to PN, *Letters*, 14 July 1939. Paul Nordoff was to become a close friend. His setting of some of her poems was performed at the Aldeburgh Festival programme in STW's honour in 1977.
4 VA, *FSHA*, p. 132.
5 *CP*, pp. 43–5.
6 *CP*, p. 45.
7 The images of VA in STW's love lyrics in *WDS* continually associate VA with the freedom of a bird, 'Sudden, dauntless and shy', and with the sky in its depth and distance.
8 *CP*, p. 46.
9 Steven Clark was the friend STW and VA had met in Barcelona in 1936; see STW to SC, *Letters*, 6 September 1937.
10 STW to PN, ibid., 1 June 1940.
11 STW, *The Flint Anchor* (1954). It falls outside the scope of this study, which focusses on the years 1930–51, the years in which both Sylvia and Valentine were most politically active. However, the novel's themes are clearly related to those of earlier works: she described it to AR as 'my work on Hypocrisy'. *PNR* 23 (1981), Vol. 8, No. 3.
12 STW to PN, *Letters*, 3 July 1940.
13 Ibid., 13 August 1940.
14 Ibid.
15 Ibid.
16 This impression may be the result of Maxwell's selection in *Letters*; the politically-committed side of STW's life, for example, is slenderly represented.
17 STW to PN, *Letters*, 17 October 1940.
18 Ibid., 17 November 1940.
19 Ibid., 5 September 1941.
20 Ibid.
21 VA, 'Letter from England', in *NR*, 2 September 1940.

22 STW to PN, *Letters*, 17 November 1940.
23 VA, 'Letter from England' in *NR*, 8 July 1940.
24 *Letters*, p. xiv.
25 STW to PN, ibid., 17 November 1940.
26 Ibid.
27 Ibid.
28 STW to Bea Howe, ibid., 4 December 1941.
29 VA to JW, 14 January 1957, Manisty Papers.
30 VA, *Further Poems* (1978), p. 25.
31 See Chapter 7.
32 STW, *CCB* (1940). It was not published in Britain until 1960.
33 See Chapter 7.
34 AT in conversation with WM. Claire Harman, too, makes this point in her review of *FSHA* in the *Powys Review* No. 17, vi, pp. 70–2.
35 STW to NC, Cunard papers, Harry Ransom Humanities Research Centre, University of Texas at Austin.
36 STW to PN, *Letters*, 5 September 1941.
37 STW to Ben Huebsch, ibid., 24 April 1946.
38 STW to PN, ibid., 9 April 1942.
39 A. Calder, *The People's War* (1969).
40 AT papers.
41 STW to NC, *Letters*, 9 April 1946.
42 The extent of Sylvia's still passionate concern with the Communist Party in the 1940s is shown in her wry but admiring comments about it to Nancy Cunard. Writing in March 1944 to Nancy, she laments that however hard they try not to, Communists always stick out, and this feature of their behaviour is a nuisance – 'it causes our high mortality rate'. She suspects the reason for it is a 'blazing self-control in a world of people not self-controlled', their reliability, and their quality of knowing where they're going. (STW to NC, 15 March 1944, Harry Ransom Humanities Research Center, University of Texas at Austin.) Her letters to Nancy up until the early 1950s are characterised by passionate disgust at the cover-ups and whitewashings of Nazi atrocities and Fascist collaboration during the war, and a blazing anger at American post-war red-hunting foreign policy.
43 STW, 'Here in this Narrow Room', in *OT*, April 1942.
44 Ibid.
45 STW, 'Fifty Girls Who Shouldn't', ibid., December 1941.
46 STW, 'The People Have No Generals', ibid., February 1941.
47 STW, Memoir of NC, in H. Ford (ed.), *Nancy Cunard: Brave Poet, Indomitable Rebel* (1968), p. 226.
48 Ibid.
49 Ibid.
50 Ibid., p. 228.

51 STW to NC, *Letters*, 28 April 1944.
52 There were a number of birth control campaigns that she might have joined in the twenties; possibly she joined the Workers Birth Control Campaign.
53 STW to NC, *Letters*, 26 July 1944.
54 STW to NC and Morris Gilbert, ibid., 9 June 1944.
55 STW to NC, ibid., 13 March 1945.
56 Ibid.
57 NC (ed.), *Poèmes à la France*, (1947).
58 Ibid., p. 58, 59.
59 STW, 'Love of France', in *OT* August 1945.
60 Ibid.
61 Ibid.
62 STW to PN, *Letters*, 17 March 1948.
63 Ibid.
64 STW to NC, ibid., 1 September 1948.
65 The Paris conference was the follow-up to the 'First World Cultural Congress for Peace', held in Wroclaw, Poland in August 1948. Four hundred delegates attended from 45 nations, including artists of the stature of Picasso. It was widely seen as a Communist front, even though writers as anti-Communist as T.S. Eliot attended.
66 STW to NC, *Letters*, 19 January 1949.
67 STW to PN, ibid., 6 June 1949.
68 Quoted in VA, *FSHA*, p. 15.
69 Ibid.
70 Ibid., p. 132.

CHAPTER 6: MATURE ART – SYLVIA:
THE WRITINGS OF THE FORTIES

1 STW to WmM, *Letters*, 20 May 1977.
2 See Claire Harman's Introduction, *CP*.
3 Ibid., p. xxi.
4 STW, *CCB*, p. 9.
5 Ibid., p. 12.
6 See also 'For love of your long legs and your proud shoulders/And the one lappet of hair hanging astray' in Sylvia's poem 'I would give you Alexander's Bucephalus', in STW and VA, *WDS*, p. 125.
7 Ibid., pp. 36–7.
8 'The Trumpet Shall Sound', in STW, *GS*, p. 68.
9 STW, 'Women As Writers', in *Journal of the Royal Society of Arts*, May 1959, p. 384. Reprinted in *CP*.
10 Hilary Spurling, review of *Kingdoms of Elfin*, 1977, reference untraced.
11 Ibid.

12 A. Calder-Marshall, 'Place Without Time', in *OT*, April 1949.
13 Ibid.
14 STW to NC, *Letters*, 9 November 1951.
15 STW, *MC*, pp. 109–10.
16 STW to PN, *Letters*, 9 April 1942.
17 STW, *MC*, p. 119.
18 Ibid.
19 Ibid.
20 Ibid.
21 STW, 'Women as Writers', p. 378.
22 STW, 'Elizabeth Gaskell', in *OT*, February 1945.
23 Ibid.
24 V. Woolf, *A Room of One's Own* (1929), p. 81: 'Do not start. Do not blush. Let us admit in the privacy of our own society that these things sometimes happen. Sometimes women do like women.'
25 STW, 'Elizabeth Gaskell'.
26 Ibid.
27 In a *Guardian* interview of 1977, Sylvia denied that anything she had ever written was a critique of society. She is quoted as saying: 'I'm sure I shouldn't know how to comment on society. It's a mystery to me.' – the kind of tongue-in-cheek reply she would make when cornered.
28 STW, 'Elizabeth Gaskell'.
29 STW, *Jane Austen* (1964), p. 5.
30 Ibid., p. 7.
31 Ibid., p. 15.
32 STW, 'Women as Writers', pp. 378–9.
33 Ibid., p. 379.
34 Ibid., p. 380.
35 Ibid.
36 Ibid., p. 383.
37 Ibid.
38 Ibid., p. 381.
39 STW, 'The Magpie Charity', in *CCB*, p. 75.
40 Ibid., p. 78.
41 STW, 'An English Fable', in *LR*, Vol. 3, August 1937.
42 STW, 'The Jungle Blossom', in *OT*, Vol. 7, No. 11, August 1948.
43 Ibid.
44 Ibid.
45 Ibid.
46 Ibid.
47 Ibid.
48 Ibid.
49 'Sylvia Townsend Warner in Conversation', *PNR* 23, Vol. 8 No. 3, p. 36.

50 STW, *CTHT*, p. 203.
51 Ibid., p. 193.
52 Hilary Spurling, review of *Kingdoms of Elfin*, 1977.
53 J. Updike, review of *Lolly Willowes* in *The New Yorker*, 1978.
54 STW to Ben Huebsch, *Letters*, 21 December 1944.
55 STW, *CTHT*, p.1.
56 Ibid., p. 310.
57 Ibid., p. 8.
58 Ibid., p. 9.
59 Ibid., pp. 242–3.
60 Ibid., p. 183.
61 Ibid., p. 249.
62 Ibid., p. 288.

CHAPTER 7: VALENTINE ACKLAND, POET

1 VA, *Later Poems*, n.d. p. 24.
2 Including a haunting nude pencil-study of her by Eric Gill that hung in the study, formerly their dining-room.
3 STW, Commonplace Book. The description is comparable to that of the handsome young man in the Introduction to *CCB*.
4 VA to JL, Lipton letters, 30 May 1935.
5 VA, 'New House', in the *London Mercury*, May 1935.
6 Ibid., reprinted in VA, *TNM* (1973), p. 15.
7 VA, 'England 1936', originally published in *LR*, 1936, reprinted in *SCWV*, p. 372. See also Chapter 3.
8 VA 'Badajoz to Dorset', *LLT*, Spring 1937.
9 VA, 'Time for a Quick One', ibid., Summer 1937.
10 VA, *TNM*, (1973), pp. 22–5.
11 STW, Commonplace Book.
12 Quoted in Chapter 5.
13 NC (ed.), *Poèmes à la France*, (1944), p. 445.
14 M. Elwin, (ed.), *The Pleasure Ground*, (1947). The anthology also contains a story by Sylvia, 'A Writer's Dream', and another by Valentine, 'A Multitude of the Heavenly Host', as well as eight of Valentine's poems.
15 Some estimates have put the possible number of poems as high as 2000, including many variant drafts. Valentine was scrupulous at her craft.
16 VA, *Further Poems* (1978), p. 49.
17 Ibid., p. 46.
18 STW, *Somerset* (1949). The tart and unexpected flavour of her commentary is apparent throughout the guide, which was dedicated to their friend Steven Clarke of Barcelona days. See, for example, the discussion on p. 55 of the decline of Wiveliscombe, a weaving-town:

> The looms were silenced. Such a calamity must have been felt all
> through the district, for cloth-making is an industry of many
> processes . . . and involves such peripheral industries as teasel-
> growing, rack, card, and bobbin-making, and transport. . .
> the drop in self-esteem must have been incalculable. Eve
> spinning had always held her head higher than Adam digging.

19 VA, *Twenty-Eight Poems* (1957), p. 10.
20 VA, 'New Paulus Silentarius', in *Poetry Quarterly*, Winter 1946/7.
   Reprinted in VA, *TNM* (1973), p. 29.
21 Ibid., p. 55.
22 VA to JW, Manisty papers.
23 STW, draft in Lower Frome Vauchurch library.
24 STW, endpaper of VA, *TNM* (1973).
25 See Chapter 6.
26 VA, 'Granny Moxon', in *The Countryman*, Winter 1949, p. 246.
27 VA, 'The Last & the First', ibid., Summer 1950, pp. 265–6.
28 VA, 'A Multitude of the Heavenly Host' in M. Elwin, *The Pleasure
   Ground*, (1947), pp. 273–6.
29 VA, 'Sunlight on the Camp' and 'When I was in Basle' in *LLT*
   (1948), pp. 53–5; (1949), pp. 211–13.
30 VA, 'Two Occasions', ibid. (1938), pp. 420–23.
31 VA, 'Urn Burial' in *Modern Writing*, ed. P. Rahv and N. Philips
   (1953), pp. 166–81.
32 Ibid., p. 177.
33 Ibid., p. 178.
34 VA, *Later Poems*, n/d op.cit., p. 5.
35 VA, *Twenty-Eight Poems* (1958), p. 7.
36 Ibid.
37 Ibid., p. 8.
38 Ibid., p. 12.
39 Ibid., 'The Guiltless Ape', p. 13. Reprinted in VA, *TNM*, p. 45.
40 Ibid., p. 14.
41 Ibid., p. 23.
42 VA, *Later Potems*, n.d. p. 24.
43 Ibid., p. 9.
44 Ibid., p. 19.
45 Ibid., p. 21.
46 Ibid., p. 19.
47 Ibid., p. 8.
48 Ibid., p. 14.
49 Ibid. Reprinted in VA, *TNM*, p. 30.
50 Manisty papers.
51 VA, *TNM*, p. 58.
52 From 'Lead, somehow, our slow minds to thy truth', ibid., p. 59.

EPILOGUE (1951–1978)

1 STW to Alyse Gregory, *Letters*, 9 March 1950.
2 See Chapter 7.
3 P. Brooks, *Salthouse: Village of Character and History*, Poppyland Publishing, 1984.
4 Ibid.
5 STW to PN, *Letters*, 31 August 1950.
6 STW to WmM, ibid., 17 March 1951.
7 STW to PN, ibid., 31 December 1950.
8 STW to PN, ibid., 27 March 1951.
9 AR, 'Plain Heart, Light Tether', *PNR* 23, Vol. 8, No. 3, (1981), p. 47.
10 VA to JW, 1957, Manisty Papers.
11 STW to PN, *Letters*, 18 October 1956.
12 AT, unpublished memoir.
13 Compare the following (unpublished) comment, from a note about three of her friends:

> Between madness and sanity there is a territory like a darkened moor, full of peat bogs and mists, with no perceptible watershed or frontier. The moisture sucks into the ground, is sucked up, & its division, whether it flows to sense or madness, takes invisibly & underground. . . . It is only a few who are transported to madness. The rest have to stumble towards it, over soggy misleading ground, & through the obstacles of being a nuisance to those who love them, & a laughing stock to strangers.

14 STW to PN, *Letters*, 18 October 1956.
15 Ibid.
16 For example, the carefully kept and extensive 'catalogue' of her sins in the years 1957–8 includes:
> 28.7.57. Inhospitable and gloomy to visitors this week. . . . Selfish and self-absorbed. . . . Good resolutions break down at least difficulty.
> 2.1.58. Tendency for everything to be referred to myself. Whether I want, or I shall be pleased, or suffer, or lose, by whatever action I have in mind . . . impossible to lose my self-centredness, because mere fact of meaning to makes me think of myself again.
> 3.1.58. Too critical of other people. . . . Self-indulgent . . . buying things totally unnecessary just because I felt I wanted them.

17 STW to George Plank, *Letters*, 6 January 1960.
18 Ibid., 11 May 1961.

19 AT in conversation with WM.
20 STW to WmM, *Letters*, 14 September 1967: 'on this island one has to go a long way to get these. . . . Ships and waves and ceaseless motion And men rejoicing on the shore did nicely for Coleridge, but men rejoicing have no charm for her [Valentine]. So it must be ultima Thule.'
21 VA to PM 1968, Manisty papers.
22 STW to WmM, *Letters*, 7 February 1969.
23 STW to M. and J. Chute, ibid., 25 October 1969.
24 STW to Janet Machen, ibid., 9 November 1969.
25 STW to WmM, ibid., 11 November 1969.
26 Ibid., 19 November 1971.
27 AT papers.
28 Produced in a card-covered, A4, stapled pamphlet for the occasion, the poems appeared in a handsome letterpress sewn edition in 1978 from Libanus Press as *Azrael & Other Poems*. (Chatto & Windus published *Twelve Poems* in hardback in 1980.)
29 STW to WmM, *Letters*, 5 May 1967.

BIBLIOGRAPHY

WORKS BY VALENTINE ACKLAND AND SYLVIA TOWNSEND WARNER

Valentine Ackland *Whether a Dove or a Seagull*, London, Chatto & Windus, 1934 (with Sylvia Townsend Warner). *Country Conditions*, London, Lawrence & Wishart, 1936. *Twenty-eight Poems*, privately printed by Clare, Son & Co. Ltd., Wells (Somerset) & London, 1957. *Later Poems*, (ed. by STW), privately printed by Clare, Son & Co., Wells and London, n/d, ?1970. *The Nature of the Moment*, London, Chatto & Windus, 1973. *Further Poems of Valentine Ackland*, Beckenham, Kent, Welmont Publishing, 1978. *For Sylvia: an Honest Account*, London, Chatto & Windus, 1985.

Sylvia Townsend Warner *The Espalier*, London, Chatto & Windus, 1925. *Lolly Willowes*, London, Chatto & Windus, 1926. *Mr Fortune's Maggot*, London, Chatto & Windus, 1927. *Time Importuned*, London, Chatto & Windus, 1928. *The True Heart*, London, Chatto & Windus, 1929. *Some World Far From Ours & Stay Corydon*, London, Woburn Books, 1929. *Elinor Barley*, London, Cresset Press, 1930. *A Moral Ending*, Furnival Books, frontispiece and forward by T.F. Powys, London, 1931. *Opus 7*, London, Chatto & Windus, (The Dolphin Books), 1931. *The Salutation*, London, Chatto & Windus, 1932. *Whether a Dove or a Seagull*, London, Chatto & Windus, 1934, (with Valentine Ackland). *More Joy in Heaven*, London, The Cresset Press, 1935. *Summer Will Show*, London, Chatto & Windus, 1936. *After the Death of Don Juan*, London, Chatto & Windus, 1938. *A Garland of Straw*, London, Chatto & Windus, 1943. *The Portrait of a Tortoise*, extracted from *The Journals and Letters of Gilbert White*, Introduction and Notes by STW, London, Chatto & Windus, 1946. *The Museum of Cheats*, London, Chatto & Windus, 1947. *The Corner That Held Them*, London, Chatto & Windus, 1948. *Somerset*, London, Paul Elek, 1949. *Jane Austen*, (British Council

Writers Series), London, Longmans, Green & Co., 1951 (1964 edition). *The Flint Anchor*, London, Chatto & Windus, 1954. *Winter in the Air*, London, Chatto & Windus, 1955. *Boxwood*, with engravings by Reynolds Stone, London, Chatto & Windus, 1957. *By Way of Sainte Beuve*, translation of Marcel Proust's *Contre Sainte Beuve*, London, Chatto & Windus, 1958. *The Cat's Cradle Book*, London, Chatto & Windus, 1960. *A Spirit Rises*, London, Chatto & Windus, 1962. *Sketches From Nature*, printed by Clare, Son & Co. Ltd., Wells (Somerset) and London, 1963. *A Stranger With a Bag*, London, Chatto & Windus, 1966. *T.H. White: A Biography*, London, Jonathan Cape with Chatto & Windus, 1967. *King Duffus and Other Poems*, Wells and London, Clare, Son & Co., 1968. *The Innocent and the Guilty*, London, Chatto & Windus, 1971. *Kingdoms of Elfin*, London, Chatto & Windus, 1977. *Azrael & Other Poems*, Newbury, Libanus Press, 1978. *Twelve Poems*, London, Chatto & Windus, 1980. *Scenes of Childhood and Other Stories*, London, Chatto & Windus, 1981. *Letters*, ed. William Maxwell, London, Chatto & Windus, 1982. *Collected Poems*, ed. Claire Harman, Manchester, Carcanet New Press, 1982. *One Thing Leading to Another*, ed. Susanna Pinney, London, Chatto & Windus/ The Hogarth Press, 1984. *Selected Poems*, afterword by Claire Harman, Manchester, Carcanet Press, 1985. (The above list does not include all STW's early and minor works, nor the reprints of the early novels. At the time of going to press, all the novels except *After the Death of Don Juan* and *The Flint Anchor* are at last in print.)

AMERICAN PUBLICATIONS

Valentine Ackland *Whether a Dove or a Seagull*, New York, The Viking Press, 1933. *The Nature of the Moment*, New York, New Directions, 1973.

Sylvia Townsend Warner *The Espalier*, New York, The Dial Press, 1925. *Lolly Willowes*, New York, The Viking Press, 1926. *Mr Fortune's Maggot*, New York, The Viking Press, 1927. *The True Heart*, New York, The Viking Press, 1929. *Opus 7*, New York, The Viking Press, 1931. *The Salutation* New York, The Viking Press, 1932. *The Rainbow*, New York, Alfred Knopf, 1932. *Whether a Dove or a Seagull*, New York, The Viking Press, 1933. *Summer Will Show*, New York, The Viking Press, 1936. *After the Death of Don Juan*, New York, The Viking Press, 1939. *The Cat's Cradle Book*, New York, The Viking Press, 1940. *A Garland of Straw*, New York, The Viking Press, 1943. *The Flint Anchor*, New York, The Viking Press, 1954. *Winter in the Air*, New York, the Viking Press, 1956. *A Spirit Rises*, New York, The Viking Press, 1962. *Swans on an*

Autumn River, New York, The Viking Press, 1966. *T.H. White: A Biography*, New York, The Viking Press, 1968. *The Innocent and the Guilty*, New York, The Viking Press, 1971. *Kingdoms of Elfin*, New York, The Viking Press, 1977. *Scenes of Childhood* and Other Stories, New York, The Viking Press. *Letters*, ed., William Maxwell, New York, The Viking Press, 1982. *Collected Poems*, ed. Claire Harman, New York, The Viking Press, 1983. *One Thing Leading to Another*, New York, The Viking Press, 1984.

FURTHER READING

Bellamy, J. & Saville, J., *Dictionary of Labour Biography*, London, Macmillan, 1972 et seq.

Branson, N., *History of the Communist Party of Great Britain*, London, Lawrence & Wishart, 1985.

Branson, N. & Heinemann, M., *Britain in the Nineteen Thirties*, London, Weidenfeld & Nicolson, 1971.

Browne, F. *Twenty Drawings by Felicia Browne*, London, Lawrence & Wishart, 1936.

Brittain, V., *Testament of Experience*, London, Victor Gollancz, 1957.

Brittain, V., *England's Hour*, London, 1941.

Bryher, (Winifred Ellermann), *The Heart to Artemis*, London, Collins, 1963.

Bruley, S. 'Socialism and Feminism in the Communist Party of Great Britain, 1920–39', unpublished thesis, London School of Economics, 1980.

Bruley, S., 'Women Against War and Fascism', in Fyrth, J. ed., *Britain, Fascism and the Popular Front*, London, Lawrence & Wishart, 1986.

Burns, E., *Spain*, London, Communist Party of Great Britain, 1936.

Calder, A., *The People's War*, London, Jonathan Cape, 1969.

Chisholm, A., *Nancy Cunard*, London, Sidgwick & Jackson, 1979.

Clark, J. et al., eds, *Culture and Crisis in Britain in the Thirties*, London, Lawrence & Wishart, 1979.

Cunard, N., *Negro*, London, Wishart & Co., 1934. (Reprinted New York, Frederick Ungar Publ. Co., 1970.)

Cunard, N. ed., *Poems for France*, London, La France Libre, 1944.

Cunningham, V. ed., *The Penguin Book of Spanish Civil War Verse*, London, Penguin Books, 1980.

Cunningham, V., ed., *Spanish Front: Writers on the Civil War*, London, Oxford University Press, 1986.

Day Lewis, C. ed., *The Mind in Chains*, London, Frederick Muller, 1936.

Dimitrov, G., *Letters from Prison*, trans. Torr, D., & Davidson, M., London, Victor Gollancz and Lawrence & Wishart, 1935.

Ehrenburg, I., *The Fall of France seen through Soviet Eyes*

(Introduction STW), London, Modern Books, 1941.

Elwin, M. ed., *The Pleasure Ground*, London, MacDonald & Co., 1947.

Farran, D., Scott, S. & Stanley, S., eds, *Writing Feminist Biography*, Manchester, Studies in Sexual Politics, University of Manchester, 1987.

Ford, H. ed., *Nancy Cunard; Brave Poet, Indomitable Rebel*, New York, Chilton Book Co., 1968.

Fyrth, J., ed., *Britain, Fascism and the Popular Front*, London, Lawrence & Wishart, 1985.

Fyrth, J., *The Signal was Spain*, London, Lawrence & Wishart, 1986.

Garnett, D., *The Familiar Faces*, London, 1962.

Geismar, M. ed., *New Masses*, New York, International Publishers, 1969.

Green, N. & Elliott, A.M., *Spain Against Fascism 1936–39*, London, Communist Party History Group, n/d.

Gregory, A., *The Cry of a Gull, (Journals 1923–48)*, Dulverton, Ark Press, 1973.

Hamnett, N., *Laughing Torso*, London, Constable & Co., 1932.

Harman, C. ed., 'Sylvia Townsend Warner 1893–1978: A Celebration', *Poetry Nation Review* 23, Vol. 8, No. 3, Manchester, 1981.

Hopkins, K., *The Powys Brothers*, London, Phoenix House, 1967.

Hynes, S., *The Auden Generation*, London, Bodley Head, 1976.

Humfrey, B. ed., *Recollections of the Brothers Powys*, London, Peter Owen, 1980.

Jameson, S., *The Defence of Freedom*, London, 1934.

Jameson, S., *You May Well Ask*, London, 1939.

Jameson, S., *Journey from the North*, Autobiography Vol. 1, London, Collins, 1969.

Lehmann, J., *Whispering Gallery*, Autobiography Vol. 1, London, Longmans Green & Co., 1955.

Liddington, J., *Selina Cooper: Life and Times of a Respectable Rebel*, London, Virago Press, 1984.

Lindsay, J., *After the Thirties: the Novel in Britain & its Future*, London, Lawrence & Wishart, 1956.

Lindsay, J., *Franfrolico & After*, Autobiography Vol. 3, London, The Bodley Head, 1962.

Lipton, J., *Poems of Strife*, London, 1936.

Low, D., *Low Again*, London, Cresset Press, 1938.

Lucas, J. ed., *The 1930s: A Challenge to Orthodoxy*, Brighton, Harvester Press, 1978.

Martin, R., & Morris, F., *No Pasaran*: Catalogue of Spanish Civil War Exhibition, Arnolfini Gallery, 1986.

Mitchison, N., *You May Well Ask: A Memoir 1920–1940*, London, Victor Gollancz, 1979.

Mitford, J., *Hons and Rebels*, London, Quartet Books, 1978.

Montefiore, J., *Feminism and Poetry*, London, Pandora Press, 1987.

Morgan, L., *Writers at Work*, London, Dolphin Books, 1931.

Morris, L. & Radford, R., *The Story of the Artists International Association 1933–1953*, Oxford, Museum of Modern Art, 1983.

Powys, L. (ed. Wilkinson, L.), *Letters of Llewellyn Powys* (Introduction by Alyse Gregory), London, John Lane The Bodley Head, 1943.

Reilly, C., ed., *Chaos of the Night*, London, Virago Press, 1984.

Renn, L., *Death without Battle*, London, 1937.

Rickword, E., (ed. Young, A.), *Literature in Society: Essays & Opinions (11) 1931–78*, Manchester, Carcanet New Press, 1978.

Rickword, E. ed., *Soviet Writers Reply*, London, Society for Anglo-Soviet Relations, 1948.

Rose, P., ed., *Writing of Women: Essays in a Renaissance*, Connecticut, Wesleyan Universty Press, 1985.

Showalter, E., ed., *The New Feminist Criticism*, London, Virago Press, 1986.

Spanish Medical Aid Committee, *The Story of the British Medical Aid Unit in Spain*, London, The News Chronicle, n/d.

Spender, S., & Lehmann, J., *Poems for Spain*, London, The Hogarth Press, 1939.

Spender, S., *Forward From Liberalism*, London, Victor Gollancz (The Left Book Club), 1937.

Spender, S., *World Within World*, London, Faber & Faber, 1951.

Spender, S., *The Thirties and After*, London, Collins/Fontana, 1978.

Strachey, J., *The Theory and Practice of Socialism*, London, Gollancz (The Left Book Club), 1936.

Symons, J., *The Thirties: A Dream Revolved*, London, Cresset Press, 1966.

Untermeyer, J.S., *Private Collection*, New York, Alfred Knopf, 1965.

Woolf, L., *Downhill All The Way*, London, The Hogarth Press, 1967.

Woolf, V., *Orlando*, London, The Hogarth Press, 1928.

Woolf, V., *A Room of One's Own*, London, The Hogarth Press, 1929.

Woolf, V., *Three Guineas*, London, The Hogarth Press, 1938.

Woolf, V. (ed. Bell, A.O.), *The Diary of Virginia Woolf*, Vol. 3, London, The Hogarth Press, 1980.

INDEX

Ackland, Ruth, 9, 12, 18, 37, 143, 145, 146, 161, 240

Ackland, Valentine: adolescence and childhood, 9–13; antiques business, 234; Bohemian life in London, 18–23; Catholicism, 20–1, 24, 233, 234, 235, 238; and Communist Party, 52–5, 57–8, 59, 60, 91, 92, 93, 152; and *Daily Worker*, 61, 101, 170; and dialectical poetry, 83; and Dorset politics, 61–2, 65–9; drinking problem, 23, 38–9, 40, 152, 153, 154; engagement and marriage, 20–1, 24; friendship with the Powyses, 24, 28; illness and death, 239–43; and Left Book Club, 81–2; and *Left Review*, 71–5, 77–80, 94, 218; and *Life & Letters Today*, 152, 209, 217, 219; relationships, with Bo Foster, 18, 21, 24, 33, 52, 238, with Elizabeth Wade White, 89, 135, 152, 173, 174, 220, 221, 222, 233) Lower Frome Vauchurch, purchase of, 156–7; and *New Republic*, 144, 147, 149, 152; and *Our Time*, 217, 218; as poet, 4, 5, 18, 26, 37, 39, 43, 44–7, 51, 73, 83, 94–5, 152–3, 154, 206–17, 223–8; and Popular Front, 82–3; pregnancy and miscarriage, 24; Quakers, 233; in Spain, Basque orphans, 91, 92, volunteer scheme for, 87–8, in Barcelona, 88–90, in Madrid, 90, 97–9, writing for, 94–5; and Sylvia Townsend Warner, in America, 134–5, meeting and life in Dorset, 26–8, 29, 30, 32, 33–4, 40–3, 51–2, 61–9, 140–1, 149–54, 156–7, 164–8, 170, 173, 231–4, 238; in France, 231, in Ireland, 229, in Italy, 171–2, and libel case, 39–40, in Norfolk, 35–9, 143–6, 229–33, in Scotland, 241; and wartime work, 151, 154; writings, articles and reviews, 73, 74, 76, 77, 79, 218; *Country Conditions*, 4, 76, 77, 78–80, 209, *For Sylvia: An Honest Account*, 4, 5, 9, 13, 22, 34, 136, 152, 154, 173, 207, *Further Poems of Valentine Ackland*, 152, 212, 227, *Later Poems*, 206, 223, 224–7, *The Nature of the Moment*, 153, 217, 227, *Twenty-Eight Poems*, 4, 213, 223–4, uncollected and unpublished stories and poems, 73, 208, 209, 216–28,

272

Whether a Dove or a Seagull,
4, 5, 43–7, 76, 212, 216
Aid-Spain Committees, 89, 93
Aldeburgh Festival, 245–6
Anarchism, 89, 95
Antonia, Gräfin von und zu
  Trauttmansdorff, 141, 244,
  246
Aragon, Louis, 71, 102, 168
ARP, 148
Ashcroft, Peggy, 91
Association of Writers for
  Intellectual Liberty, 84, 86, 87,
  92, 93
Atholl, Duchess of, 93
ATS, 162
Auden, W.H., 97, 98, 102

Bentley, Phyllis, 193
Binder, Pearl, 71, 84, 103
Bloomsbury, 1, 16
Bowen, Elizabeth, 180
British Medical Association, 82
Brittain, Vera, 1, 61, 80, 96, 103
Browne, Felicia, 90, 100
Bryher (Winifred Ellerman), 15,
  16, 209
Buck, Dr Percy, 14
Bush, Alan, 175, 246

Calder-Marshall, Arthur, 180
Carnegie Foundation, the, 13, 14
Catholic Church, the, 20–1, 24,
  233, 234, 235, 238
Chamberlain, Neville, 94, 158
Churchill, Winston, 158
Chute, Marchette and Joy, 241
Clarke, Steven, 98, 140
Cleall, Mrs, 246
Comintern, the, 158
Communism, 95, 100, 103
Communist Party of Great
  Britain, the, 52, 55, 57–61, 66,
  67, 69, 72, 82, 87, 167, 191,
  246; and Spain, 88, 90, 91, 93,
99; and the war, 150, 157–60,
  163
Communist Party Writers Group,
  171
Cunard, Nancy, 3, 71, 73, 87,
  123, 154, 164, 165, 166, 171,,
  212; *Poèmes à la France*, 164,
  168; *Authors Take Sides on the
  Spanish War*, 102, 164

Day Lewis, Cecil, 59, 85
Dimitrov, Georgi, 54, 195
Dorset Peace Council, 60, 80, 81
Douglas, Norman, 48, 166

East Chaldon, 26, 63, 64
Engels, Friedrich, 116

Fleta, Asunción Lou, 94, 98
Foster, 'Bo', 18, 21, 24, 33, 52,
  238
Franco, General, 89, 103, 124
Frankfort Manor, 35, 37, 39, 40,
  177
Fyrth, Jim, 61, 66

Garcia, Ramona Siles, 90, 91
Garnett, David, 3, 14, 23, 24, 28,
  100, 243
Gide, André, 60, 84, 86, 99
Gilbert, Morris, 164
Gill, Eric, 18
Goat, Georgy, 64, 65
Gollan, Elsie, 90
Gollancz, Victor, 81, 82
Great Eye Folly, 229–31
Green, Nan, 90, 92, 100
Gregory, Alyse, 24, 28, 40, 229

Hamnett, Nina, 22, 23
Harrow School, 3, 16
Heinemann, Margot, 7, 59
Holtby, Winifred, 71, 84
Howe, Bea, 12, 14, 16, 34, 164,
  173, 244

Huxley, Aldous, 46, 48, 84

International Association of Writers for the Defence of Culture, 84, 85, 86, 90, 97
International Literature, 122
International Brigade, 66, 93, 99
Ireland, John, 175, 246

Jameson, Storm, 1, 51, 52, 71, 84, 86, 103
John, Augustus, 18, 22
Jubilee, the, 61, 62

Lansbury, George, 61
Laski, Harold, 81
League of Nations Union, 92
Left Book Club, 67, 70, 81, 82, 160
Left News, 70, 195
Left Review, 70, 71, 73, 74, 82, 85, 102
Lehmann, John, 75, 97, 98, 100, 104, 122
Lehmann, Rosamund, 103
Lindsay, Jack, 73, 160, 161, 193
Lipton, Julius, 44, 61, 62, 63, 65, 67, 73, 77, 83, 207
Lipton, Queenie, 63, 73, 82
Lloyd, A.L., 71, 97
Lower Frome Vauchurch, 43, 140, 141, 145, 156, 157, 173

Macaulay, Rose, 51, 103
Mackenzie, Compton, 84
Malraux, André, 97
Manisty, Peg, 142, 227, 228
Maxwell, William, 26, 61, 135, 140, 148, 150, 241, 243, 246
Medical Aid For Spain, 88
Miss Green's Cottage, 29, 30, 32, 33, 35, 167
Mitchison, Naomi, 1, 71, 84, 91, 103
Mosley, Oswald, 54

Moxon, Granny, 50, 63, 218, 219
Muntz, Betty, 24, 170

National Council for Civil Liberties, 70
National Joint Committee for Spanish Relief, 91
Neruda, Pablo, 97, 102
New Yorker, The, 135, 145, 156
Nordoff, Paul, 136, 143, 146, 147, 171, 211, 231, 235, 244, 246

Our Time, 82, 157, 159–63, 168, 170, 176, 180, 191–3, 202, 217, 218

Paris Peace Congress, 171
Parker, Dorothy, 171
Parsons, Ian, 100
Peace Pledge Union, 55
Pears, Peter, 175, 243
Picasso, Pablo, 91
Pitman, Jim and May, 37, 65, 167, 168
Popular Front, 59, 81, 82
POUM, 95
Powys, John Cowper, 92
Powys, Katie (Philippa), 24
Powys, Llewellyn, 24, 40, 177
Powys, T.F., 16, 22, 24, 26, 28, 29, 46, 47, 48, 49
Powys, Violet, 26
Priestley, J.B., 60, 71, 193

Quakers, 233

Rattenbury, Arnold and Sim, 1, 53, 61, 160, 171, 231, 246
Red Cross, 149
Reichstag Fire Trial, 54
Renn, Ludwig, 153, 178
Rickword, Edgell, 66, 70, 71, 73, 84, 98, 193

Rickword, Jonnie, 124

Sackville West, Vita, 103
Shepherd, Revd Dick, 55
Slater, Montague, 70, 71, 193
Soviet Union, 57, 60, 89, 99, 103, 159, 195, 235; agriculture, 58; literature, 58; Society for Cultural Relations with, 193; treason trials, 60; in wartime, 158, 163
Spanish Civil War, 87–103
Spender, Stephen, 66, 97, 98, 99, 100, 102, 104
Spurling, Hilary, 179
Stead, Christina, 84, 85, 86
Strachey, John, 54, 97

Tomlin, Stephen 'Tommy', 16, 29, 170
Trotskyists, 60, 95
Turpin, Richard, 20, 21, 24, 28

Untermeyer, Jean Starr, 30, 32

Wade White, Elizabeth, 33, 89, 135, 137, 152, 173, 174, 220, 221, 222, 233
Wang, Professor Shelley, 92
Warner, George Townsend, 3, 6, 7, 13, 16
Warner, Nora Townsend, 3, 7
West Chaldon, 41
West, Rebecca, 51, 103
World Peace Council, 171
Warner, Sylvia Townsend:
adolescence and childhood, 6, 7; and Aldeburgh Festival, 244–6; and America, 134–5; American Academy of Arts, 246; Anarchism, love of, 89; and AWFIL, 84, 86–7, 92, 93; and Buck, Dr Percy, 14; and Communism, 100; CP, membership of, 52–5, 57–8, 59, 60, 91–3; and *The Countryman*, 57–8, 75–6, 103; and *Daily Worker*, 61, 69; and Dorset politics, 61–2, 65–9, 80–1, 83–4, 90, 97–8; France, love of, 168–9; and IAWDC, 8–6, 90, 97–9; and Left Book Club, 81–2; *Left Review*, 71–5, 96, 97; likes and dislikes, 48–9, 244; in London, 13–8; Lower Frome Vauchurch, 140–1, 155, 157, 243, 246; and Miss Green's cottage, 29, 30, 32, 33, 35, 167; and music, 13, 14, 15; National Joint Committee for Spanish Relief, 91; and *New Yorker, The*, 135, 145, 156; old age and death, 244–6; opera libretto, 147, 246; political scrapbook, 55–7; and Popular Front, 82–3; and Powyses, 26–9; and Reichstag Fire Trial, 54; religion, 229; Royal Society of Literature, the, 246; and Spain, 87–90, 94–5, 97–9, 101–3, 104, 122–4; and speeches, 69, 80–1, 82; and treason trials, 66; and Valentine Ackland, in America, 134–5, Dorset, meeting and life together, 26–8, 29, 30, 32, 33–4, 40–3, 51–2, 61–9, 140–1, 149–54, 156–7, 164–8, 170, 173, 231–4, 238, in France, 231, in Ireland, 229, in Italy, 171–2, and libel case, 39–40, in Norfolk, 35–9, 143–6, 229–33, in Scotland, 241; warwork, 151, 153; and WVS, 142, 167; writers' conference, 58, 135; writings, *After the Death of Don Juan*, 123–34, 169, 191; *Azrael*, 190; *Cats Cradle Book*, 37,

153, 155, 176–8, 192–4;
Collected Poems, 137, 175,
176; *The Corner That Held
Them*, 155, 191, 195,
196–205; *The Espalier*, 3, 29;
The Flint Anchor, 105, 144,
181, 186, 195, 231; *A Garland
of Straw*, 147, 155, 178–80,
181; *Jane Austen*, 185–7; *King
Duffus*, 190; *Kingdoms of
Elfin*, 4, 125; *Lolly Willowes*,
3, 29, 105–8, 191; *Mr.
Fortune's Maggot*, 47, 108,
147; *More Joy in Heaven*, 51;
The Museum of Cheats, 147,
155, 178, 181–3; *Opus 7*,
48–9; *One Thing Leading to
Another*, 21; *Proust, Contre
Sainte-Beuve*, 238; *The
Salutation*, 35, 47, 137, 186,
190; *Stranger with a Bag*, 186;
Summer Will Show, 37, 59,
104–5, 108, 109–24, 127, 134,
191; *T.H. White: A Biography*,
4, 238, 240; *Time Importuned*,
29; *The True Heart*, 47, 108,
109, 186; *Twelve Poems*, 190;

Whether a Dove or a Seagull,
35, 49–51, 121; *Women as
Writers*, 183, 187–90
Warren, Dorothy, 22
Watson, Mary, 160
West Chaldon, 41
West, Rebecca, 51, 103, 214
Williams Ellis, Amabel, 54, 71,
74, 84, 98, 214, 241
Williams Ellis, Clough, 214, 241
Williams, Sir Ralph Vaughan,
15
Wintringham, Tom, 69, 70, 71,
73, 83, 97
Women's Voluntary Service, 142,
145, 167
Woolf, Leonard, 57
Woolf, Virginia, 29, 54, 70, 187
Woollcombe, Joan, 9, 12, 20,
145, 151, 155, 156, 234, 238,
240
World Peace Council, 171
Writers Against Fascism and for
Collective Security, 70
Writers' International, 70

Young Communist League, 66

Some Pandora titles you will enjoy:

ELLEN AND EDY
A biography of Ellen Terry and her daughter, Edith Craig, 1847–1947
Joy Melville

Ellen Terry lived during the reign of Queen Victoria when women were required to live according to the strictest of moral codes. She broke the rules of that code, marrying three times, living with her lover, Edward Godwin by whom she had two illegitimate children. Yet, paradoxically, she demonstrates in her life and in her beliefs the concerns of her age and, despite her huge public fame – modern equivalents might be Madonna or Meryl Streep – she has remained an enigmatic figure. Her daughter, Edith Craig was a talented theatre producer and constume designer, a suffragette who founded the Pioneer Players and who lived for most of her life with another woman, Christopher St John. Joy Melville focuses on the everyday lives, and the loves, of Ellen and Edy. Whilst she follows Ellen's adventures in England and America and her relations with, among others, Edward Godwin, Henry Irving and George Bernard Shaw, this is above all the story of the stormy, mutually possessive, but ultimately strong and loving bond between a remarkable mother and daughter. Edith Craig emerges for the first time as a person worthy of attention in her own right, and the biography is enhanced by carefully chosen and illuminating illustration.

Paper   £4.95   Biography/Life and Times   0 86358 252 4

JANE AND MAY MORRIS
A Biographical Story 1839–1938
Jan Marsh

'Why should there be any special record of me when I have
never done any special work?'
Jane Morris.

'I'm a remarkable woman – always was, though none of you
seemed to think so.' *May Morris.*

As the wife of William Morris and icon of the Pre-Raphaelites,
Jane Morris's fame is reflected against that of a famous
Brotherhood. Her daughter May has also been allotted a walk-on
part in all that has been written about those men – notably
William Morris, Dante Gabriel Rossetti, George Bernard Shaw –
who feature in Jan Marsh's story. This time, however, it is the
women who take centre-stage. This story of the lives of
celebrated mother and daughter spans a century. It is a
fascinating tale told with narrative zest, illuminating the
relationships of both with the women around them. It reveals
them as women of their times and, scrupulously researched,
gives us new insights into the artistic movement and the society
in which they lived. Carefully chosen illustrations complete the
picture of Jane and May Morris.

Paper   £4.95   Biography/Life and Times   0 86358 026 2

WOMAN OF LETTERS
A Life of Virginia Woolf
Phyllis Rose

Woman of Letters received considerable critical acclaim when it was first published in 1978. Now available as a Pandora paperback, Phyllis Rose's compelling biography assesses the way Virginia Woolf's past reverberates in her novels and places her feminism at the centre of her emotional and intellectual life.

Phyllis Rose tells the story of Virginia Woolf's life as Woolf herself might have perceived it; she revises the image of Woolf as an isolated technician unconcerned with social reality, giving us instead the picture of a woman immersed in issues that have become, if anything, more pressing since her death.

'Phyllis Rose writes with considerable insight and feeling of Woolf's attitudes to herself as a woman and of the possibility of being a woman writer.' Margaret Drabble, *New Statesman*

'An admirable book.' Frank Kermode, *New York Review*

Paper   £4.95   Biography/Life and Times   0 86358 066 1

CHINA CORRESPONDENT
Agnes Smedley

Agnes Smedley, feminist, socialist and author of the acclaimed classic *Daughter of Earth*, travelled to China in 1928 and lived and worked there through the war-torn decade of the 1930s.

China Correspondent (first published as *Battle Hymn of China*) is her gripping story of a nation in turmoil and a woman on the front line, long held to be a masterpiece. A mixture of autobiography, travel narrative and war reporting, it is a fast-moving unfolding of events which none the less never loses its sensitivity to the individuals caught up in them. Agnes Smedley (acting as war correspondent for the *Manchester Guardian*) travelled with the Red Army as a medic, knew Mao Tse-tung and Chou En-lai and witnessed the emergence of the new China with a particular feeling for the massive changes in women's lives.

Paper   £4.95   Travel/Autobiography   0 86358 036 X 366

AUTOBIOGRAPHY OF A CHINESE GIRL
Hsieh Ping-ying

With an Introduction by Elisabeth Croll

This is the story of Hsieh Ping-ying, a Chinese girl born at the beginning of this century who rejected the traditions of the old order and eventually became one of China's leading women writers.

At school, she unwrapped the binding on her feet so that she could run freely with the other children. As a young woman she went into the army in order to escape an arranged marriage. As an adult she was charged with being a Communist and imprisoned.

Hsieh Ping-ying's story takes us back to the heart of pre-revolutionary China. She describes her relationship with her family – with her mother and with her grandmother – and the difficulties she faced rejecting traditional restraints in order to live as an independent woman.

Paper   £4.95   Autobiography   0 86358 052 1 224